ALSO BY RICHARD BROOKHISER

America's First Dynasty: The Adamses, 1735–1918

Alexander Hamilton, American

Rules of Civility

Founding Father: Rediscovering George Washington

The Way of the WASP

The Outside Story

Gentleman Revolutionary

· GOUVERNEUR MORRIS ·

THE RAKE

WHO WROTE

THE CONSTITUTION

RICHARD BROOKHISER

FREE PRESS
NEW YORK TORONTO LONDON SYDNEY SINGAPORE

*f*P

Free Press
A Division of Simon & Schuster, Inc.
1230 Avenue of the Americas
New York, NY 10020

FREE PRESS and colophon are trademarks
of Simon & Schuster, Inc.

For information regarding special discounts for bulk purchases,
please contact Simon & Schuster Special Sales at
1-800-456-6798 or business@simonandschuster.com

Designed by Chris Welch
Manufactured in the United States of America

1   3   5   7   9   10   8   6   4   2

Library of Congress Cataloging-in-Publication Data is available

ISBN 0-7432-2379-9

THIS BOOK IS DEDICATED TO

KENNETH WALD

Acknowledgments

I would like to thank the staffs of the Library of Congress, the New York Public Library, the Special Collections of Rutgers University, and the Alderman Library at the University of Virginia, for their help with unpublished documents. Mary Ellen Jones of the St. Lawrence County Historical Association, and Russ Sprague gave me valuable information about Gouverneur, New York. The Reverend Martha Rollins Overall, priest of St. Ann's Church of Morrisania, kindly showed me the church Gouverneur Morris II built and the graves of his parents.

Linda Bridges, Alan Pell Crawford, Charles Kesler, Susan Shapiro and David Zincavage gave useful assistance. I am especially grateful to Forrest and Ellen McDonald. *City Journal* and its editor, Myron Magnet, let me write a piece about my great New Yorker. My wife, Jeanne Safer, let me have a wonderful line about the skins of the eighteenth-century poor.

I would like to thank my editor, Bruce Nichols, and my agent, Michael Carlisle.

Contents

Part 3 The Brink of Revolution

A Note on Money and Spelling

I have tried to provide islands of modern value in the rush of currency that flowed through Morris's life as a private businessman and a public financier. In his youth the American colonies kept their accounts in pounds, with 20 shillings to the pound and 12 pence to the shilling. (The pound sterling of England was worth almost twice as much as any of the colonial pounds.) But the most common colonial coin was the Spanish dollar, which was worth 4 shillings 6 pence sterling, or about 8 colonial shillings. The pre-revolutionary French livre (equal to 20 sous) was worth about 9 pence sterling. Morris lived through several periods of inflation, at home and abroad.

English was spelled and punctuated differently in Morris's lifetime. Eighteenth-century capitalizing survives in the Constitution: "We the People of the United States, in Order to form a more perfect Union . . ." My compromise between readability and period flavor has been to modernize most of the punctuation, and to leave most of the spelling in its original form.

Introduction

$\mathscr{A}$ BIOGRAPHER can feel a moment's hesitation when it comes to introducing his subject, for every traditional means has its drawbacks. If the hero appears *in medias res*, in the midst of some great action, the reader may feel manipulated, even coerced: his attention is being claimed before it has been earned. If the story of a life begins where the life does, in a cradle, then the reader might experience a sense of delay: he wished to read about great men, not infants. For the biographer of Gouverneur Morris, it is perhaps best to let him be introduced by a woman.

In 1795, Harriet de Damas, a French countess, wrote a portrait of a tall, handsome American who had become a fixture of Parisian society.[1] Gouverneur Morris had come to France in 1789, age thirty-seven, as a businessman; three years later, he was appointed the American minister to that country. Mr. Morris had a French first name (his mother's maiden name), which Americans insisted on pronouncing "Gov-er-*neer*"; he had learned French as a child, and wrote it well enough to produce papers on French politics, or little poems for his friends.[2] Mme de Damas called his spoken French "always correct and vigorous," though other Frenchwomen teased him for his mistakes. Mr. Morris cut a figure for many reasons: his impressive bearing (the French sculptor Jean-Antoine Houdon used him as a body double for a statue of George Washington); his wit; his severely elegant clothes and carriage, so different from French silks and colors; and what was severe in a different way, his wooden left leg. When he arrived at a party, the servants watched him; the guests watched him; he watched himself, mindful of the impression he made.

"Superficial observers," wrote Mme de Damas, ". . . might be acquainted with Mr. Morris for years, without discovering his most eminent qualities. Such observers must be told what to admire." The Frenchwoman confronts a difficulty with her portrait head-on: she had known Mr. Morris for only a small part of his life, since his first thirty-seven years had been spent in America. But she plunged ahead confidently.

The superficial observers of his early life "regard Mr. Morris as a profound politician," and indeed he had been involved in politics, often of the most eventful kind. When he was twenty-three years old the American Revolution began, and he watched it pull society and family asunder (one of his elder half brothers signed the Declaration of Independence; another half brother was a general in the British army). He left American towns a step ahead of marauding British armies, and when Morris visited his mother, who supported the crown throughout the war, he had to get passes from both sides to cross their lines. He eventually followed his patriot half brother into the Continental Congress, where he helped accomplish great things, but also engaged in endless petty wrangling. ("We had many scoundrels" in Congress, he would remember as an older man.)[3]

When he was still a young one, age thirty-five, Mr. Morris drafted the Constitution of the United States. The proceedings of the Constitutional Convention were secret, to allow the delegates maximum freedom to speak their minds, so Mr. Morris's role on the Committee of Style was not generally known. But in later years he admitted to a correspondent that "that instrument was written by the fingers which write this letter."[4] Years after Morris's death, an elderly James Madison told an inquiring historian that "the *finish* given to the style and arrangement of the Constitution fairly belongs to the pen of Mr. Morris."[5] James Madison, the careful and learned theorist, is commonly called the Father of the Constitution, because he kept the most complete set of notes of the debates, and made cogent arguments for ratification after the debates were done (he wrote one third of the

Federalist Papers). But Gouverneur Morris, who put the document into its final form and who wrote the Preamble from scratch, also deserves a share of the paternity. The founders were voluminous writers, and much of their writing is very good, but few of them had the combination of lightness and force that generates a great style. Jefferson had it; Franklin had it; Thomas Paine, the passionate and ungainly English immigrant, had it. The only other one of their number who hit that note consistently was Morris. "A better choice" for a draftsman "could not have been made," Madison concluded.[6]

Mme de Damas and her French friends certainly knew about Mr. Morris's political activity: it was one facet of his social cachet, a point of interest like his wardrobe and his leg. A more striking feature of their friend was his manner. Mme de Damas called him "the most amiable" of men. "His imagination inclines to pleasantry, and being abundantly gifted with what the English call *humor*, united to what the French name *esprit*, it is impossible not to be delighted. . . ." Humor and *esprit*: Mr. Morris delighted in the incongruities and follies of life, including his own, and his comments—quick, shapely, and bold—communicated that delight to others. Women found him especially pleasing, perhaps because he took special pains to please them. "Govr Morris kept us in a continual smile," was how one young lady put it.[7] His women friends did more than smile. At the cardtable of the sexes, his wit and looks always trumped his disability, and the one-legged American left a trail of lovers on two continents.

Mr. Morris's good company went beyond good times. When the French Revolution, more stressful than the American, began to suck his glittering friends into poverty, exile, and danger, he gave many of them refuge, and saved several of their lives. Mme de Damas was not one of his lovers, but he did save her life.

But more important than Mr. Morris's career or his behavior was his nature. "Nothing really worthy of him," wrote Mme de Damas, "will be said by any one, who does not ascend to the source of all that is great and excellent in his character." That, she decided, was "a belief that God can will nothing but what is good." This gave him confidence, charity, and hope. "Ever at peace with himself . . . seldom ruffled in his temper, not suffering men or events to have a mastery over his spirit, he is habitually serene, alike ready to engage in the most abstruse inquiries, or to join in the trifles of social amusement." Gouverneur Morris took his life as it came. "He conceives it to be following the order of Providence to enjoy all its gifts. 'To enjoy is to obey.' And upon the same principle he submits, with a modest fortitude, and sincere resignation, to the ills inflicted by the same hand." Living among tottering thrones and shaky republics, Mr. Morris showed the gift of poise.

Gouverneur Morris belonged to that band of brothers that we now call the founding fathers. Some were his friends: he knew and worshipped George Washington for almost twenty years; he knew and squabbled with Paine for almost as long; he was at Alexander Hamilton's deathbed. Some of them were enemies: he thought James Madison was a fool and a drunkard. He knew them all, and was one of their number. The founding fathers-to-be were guided by the pursuit of greatness. They measured themselves by their service to the country they were making. Mr. Morris was moved by the same tidal pull of public good. "This is the seed time of glory," he wrote in one of his sweetest phrases.[8] The second half of his life, after Mme de Damas finished her portrait, had two great public occasions in store for him. He was one of those New Yorkers who pushed early and hard for what became the Erie Canal, a project that made the paper structure of national union economically vital. At the same time, and paradoxically, he was one of those northerners who decided, during the War of 1812, that the nation should be broken up, and the Constitution scrapped. Other Americans would come to the same conclusion, from abolitionists calling the Constitution a deal with the devil to southerners arguing that it gave them a right to secede. But Morris's abandonment of the document he had written is more astonishing than later repudiations.

Yet Mr. Morris, alone among the founding fathers, thought that his private life was as important as his public life. Being a gentleman mattered as much to him as being a great man. When public life was not going well, he could go home—not to bide his time before his next opportunity, or to enjoy the retirement on a pedestal of a Cincinnatus, but because he enjoyed farming, reading, eating, fishing, making money, and making love as much as founding a state. "A characteristic trait, which I must not forget," wrote Mme de Damas, "is his faculty and habit of applying his mind to a single object, of suddenly collecting the whole force of his attention upon one point." That point might be a stumbling economy, or an imperfect constitution; it might also be the parade of domestic life. "He is fond of his ease, does his best to procure it, and enjoys it as much as possible. He loves good cheer, good wine, good company." Mr. Morris's ability to switch from public to private life—his inability ever to banish his private frame of reference, even in the midst of public business—did limit his effectiveness as a public man. He lacked the persistence of the other founders. He could focus on one political idea, but soon he might be focusing on another. One delegate to the Constitutional Convention called him "fickle and inconstant," a charge that rang down the years.[9] But this limitation brought benefits. In an era when American politics was as poisonous as it would ever be, he was remarkably free from rancor. Though a war would finally drive him to it, once the war ended, rancor receded. Even James Madison could not long disturb his peace of mind.

Mr. Morris had many reasons to be happy. He was born to privilege, he worked hard to make himself rich, and he was successful in politics, business, and love: after all his affairs, he married a devoted and intelligent woman (accused, it is true, of being a double murderess, though the accuser, her brother-in-law, was commonly supposed to be somewhat insane). But Mr. Morris also saw many things that could have made him gloomy, bitter, perplexed. He witnessed two revolutions, up close and on the ground, one more turbulent than we remember, the other as turbulent as any has ever been. He fled a town that was about to be burned to the ground, and he saw a corpse that had just been torn apart by a mob. His own body was not only missing a leg, but most of the flesh of one arm. Pessimists and misanthropes have been made of less.

In 1936, as Europe slid to war, William Butler Yeats wrote that there is a gaiety in art, even tragic art, that transfigures the dread of life. Gouverneur Morris was no artist, unless living is an art. He carried his gaiety within himself. It was, we might say, constitutional.

GAIETY TRANSFIGURING ALL THAT DREAD,

—W. B. Yeats, "Lapis Lazuli"

CHAPTER ONE

Past and Youth

INCE GOUVERNEUR Morris bore his mother's maiden name, and since pleasing, pursuing, and avoiding commitments to women would occupy much of his attention as an adult, it would be interesting to know more about Sarah Gouverneur Morris, the first woman in his life. As it is, the little we do know about her life story and her background provides several clues to what she must have been like.

The Gouverneurs were a family of Huguenots, or French Protestants, who had been driven by religious strife in their homeland to Holland in the 1590s; from there, in 1663, they went to the Dutch colony of New Amsterdam. Sarah Gouverneur, who belonged to the third generation of the family in the New World, retained enough of a French identity to send her only son briefly to a French school. But her own mother, Sarah Staats, sprang from the Dutch who had founded the colony of New Amsterdam and who had been running it for forty years when the Gouverneurs arrived.

The Gouverneurs and the Staatses thus represented something that existed nowhere else in the Thirteen Colonies—an old world of European settlement that preceded the arrival of Englishmen. Since New Amsterdam was a commercial venture based on the getting and spending of the fur trade, she had neither the time nor the desire to cultivate spokesmen; her first literary champion, Washington Irving, only appeared many years after the old world had vanished. Irving's histories and stories about Rip Van Winkle, the headless horseman, and St. Nicholas, the patron saint of Christmas, embroidered every factual detail that he did not invent out of whole cloth; but with the insight of art, he captured important facets of a lost psychology. The people of New Amsterdam were private, stubborn, and conservative. Their women were powerful figures in the household, enjoying rights of property ownership and inheritance that were denied their English sisters (in "Rip Van Winkle," Irving makes a joke out of female independence: poor Rip is hen-pecked). The men and women of New Amsterdam, finally, were losers: England had conquered them in 1664, renaming the city and the colony New York, and English customs and language steadily displaced all rivals as time wore on. Sarah's Dutch grandfather, Dr. Samuel Staats, had briefly moved back to Holland rather than "make himself an Englishman."[1]

In 1689, twenty-four years before Sarah was born, the old world had its last hurrah in New York: Jacob Leisler, a German merchant, led a confused rebellion against the English governor that was supported by most of the city's old families, including the Gouverneurs and the Staatses. After almost two years, Leisler was besieged by troops from England, convicted of treason, and drawn and quartered. Power returned to its new channels, and assimilation proceeded apace—which made the descendants of the old world all the more private and stubborn. Sarah Gouverneur Morris would show such traits over the course of her long life.

Her son's paternal ancestors, the Morrises, were by contrast winners in the lottery of the British Empire. To the brashness that typically attends success, they added a quirky extroversion of their own. The Morrises were a family of originals.

The first Morrises to settle in North America were a pair of Welsh brothers, Lewis and Richard. They fought on Cromwell's side in the English Civil War; after taking one royalist stronghold, they adopted as their family crest a burning castle, with the motto *Tandem vincitur* (Finally conquered). After the Restoration, they moved to Barbados, an English Caribbean colony that was filled with Civil War veterans and refugees. From there they moved in the 1670s to New York: a logical next step, since the new English colony had become a hub for processing the sugar the plantations grew, and for shipping staples to the planters. In 1671, Richard Morris had a son, whom he named Lewis. When Richard died four years later, the elder Lewis, who had no children of his own, became his nephew's guardian.

The Morris family did very well in New York. They bought 500 acres (later expanded to 1,900) from a Dutch farmer named Jonas Bronck, lying ten miles north of the city, stretching east from the Harlem River to Long Island Sound. Centuries later Broncks' land would give its name to the Bronx; the Morrises named their new estate "Morrisania." The elder Lewis Morris also bought 3,500 acres in New Jersey. Altogether he had a grist mill, a sawmill, an iron mine, a sloop, and forty-one slaves.

He and his nephew did not at first get along. The elder Lewis hired a Quaker tutor, Hugh Copperthwaite, whom the younger disliked. One day the boy hid himself in a tree beneath which Copperthwaite was used to pray. As the Quaker was addressing the Lord, young Lewis called his name. "Here am I, Lord," said Copperthwaite, "what wouldst Thou with me?" "Go," the voice answered, "preach my gospel to the Mohawks, thou true and faithful servant."[2] The tutor was preparing to leave on his mission when the trick was exposed, and Lewis's guardian exploded. The boy ran away to Jamaica, supporting himself as a scrivener, or copier of documents, until he finally came home, reconciled with his uncle, and settled down. When the elder Lewis died in 1691, the younger inherited all his bustling property.

The new owner of Morrisania directed his considerable energies into politics. The politics of New York, after Leisler's rebellion, was defined by alliances of prominent families competing with each other for office, and for the favor of governors appointed in London. In 1697, Morrisania was designated a manor—a quasi-feudal status enjoyed by the estates of a dozen other wealthy New Yorkers (Rensselaerwyck, the manor of the Van Rensselaer family, covered 1,100 square miles). In the early eighteenth century the lord of the new manor began holding office—first in the colonial Assembly, the elective branch of the legislature, then as Chief Justice of the Supreme Court. In the latter role he became involved in one of the most famous political trials of the colonial period.

In 1732, the new governor of New York, William Cosby, a professional placeholder who looked on his offices as opportunities for en-
richment, brought a suit for what he claimed were arrears in his salary,
and asked the Supreme Court of the colony to erect a special court to
hear his case. When Judge Morris wrote a caustic opinion rejecting
the maneuver, Cosby removed him from the bench. This was a declaration of political warfare. Morris and his allies hired John Peter
Zenger, a poor German printer, to edit a new newspaper in New York,
the *Weekly Journal,* to compete with the established, pro-Cosby paper,
the *Gazette,* and to act as their mouthpiece. The *Weekly Journal* published English political tracts and abusive poems, and called Cosby
and his supporters "monkeys" and "spaniels." Cosby complained of
Morris's "open and implacable malice,"[3] and had Zenger arrested for
seditious libel. Under the common law of seditious libel, any publica-
tion that, in the view of a judge, held the government up to contempt
was illegal. The only function of a jury in a seditious libel trial was to
decide whether the accused had actually printed the offensive mater-
ial. The situation was not a happy one for defendants. The Morris
party, however, brought in Alexander Hamilton, an eloquent lawyer
from Philadelphia (no relation to the future Treasury secretary), who
urged the jurors to vote their consciences. "It is not the cause of a poor
printer, nor of New York alone, which you are trying. No! . . . It is the
cause of liberty."[4] Zenger won his freedom, and Hamilton was given a
5 1/2-ounce gold box and a party at the Black Horse Tavern. In the
next Assembly elections, "the sick, the lame and the blind were all carried to vote" and the Morrisites swept the Assembly.[5]

The Zenger verdict set no legal precedent, since it was sheer jury
nullification. Judge Morris did not intend to lead a popular party; tart,
opinionated, and tactless, he was "not fitted to gain popularity,"[6] and
when London, to get him out of New York, offered him the governor-
ship of New Jersey, he happily accepted, and ran the province with a
firm hand. Morris lacked the principles of a later generation, but he
had a principle of his own: that he and his interests were not to be tri-
fled with.

He lived hard, in the eighteenth-century manner. When he went on a lobbying trip to London, his wife told their younger son, who went along, "Don't let your father sit up late and drink too much wine."[7] The son failed in this task. The older man read as hard as he drank, accumulating a library of over two thousand books—vast by American standards. His fancy stimulating the fancy of others, he became a magnet for tall tales, some of them possibly true. He was supposed to have designed and built a sloop on his New Jersey property, ten miles inland, but because he never considered how to bring it to the water, it rotted where it lay. His will offers verifiable proof of singularity. If any man was "inclined to say anything" at his funeral, wrote Morris, "he may, if my executors think fit." But Morris wished for no mourning. "When the Divine Providence calls me hence, I die when I should die, and no relation of mine ought to mourn when I do so."[8]

 LEWIS MORRIS, governor and former judge, died in 1746, leaving his properties, his library, and two sons: yet another Lewis, and Robert Hunter. Their father trained them to argue as boys, encouraging them "to dispute with one another for his diversion" after dinner.[9] Both sons held public office, and both approached public life in a contentious spirit. When Robert Hunter Morris became deputy governor of Pennsylvania, he was advised, by Benjamin Franklin, a leader in the colonial Assembly, that he would have a "very comfortable" time, if only he avoided disputes. "My dear friend," Morris replied, ". . . you know I love disputing. It is one of my great pleasures."[10] Yet Robert Hunter Morris had the art of carrying on political wrangles without personal acrimony. Franklin remembered that even when their official exchanges were "indecently abusive," Morris "was so good natured a man that . . . we often dined together."[11] Robert Hunter Morris left four children, all illegitimate, and died of a heart attack while dancing with a clergyman's wife at a village ball.

Robert's elder brother, Lewis, also followed what had become the family profession of politics. This Lewis Morris, like his father, served in the New York Assembly, and later became Judge of the Court of Admiralty, with jurisdiction over New York, New Jersey, and Connecticut (New York City, the centerpiece of his domain, had become, thanks to its West Indies traffic, one of the largest ports in the Thirteen Colonies). But in him the family traits of feistiness and oddity took a darker turn. "Instead of a hat," he "used to wear upon his head a Loon's skin . . . with all its feathers on." [12] It seems that Judge Morris wore this costume both in society and in court. Since loons are famed for their crazy laughing calls, the judge's cap must have been all the more striking. This is stranger than building a boat in the woods or siring a family out of wedlock. A landlocked boat bothers nobody, and illegitimacy was not uncommon in the eighteenth century. A loon-skin hat proclaims that the wearer is unique, and that his fellows are beneath his consideration. It is a declaration of independence, and insouciance.

The third Lewis Morris married Katryntje (or Tryntje) Staats, daughter of Samuel Staats, the New Amsterdam doctor who had not wanted to become an Englishman. By her he had a daughter, Mary, and three sons—a fourth Lewis, Staats Long, and Richard. Mrs. Morris died in 1731, and Lewis remained a widower for fifteen years. But in 1746, after his father died and he became lord of the manor of Morrisania, he married Sarah Gouverneur, who was fifteen years his junior, and his first wife's niece.

In an age of high mortality, people frequently had second and third spouses, and men frequently took younger ones; in a subworld as small as the descendants of New Amsterdam, the entanglements of intermarriage were almost unavoidable. However unremarkable Lewis's second marriage was for that time and place, his children resented it, fearing particularly the appearance of a half brother who would divide their inheritance. Lewis and Sarah's first two children were girls—Isabella, born in 1748, and Sarah, born in 1749. But on January 31, 1752, at 1:30 in the morning, came a son, who was christened Gouverneur. The parents had two more girls—Euphemia, born in 1754, and Catherine, born in 1757—then stopped reproducing.

Lewis Morris died in 1762, when Gouverneur was ten. His will was a cri de coeur, expressing troubled feelings about his family and himself. He highlighted the dissension that his second marriage had caused by trying to allay it. "[I]t is my desire that all my children use their best endeavors to cultivate a good understanding with each other [and] that they be dutiful to" Sarah.[13] He expressed his displeasure with the education he had given his three older sons. Lewis, Staats Long, and Richard had all been sent to Yale College, which had been founded in neighboring Connecticut at the beginning of the century. But in 1746, the eventful year in which their father inherited Morrisania and took a second wife, he pulled all of them from school. In his will, he condemned Connecticut, declaring that "low craft and cunning" were so "interwoven" in the character of its people "that all their art cannot disguise it from the world, though many of them under the sanctified garb of religion"—Yale was a Congregationalist college— "have endeavored to impose themselves on the world for honest men."[14] Evidently he believed that someone at Yale had cheated him somehow, not a feeling unknown to the parents of college students. But how many proclaim it in their wills?

He saw great promise in his son Gouverneur. This was a perception that was widely held. One New Yorker who knew all the Morrises wrote that Gouverneur "has more knowledge (though still a youth) than all his three other brothers put together"[15]—this, even though the sons of the first marriage were all successful men: Lewis was third lord of the manor, Staats Long an officer in the British army, and Richard a rising lawyer. But Lewis Morris found the family spark only in his last son, and he was determined that it be nurtured. "It is my desire," he directed, "that my son Gouverneur Morris have the best education that is to be had in Europe or America."[16]

In his own life Lewis Morris saw only failure. "My actions have been so inconsiderable in the world that the most durable monument will but perpetuate my folly. . . . My desire is that nothing be mentioned about me, not so much as a line in a newspaper to tell the world I am dead. That I have lived to very little purpose my children will remember with concern when they see the small pittance I have left them, for children judge the wisdom, goodness and affections of their parents by the largeness of the bequests coming to them. But what I have left them is honestly acquired, which gives me a satisfaction that ill got thousands cannot bestow."[17] Even as the loon-skin hat outdid the family eccentricities, so this bitter cup of despair, hostility, and pride exceeded the whimsical language of Morris's father's will. The clause is absurd as well, for the "small pittance" he complained of was still, even shorn of the New Jersey acres, which had gone to Robert Hunter Morris, a fine estate. Lewis Morris died focused on his failures, convinced that the world would ignore his virtues, and placing all his hopes in a ten-year-old boy.

Lewis divided his estate among his heirs. Morrisania was split in two by a south-running brook; the western portion, 500 acres, and the title of lord of the manor, went to the eldest son, Lewis. Sarah Gouverneur Morris was given a life interest in the 1,400 acres to the east: the land and its income were hers to enjoy, though she could not sell it. At her death, it would pass to Staats Long, at which time he would give Richard and Gouverneur £2,000 apiece (perhaps $90,000 in modern money); the daughters would get £600 each (about $27,000). In the division of personal property, Gouverneur got a slave, and his father's shaving box, seal ring, and a pair of gold buttons that his father had worn daily.

Gouverneur Morris's inheritance thus presented him with a variety of options. If he took after his mother and her family, he might show a stubborn independence. If he took after the Morrises, he would be intelligent, flamboyant, and unusual (depression was also a possibility). His Morris heritage certainly accustomed him to politics: when he was a young man, a cousin would write him that if he failed to "dabbl[e]" in it, he would "impeach . . . [his] mother's continency."[18] He was also accustomed to politics at the highest level; Morrises had made the governor of one colony miserable, and had governed two others. Many of the men who would lead the American Revolution were steeped in politics (Samuel Adams, Benjamin Franklin); others were politically active rich men (George Washington, John Hancock). Morris was one of the few to spring from the governing elite. He would also know, if he were wise, that his place in this elite was not guaranteed. Quite apart from the fluctuations in the fortunes of powerful New York families, he was only the last sprig of the Morrises, a fourth son. His monetary inheritance, though tidy, would be long delayed, and he could claim no portion of Morrisania. If he wished to play a part like those his father, uncle, and grandfather had played in the world, he would have to use his opportunities to make his way.

Gouverneur Morris grew up in the manor house, which stood on the eastern half of the estate on a hill overlooking Long Island Sound. As an adult, he would write of the "brilliance in our atmosphere";[19] in a letter to a European friend, he called the climate of Morrisania *"riant* [laughing]."[20] The rivers provided the easiest pathways to New York, or to nearby towns; from Morrisania to the Jersey shore of New York Harbor was a leisurely three-hour sail (an unleisurely one-hour drive today). The manor house had nine rooms and two stories, with a balcony over a porch. The parlor, where Judge Morris sometimes heard Admiralty cases, was done in black walnut and mahogany.

Young Morris did not spend as much time there as he would have liked, for his education took him away from home when he was still a boy ("I have been somehow or other hurried through the different scenes of childhood," he would write when he was twenty).[21] He was sent to a school in New Rochelle, New York, a town ten miles out on the Sound. New Rochelle had been settled by Huguenot refugees in 1688, and Gouverneur's school was run by a Swiss Huguenot minister, who taught his pupils French and the "useful sciences."[22] In 1761, when he was nine years old, he was sent to an institution of continental reputation: the Academy of Philadelphia, founded ten years earlier by Benjamin Franklin. The Academy was housed in a structure that had been built to hold the overflow crowds from the preaching of George Whitefield, the barnstorming evangelist. Morris came with the recommendations of a child of the elite: his sponsor at the school was Thomas Lawrence, a trustee, and former mayor of Philadelphia, who also happened to be the husband of his half sister Mary. The purpose of the Academy was college preparation, and after three years there, in 1764, Morris escaped the snares of Yale, Connecticut, and Congregationalism by entering King's College, an Anglican institution, in New York. The college, which had been founded in 1754, stood on the northern verge of town, overlooking the Hudson River.

Both the Academy and King's were founded to incarnate the latest in eighteenth-century educational ideals; the learning they imparted was to be practical, comprehensive, and freed from the domination of Greek and Latin. Franklin wanted a curriculum grounded on English, history, and natural science, while the first president of King's hoped his students would learn about surveying, husbandry, meteors, and stones.[23] But by the time Morris arrived at each school, the curriculum had shifted back to the standard channels of the classics. Morris would have been a freak among his peers if he had not learned his Caesar and Cicero, his Homer and Xenophon. Perhaps the merrily stoical Horace helped shape his worldview.[24] The exposure to Greek and Latin, on top of his youthful French, surely developed his skill with languages. All his life he would amuse his friends by dashing off tripping little poems; when he acquired French and German friends, he would amuse them with poems in their own tongues. His other skill, which shone in his student days, was mathematics; his first biographer wrote that he used to "amuse himself with rapid calculations in his mind."[25] For the rest, Morris and his classmates tormented the teachers who could not command their respect, throwing books at the head of the Latin master at the Academy, and slandering the morals of the mathematics and natural sciences professor at King's.

*I*N AUGUST 1766, when Morris was fourteen, his hurry through the scenes of childhood was rudely interrupted. While he was home from King's, he accidentally upset a kettle of boiling water on his right arm and side. "You have doubtless heard," wrote one family friend to another, "of the melancholy accident that befell Master Gouverneur last Sunday. I set up with him last night. He rested much better than he had done before . . . though his arm seemed too free from pain for so great a wound, which you know is the first symptom of a mortification."[26] Another friend who had been with him when the accident occurred remembered that he "had borne the torture with a fortitude that would have done honor to an Indian brave."[27] So severe was the burn that his nerves had probably been damaged; years later, William Pierce, a fellow delegate to the Constitutional Convention, would describe Morris's right arm as having "all the flesh taken off."[28] If the wound had become gangrenous, as the family friend feared, then the arm would have had to be amputated. But eight days after that worried letter, the same correspondent added, as a postscript to another note, that "Gouverneur is like to do well."[29]

As an adult, Morris was a man of imposing physical stature, standing over six feet tall. He was also active. He had rambled through the fields and woods of Morrisania as a boy; as a man, he paddled through the swamps of upstate New York and shot the rapids of the St. Lawrence. Here, at the threshold of his manhood, was a disfigurement. Did it keep him out of the army? One half brother was already a British officer, and his other two would serve as generals in the American militia. His nephews, the sons of Lewis Morris, also served in the American army and navy. Gouverneur Morris himself responded imaginatively to things military all his life, drawing up plans of campaign for wars on two continents, and employing military images in his workaday prose (George Washington, the greatest American commander of the age, hardly ever used them). Yet Morris never wore a uniform, nor fought in battle. Neither, of course, did many other civilians, well launched in their careers. Did Morris, given his wound and his proclivities, feel a lack?

Morris's injury did not diminish his attractiveness to women. He rarely paid for sex; "I like only the yielding kiss," he wrote, "and that from lips I love."[30] His lovers were intelligent, appealing, and enthusiastic. Darkness and the elaborate outfits of the eighteenth century could conceal much. What did his women friends think of his arm? Surely they felt it. Did he allow them to see it?

These questions are unanswerable, for Morris matched the fortitude of an Indian brave with a brave's silence. In his case, silence was supported by his own particular equanimity. All his life he would face bad things—and he faced an unusual number—with buoyancy and even-heartedness; this was the first instance.

Gouverneur took more than a year off from King's College to recuperate, but his mind was so quick that once he returned he made up for lost time and graduated with his class in 1768. He gave the commencement address, on the theme of "Wit and Beauty." The sixteen-year-old made an interesting variation on the social contract theories of Hugo Grotius and Samuel Pufendorf, the political philosophers of natural law that students at King's read. "Philosophers who find themselves already living in society say that mankind first entered into it from a sense of their mutual wants." But Morris was skeptical of this calculating rationalism; ". . . the passions of barbarians must have had too great an influence on their understandings" for them "to commence this arduous task." Before men could live together, their passions had to be tamed by another passion—the lure of beauty. "Reason unassisted by Beauty would never have smoothed away" man's primordial "ferocity."[31] Without reading too much into a youthful performance, we can credit Morris with having experienced something ferocious, and with finding the means within his temperament to smooth it.

Part 1

The American Revolution

CHAPTER TWO

War Comes

AFTER GRADUATING from King's, Gouverneur followed his father, grandfather, and half brother Richard in becoming a lawyer, apprenticing himself as a clerk to William Smith, Jr., who lived at the southern end of Broadway in New York City.

The city then clung to the southern tip of Manhattan island. At the tip of the tip stood a large fort, Fort St. George, containing the governor's house. The built-up waterfront lay along the East River where, behind a comb of piers and slips, the houses extended for more than a mile. On the North (or Hudson) River side of the island, the city still showed gaps and green spaces. A 1771 census counted a population of 21,835, less than the population of present-day Poughkeepsie; one sixth of them were slaves. Beyond the city limits lay a pleasant landscape, sometimes rolling, sometimes steeply hilly, of woods, farms, and salt marshes.

Dutch ways still persisted in Brooklyn, Flatbush, and other villages of Long Island; on Manhattan, the northbound Post Road passed the estates of the Stuyvesants, descendants of the last Dutch governor. But the merchants, artisans, sailors, and soldiers of New York were English, by birth or assimilation; all their quarrels (and there were many) were internecine. Peter Van Schaak, a friend of Morris's from King's College who also clerked for Smith, would say, when he had acquired experience of English life, that the manners of New York were those of a provincial English town.

Like any other aspiring lawyer of his day, Morris spent the years of his clerkship drudging in the thickets of English common law, which seemed all but pathless. Smith prepared a study guide for his clerks, but it barely organized the confusion. "[H]ow many hours have I hunted," wrote Van Schaak, "how many books have I turned up for what three minutes' explanation from any tolerable lawyer would have made evident to me!"[1] In October 1771, at the age of nineteen, Morris was sworn in as a lawyer, after which his new colleagues drank his health at Fraunces Tavern.

Morris's mind, versatile and quick, which handled numbers and words with equal ease, took to the law as well, and he made a good start in his profession. His manner must have strengthened his arguments: his voice was strong and rich, and the same man who found him smarter than his siblings also called him "witty, genteel, polite, [and] sensible."[2] On occasion he earned fees of £200 and £300 ($9,000 and $13,500); his mother and his half brother Lewis, the manor lord, gave him their business. He was invited to join the Moot, a lawyers' club which took its name from a legal debating society at London's Inns of Court, and which brought together all the ornaments of the small world of the New York bar. His mentor, Smith, and his half brother Richard (who had succeeded their father as Judge of Admiralty Court) were members. So were several representatives of the large, rich, and politically prominent Livingston family. The family motto was *Si je puis* (If I can), and Livingstons had been doing all they could for themselves in New York since the 1670s, when the first of them to settle in the New World had married a Van Rensselaer.

Robert R. Livingston (the R. stood for a second "Robert," to distinguish him from other Robert Livingstons in different branches of the family) became Gouverneur Morris's lifelong friend. He had grown up at Clermont, a Hudson Valley estate that, even though it was not a manor, was far grander than Morrisania. Tall and easygoing, Robert had intelligence, talents, and energy enough to impress the world, without overshadowing his main claim on its attention, which was that he was a Livingston. Besides Gouverneur Morris and Livingston, the junior members of the Moot included Peter Van Schaak, a sweet-natured young man from Kinderhook whom William Smith called "the first genius of all the young fellows,"[3] and John Jay, Robert Livingston's law partner. Jay, a native New Yorker, was the son of a rich merchant who was one of the owners of the public bowling green opposite the fort. When Jay was six, his father noted that "Johnny is of a very grave disposition and takes to learning exceedingly well."[4] All his life he would be proud, serious, and brilliant. Outside the Moot, Morris, Livingston, Jay, Van Schaak, and other young men also formed a Social Club, spending their Saturday nights at Fraunces Tavern, which served the public, then as now, at the corner of Broad and Pearl streets.

As soon as Morris had a foothold in this New York world, he thought of leaving it. All his life he would be accused of fickleness. Perhaps the hurry of his childhood set the pattern of changeability. In his youth he shuttled from Morrisania to New Rochelle to Philadelphia to New York. Now he proposed to spend a year in London, and two months after his twentieth birthday, he wrote William Smith a letter, both charming and revealing, asking his advice.

"The advantages I expect" from a year abroad, he wrote, "are shortly these. I hope to form some acquaintances, that may hereafter be of service to me; to model myself after some persons who cut a figure in the profession of the law; to form my manners and address after the example of the truly polite; to rub off in the gay circle a few of those many barbarisms which characterize a provincial education; and to curb that vain self sufficiency which arises from comparing ourselves with companions who are inferior to us." Morris's breezy explanation of the source of his vanity suggests that he would have trouble curbing it.

"There are many dangers," he admits, "which it is alleged attend a young man thrown from under his parents' wings upon the gay stage of pleasure and dissipation, where a wanton circle of delusive joys courts his acquaintance, and an endless variety of objects prevents satiety and removes disgust." This warning against the snares of London life sounds more like an advertisement: *dangers* and *delusive* hardly balance *pleasure, joys,* and *endless variety.* Morris then confesses that he has "naturally a taste for pleasure," but argues that his good taste will steer him away from "low pleasures." He concludes with a plea cast as an assertion: "I still have some time left before I tread the great stage of life."[5]

Smith wrote his protégé a good-humored but serious reply, based on family history. "Remember your uncle Robin [Robert Hunter Morris]. He saw England thrice. No man had better advantages, either from nature or education. He began with a figure of 30,000 pounds [over a million dollars]. He did not leave 5000 pounds. I know others that never saw the east side of the great lake, who had no other friends than their own heads and their own hands, to whom your uncle was in bonds. What! *Virtus post nummos?* [a line from Horace—Virtue after money] . . . Spare your indignation. I too detest the ignorant miser. But both virtue and ambition abhor poverty, or they are mad."[6] Morris should stay home, with his nose to the grindstone.

Morris took this good advice, perhaps because, mindful of his circumstances as Smith was, he already believed it. He would spend most of the next two decades working, until he had made for himself the fortune that his father and his uncle had enjoyed.

But he did not postpone his pursuit of pleasure, even if he postponed his travel plans. Older men were not the only people who found him witty and genteel. Morris befriended the daughters of William Livingston, a politician, member of the Moot, and cousin of Robert, who moved his base of operations in 1770 across the harbor to Elizabethtown, New Jersey. Everyone loved the lovely Livingston girls. Morris wrote a vignette of seventeen-year-old Sally Livingston holding court: one admirer sitting "sidelong on his chair with melancholic and despondent phiz prolongated unto the seventh button of his waistcoat . . . another with his elbows fastened to his short ribs . . . in the midst of all this sits Miss with seeming unconsciousness of the whole. . . . The rosy fingers of pleasure paint her cheeks."[7] John Jay was the lucky suitor who won her. Alexander Hamilton, a poor but promising West Indian sent by island patrons to King's College in 1773, courted Kitty Livingston, writing to her about the "roseate bowers of Cupid" and the "complex, intricate and enigmatical" nature of woman.[8] Morris had discovered Kitty first. He sent her poems: "Ease at length my troubled breast/ Sweet tormentor now be kind." He told her "how uncomfortable" his "hopeless passion" was.[9] When she did not reciprocate, he admitted that "I am (as you know) constitutionally one of the happiest of men." Gouverneur's cousin, Robert Morris, son of his improvident uncle, rallied him on his taste for "youth, beauty, claret wine and company."[10] This was gentle enough teasing, but if there was also a note of envy of Gouverneur's capacity for enjoyment, it would not be the last to come his way. Gouverneur's final attitude toward his lost Miss Livingston was gracious. "A heart like yours deserves to be happy, and depend upon it, it will be so."[11]

One distraction Morris did not yet allow himself was politics. The politics of the city and the colony revolved, as it had for decades, around the rivalries of powerful families, and old allies and enemies of the Morrises still set the agenda. When Governor Cosby had removed Gouverneur's grandfather Lewis from the Supreme Court bench, the man he replaced him with was James DeLancey, the son of a Huguenot merchant. Thirty-five years later, the DeLanceys still ran one faction. Their opponents were led by Gouverneur's acquaintances, the Livingstons and William Smith, Jr. These two elite parties had divergent interests: the DeLanceys represented merchants, and the Anglican Church (they had supported the creation of the Anglican King's College). Smith and the Livingstons spoke for the great landowners, and for other Protestants (hence their nickname, the Presbyterian Party). Since the Stamp Act of 1765—London's failed attempt to raise money from its North American colonies by taxing legal documents—New York had also a party of radical Liberty Boys, sailors, artisans, and nouveaux merchants, who set themselves up as champions of colonial rights and who threw their weight to whichever of the established factions most courted them. Each group advanced its cause by the traditional means of New York politics—parades, newspapers, slander, and fists. "We have by far the best part of the bruisers on our side," said one of the Livingston faction during a rough Assembly election.[12] This rowdy and comfortable system was part of Morris's legacy, an item in his inheritance like eccentricity or his father's shaving bowl; for that reason, perhaps, he could take it for granted. "Politics I dislike, and only look on with pity," he wrote in January 1774, "exclaiming with Hamlet, 'What's Hecuba to him, or he to Hecuba?'"[13]

Only four months later, the world of New York politics was repolarized. A tea tax, as hateful as the Stamp Act, had provoked the Liberty Boys of Boston to dump a shipment in the harbor. As punishment, in April 1774 Britain closed the port of Boston, and sent a military governor at the head of four regiments to rule. When word reached New York early in May, meetings were held to elect a committee of protest and response. Morris attended one of them, at Fraunces Tavern, and looked on with interest.

"I stood in the balcony," Morris wrote a friend, "and on my right hand were ranged all the people of property, with some few poor dependants, and on the other all the tradesmen . . . who thought it worth their while to leave daily labor for the good of the country." These were the familiar parties in New York politics: Livingstonites and DeLancey men (people of property), Liberty Boys (tradesmen). But their old system was cracking up. "The mob begin to think and to reason. Poor reptiles! It is with them a vernal morning, they are struggling to cast off their winter's slough [or skin], they bask in the sunshine, and ere noon they will bite, depend upon it. The gentry begin to fear this." So did Morris. "I see, and I see it with fear and trembling, that if the disputes with Britain continue, we shall be under the worst of all possible dominions"—that of "a riotous mob."[14]

Morris wrote with the sharp conservatism of the young, if they are conservative at all. In the eighteenth century, "mob" (short for *mobile vulgus,* the fickle crowd) was a new word, meaning both an unruly crowd, in the modern sense, and the common people as a whole. A riotous mob, to Morris's mind, was simply a calamity, deserving neither respect nor efforts to understand its motives. A peaceful mob—the ordinary populace in its daily life—could never govern, since it was always manipulated by its betters, or at least by those who were more cunning. In the same letter, Morris switched metaphors from reptiles to sheep. "The bellwethers"—belled male sheep that lead a flock—"jingled merrily, and roared out liberty, and property, and religion, and a multitude of cant terms, which everyone thought he understood, and was egregiously mistaken. For you must know the shepherds kept the dictionary of the day, and like the mysteries of the ancient mythology, it was not for profane eyes or ears . . . the simple flock put them-

selves entirely under the protection of these most excellent shepherds."[15] Morris at age twenty-two was not a democrat, nor would he
ever become one.

But Morris did believe in rights. He believed in his own rights, because he was an aristocrat, whose family had wielded power for seventy years; and because he was consistent and fair-minded, he believed
in extending his own rights to others. His grandfather Lewis Morris
had used John Peter Zenger as a journalistic bruiser, and Zenger's trial
as a piece of political theater. But Gouverneur Morris viewed the
Zenger case innocently, as a defense of a free press; in one of those
beautiful phrases that he regularly produced, he called Zenger's ac-
quittal "the morning star" of "liberty" in America.[16]

In the present situation, Morris wrote, political necessity seemed to
call for a compromise: the colonies should tax themselves and provide
for their own defense, while England, the imperial center, should reg-
ulate trade. Its greed would be tempered by prudence. Will England
try to "draw all the profits of our trade into her coffers[?] All that she
can undoubtedly. But unless a reasonable compensation for his trouble
be left to the merchant here, she destroys the trade, and then she will
not profit from it."[17]

The May meetings in New York City elected a Committee of Fifty-
One, which included Jay and Van Schaak, and which encouraged the
formation of similar committees elsewhere in New York. In September, in response to a call from Massachusetts, committees throughout
the colonies sent delegations to Philadelphia to discuss their griev-
ances. Jay went as a delegate from New York, William Livingston as a
delegate from New Jersey. The Continental Congress agreed to an
embargo on trade with the mother country, to be enforced by a Continental Association, and narrowly defeated a proposal to reform the
empire by establishing an American house of Parliament.

The firebrands in Philadelphia, for embargo and against compromise, had come from Massachusetts and Virginia. Massachusetts was
suffering, and its history of religious dissent made all but employees of
the crown susceptible to radical arguments. The gentry of Virginia,
who were as grand as any Hudson Valley landowner, instead of fearing

the common people like Morris, identified themselves with them; they could afford to do so, since the "reptiles" in their colony were black slaves, who would never slough off their skins. The New York delegates had supported both the aggressive embargo and the failed political compromise—a seemingly moderate position that disguised sharp political divisions at home. Most of the farmers in lower New York were deeply suspicious of the embargo, as an attempt by local merchants to gouge them. Samuel Seabury, an Anglican clergyman in Westchester County, played on their fears in a pamphlet attacking the Continental Association as a "venomous brood of scorpions." He was answered by a young member of the emerging patriotic party, Alexander Hamilton, the immigrant at King's College. "The sacred rights of mankind . . . are written, as with a sunbeam, in the whole volume of human nature, by the hand of the Divinity itself. . . ."[18] But the patriots, strongest in New York City, were themselves divided between those who thought that their sacred rights could be secured by reform and those (still only a handful) who wanted more drastic measures.

Before it adjourned in October 1774, the Continental Congress had called for another session to meet in Philadelphia the following May. The new meeting was preceded by a bloody crisis. British troops, searching the countryside around Boston for illegal stores of weapons, had fired on local militia at Lexington and Concord. The news reached New York at the end of April 1775. "It is impossible to describe the state of the town," wrote Morris's mentor, William Smith, Jr. ". . . Tales of all kinds invented, believed, denied, discredited. . . . The taverns filled with publicans at night. Little business done in the day. . . ."[19]

The divisions in New York ran through Morris's family. Lewis the manor lord sided with the patriots. Richard resigned his judgeship rather than continue to serve under the British, though he would not yet actively join the patriotic side. Staats Long, who had moved to England and married the Duchess of Gordon, was by this time the colonel of a regiment in the British army; when hostilities broke out, he offered to resign, but the War Office assigned him to garrison Minorca in the Mediterranean, so that he would not be forced to fight on his native soil.

Two of Morris's Gouverneur uncles, both West Indies merchants, sent cannon to the patriots from their storehouse on Curacao. But Sarah Gouverneur Morris was loyal to the king, and remained so throughout the war. Of Morris's married sisters, Euphemia had a loyalist father-in-law; Catherine and Isabella had loyalist husbands. Isaac Wilkins, Isabella's husband, had a run-in with Lewis Morris, his patriot brother-in-law. Wilkins sat for Westchester County in the New York Assembly, where he and other loyalists blocked the sending of any delegates to the Second Continental Congress. The cause of protest and reform was thus left to committees that were outside the law. When a meeting was called in April at the courthouse in White Plains to select delegates for a "Provincial Congress," Wilkins and a handful of loyalists, including Samuel Seabury, marched in from the pub where they had been caucusing to protest the "disorderly proceedings" and sang a chorus of "God Save the King." Wilkins would pay for this gallant demonstration; patriotic marauders, called "cowboys," would drive him out of his house, and force Isabella to live at Morrisania with her mother. Once the loyalists had left the meeting in White Plains, Lewis Morris and the patriots who remained elected a slate of delegates to the Provincial Congress, including Gouverneur Morris. He had cast his lot with his half-brother and the most clamorous traditions of his forefathers, and against his mother and his sisters.

New York's first Provincial Congress met at City Hall, on Wall Street at the head of Broad Street, in May 1775. The twenty-three-year-old Morris impressed the older delegates. One called him a "fine young fellow," who "cuts a figure."[20] Another said that he understood knotty issues "as it were by intuition."[21] The Provincial Congress nominated delegates to the Second Continental Congress (Jay, Robert R. Livingston, and Lewis Morris were among those picked); it also took on itself the responsibility of governing New York. Troops had to be raised; money had to be issued; loyalists had to be dealt with. There were also the British, who still occupied Fort St. George at the tip of Manhattan.

One irksome loyalist was James Rivington, a printer with a shop on Hanover Square. Rivington published a newspaper, the *New York*

Gazetteer, and a good deal of loyalist propaganda, though he had also printed Alexander Hamilton's replies to Samuel Seabury. In May a patriot mob threatened him, after which he signed a loyalty oath to the patriot cause.

Morris urged that the "unfortunate printer" be treated charitably. "Magnanimity," he wrote one patriot, "will dictate . . . the true line of conduct." "Not one month ago," he reminded another, patriotism "was branded with infamy. Now each person strives to show the excess of his zeal by the madness of his actions." He ended this letter with a credo: "I plead the cause of humanity to a gentleman." Gentlemen should settle public affairs, and they should settle them humanely.[22]

Roman Catholics were as unpopular in New York as reckless printers. Catholics had been falsely accused of fomenting a slave revolt in the 1740s, and they were still the only sect forbidden to have clergymen or a place of worship in the city. More recently, Britain's policy of supporting Catholicism in its Canadian dominions had alarmed Protestants throughout the Thirteen Colonies, and the Provincial Congress condemned the "establishment of Popery along the interior confines of the old Protestant Colonies." Morris did not share his colleagues' fear. "That foolish religious business," he wrote of the no-Popery declaration, ". . . would do as well in a high Dutch Bible as the place it now stands in."[23] Religious polemics belonged in the pulpit not the legislature.

Morris's humanity struck some patriots as craven. In June 1775, the British pulled their last troops in New York City—one hundred men of the Royal Irish Regiment—out of the fort, intending to place them aboard the *Asia,* a 64-gun warship moored in the harbor. The Provincial Congress had agreed to let the soldiers go peacefully, but a party of Liberty Boys stopped them at Broad Street and seized five wagons of weapons. Morris, who happened to be passing by, tried to prevent the seizure. "To be opposed by Mr. Morris staggered me," wrote one patriot.[24] Staggered or not, the patriots kept the arms, though the Provincial Congress, at Morris's urging, eventually returned them to the enemy.

New York was in a revolution, but the goals and the battlelines were not yet clear. The patriots had set up parallel institutions: they were waging economic warfare on England, and preparing to wage actual warfare. But independence had not yet been declared; George III was still their sovereign, and a gilded statue of him stood on the bowling green. (The more prudent patriots also didn't want the city bombarded and burned by the *Asia*'s guns.) Morris felt he was in the midst of an "unnatural quarrel between the Parent and the Child," and still hoped there might be a reconciliation. But he knew that if hope failed, there must be "an appeal to the God of Battles."[25]

This deity did not smile on him. In the fall of 1775 New York sent an army to invade Canada, hoping to deprive the British of a potential base. Morris was not pleased by the quality of it—"for the most part the soldiers from this town [are] not the cream of the earth but the scum."[26] In November, the Provincial Congress, plagued by bad attendance—the population of the city itself was plummeting as loyalists fled—called for new elections. Morris was not returned; the new Westchester delegation included four officers. When the Canadian invasion ended bravely but disastrously in a blizzard under the walls of Quebec, New York prepared for the British counterstroke. In February 1776, Morris applied to be the colonel of a newly raised regiment. This was the only time he would volunteer for military service, and he was not accepted. The position went instead to a militiaman who was a shoemaker in private life, and Morris refused to serve as lieutenant colonel under him. The letter he sent his half brother Lewis is a combination of pique, self-knowledge, and regret: ". . . a herd of mechanicks are preferred before the best families in the colony . . . my little abilities [are] more adapted to the deliberations of the cabinet than the glorious labours of the field."[27]

Morris was reelected to the Provincial Congress—New York's third—in May 1776. He arrived late for his duties, having had to console his sister Catherine, whose husband had been jailed for loyalism. Late though he was, Morris got one of the most fortunate assignments of his life: he was named to a secret committee to deal with George Washington.

Washington had been named commander in chief of the Continental Army the previous June, and sent to besiege the British in Boston. Thanks to his artillery dispositions, the British had evacuated Boston in March 1776. They were sure to strike again, however, and New York was a likely target. Washington and eight thousand men had arrived to defend the city in April.

Unlike most Americans, Gouverneur Morris would not have been impressed merely by Washington's height: they were the same size. Morris had a far better education—Washington's consisted of some tutoring and some country schooling—and a quicker tongue and pen. The Morrises were a more impressive family; several Washingtons, including George, had served in the Virginia House of Burgesses, but none of them had been appointed to the Governor's Council, the true mark of the elite in Virginia; none of them had been governors. But Washington was the one man in his life that Morris never failed to respect. Washington was twenty years older than Morris—just close enough for the outer edges of friendship, well within the normal range of paternity (Morris's own father had been fifty-four years older than his youngest son, almost a grandfather). When Morris met him, the commander in chief was forty-four—an incarnation of principle, firmness, and manly power.

What did Washington see in Morris? The most famous story about the two of them also involves Alexander Hamilton, who would enter their lives later. According to the story, Hamilton bet Morris a dinner that he would not go up to Washington, slap him on the back, and say, "My dear general, how happy I am to see you look so well." [28] Morris slapped the General and won his bet, but reported that the look of reproof he got was the worst moment in his life. The founding father rebuked two founding youths. There are problems with this story: when it first appears, it is already in two versions, occurring at different times. There is also a third story of Morris slapping another officer, Baron von Steuben. The protean story took hold because people thought that Morris, proud and pert, might do such a thing. Maybe Morris never did. But surely one of the reasons Washington enjoyed the younger man's company (in addition to his devotion) is that Morris had these relaxed and confident qualities.

One of Morris's assignments in June 1776 was to hear evidence of a plot on Washington's life. New York loyalists, expecting a British attack, were supposed to have planned an uprising. Thomas Hickey, a member of Washington's military bodyguard, was to have killed him with a poisoned dish of peas. Hickey was hanged in a field near the Bowery, before a huge crowd. The exposure of the plot was a signal for a general roundup. One loyalist wrote that his fellows "were pursued like wolves and bears, from swamp to swamp, from one hill to another . . . numbers were taken, some were wounded, and a few murdered."[29] Other suspected loyalists were listed for further investigation.

Morris, who sat on a committee of inquiry with John Jay, found that one of the suspects whose name came before him was his half brother Richard. Richard Morris pledged to support the Provincial Congress, and thereby became patriotic enough. Yet another suspect was William Smith, Jr.

Late in June, Morris signed a summons to his mentor, directing him to appear before the committee and show "why you should be considered as a friend to the American cause." Smith's reply was addressed to "Gouverneur Morris, one of the Committee & formerly a clerk in my office." He explained that while he was a friend to American "rights and liberties," he considered "the two countries"—America and Britain—to be linked "under a great covenant." Morris wrote back, appealing to Smith's desire for future "offices and honors"; appealing to his idealism (a "sweet consciousness of integrity . . . warms the bosom of that man who risks all for the benefit of mankind"); appealing most of all to the fact that "the ties between Britain & America are haggled away by the sword of war."[30] Morris's mentor was not persuaded. He stayed loyal to the crown, eventually becoming Chief Justice of Quebec.

Time and experience had pushed Morris over the line of independence. "It already exists in everything but in name," he told the Provincial Congress in an oration of which only fragments survive. "Coining money, raising armies, regulating commerce, peace, war, all these things you are not only adepts in, but masters of . . . I see no reason why Congress is not full as good a word as . . . Parliament, and it is a mighty easy matter to please people, when a single word will effect it."[31] This was the voice of Morris the realist. But his imagination had also been stirred.

> By means of that great gulph which rolls its waves between Europe
> and America ... by the productions of our soil, which the Almighty
> has filled with every necessary to make us a great maritime people,
> by the extent of our coasts and those great rivers which serve at once
> to open a communication with our interior country, and teach us the
> arts of navigation ... finally by the unconquerable spirit of freemen,
> deeply interested in the preservation of a government which secures
> to them the blessings of liberty and exalts the dignity of mankind;
> by all these I expect a full and lasting defense against any and every
> part of the earth.[32]

Many patriots spoke in this exalted strain; Washington habitually referred to America as a "rising empire." But Morris had distinguished himself in his young career as witty, cynical, and hardheaded. He was all these things; yet there were also romantic chords in his nature which vibrated powerfully when struck.

Washington and the Americans were not masters of war yet. On July 9, the Declaration of Independence, passed by the Continental Congress in Philadelphia, was read in New York. (Robert R. Livingston had been on the drafting committee, though he had done none of the work.) Three days later, General Sir William Howe and Admiral Lord Richard Howe sailed through the Narrows between Staten and Long Island and into the inner harbor with hundreds of ships and 32,000 men. Washington's forces by this time had risen to 19,000 men, but they were almost all raw militia; the Howe brothers' troops were British and Hessian professionals. The battles of the Duke of Marlborough and Louis XIV in Europe, where troops could be more easily provisioned, had involved masses of men three or four times as large; but Britain had never assembled a sea-land operation as great. The Provincial Congress had already adjourned, and reconvened (as the Fourth Provincial Congress) in White Plains. In late August, the British began to drive the Americans from the New York area like deer. One quarter of the captured city burned, in a fire set by accident or patriotic arson; grateful loyalists were happy to return even to the ruins.

The Fourth Provincial Congress fled yet again, to the Dutch Reformed Church in the village of Fishkill, fifty miles north of the city on the eastern side of the Hudson. For three months, from early September to early December, Morris was truant, staying with his sister Euphemia and her husband in northern New Jersey. "A series of accidents too trifling for recital have prevented me the pleasure of attending," was the only explanation he offered his colleagues.[33] They were not pleased. Robert R. Livingston wrote that Morris was enjoying "his jest and his ease while his friends are struggling with every difficulty and danger. . . ."[34] In truth, the Provincial Congress was not struggling too hard; absenteeism deprived it of quorums more often than not. Considering the troubles that had befallen his family, Morris may have felt entitled to spend some time with them.

Morris resumed his duties in Fishkill early in December 1776; shortly thereafter he learned that his sister Catherine had died at Morrisania. Now it was his family that felt abandoned. He wrote his mother, who was behind enemy lines—she thought them friendly lines—a letter gravely balancing private and public.

"There is one comforter, who weighs our minutes, and numbers out our days. It is He, who has inflicted upon us the weight of public and private calamities, and He best knows when to remove the burthen. I am sorry it is not in my power to see you at present. I know it is your wish that I were removed from public affairs. . . . But I know it is the duty of every good citizen or man to preserve that post, in which by a superior order he is placed." The distinction between *good citizen* and *(good) man*, so lightly made, deserves comment. Morris believed that each had a duty to serve, but in distinguishing between them, however passingly, he refused to let all of the obligations of manhood be swallowed by those of citizenship.

"What may be the event of the present war, it is not in man to determine. Great revolutions of empire are seldom achieved without much human calamity; but the worst which can happen [to a patriot] is to fall on the last bleak mountain of America, and he who dies there, in defence of the injured rights of mankind, is happier than his conqueror, more beloved by mankind, more applauded by his own heart." The imperial vision of his oration in the Provincial Congress had become a desolate image of failure; even so, it was lit by his ideals.

"My love to my sisters, to Wilkins, whose integrity I love and respect [this, of his loyalist brother-in-law] . . . and such others as deserve it. The number is not great." Wit returned in the end.[35]

CHAPTER THREE

The Young Men's Constitution

A FTER HIS DEFEATS in New York in the summer and fall of 1776, George Washington stabilized the patriot cause with winter victories in New Jersey. But the British controlled the mouth of the Hudson, and Westchester County was a lawless no-man's-land. The Provincial Congress decided in February 1777 to move twenty-five miles further north, and across the river, to Kingston. The town of Kingston sat on a bluff, with the blue Kaatskil Mountains in the background, in the remote, still-Dutch heartland of upper New York. The legislators met in a stone building that was already one hundred years old, with a prison in the basement. It stank so that Morris asked if lawmakers could smoke, to drive out the "disagreeable effluvia."[1]

The Fourth Provincial Congress had been empowered by the voters of New York to act as a Convention for writing and ratifying a state constitution, though a lack of quorums had prevented it from accomplishing anything as yet. In Kingston, John Jay was asked to prepare a draft, which he presented to the body in March, and Morris was to acquire his first experience of constitution making.

Many of the prime movers in the Convention were young men: Jay was thirty-one; Robert R. Livingston, returned from the Continental Congress, was thirty; Morris was only twenty-five. But they were intelligent and, for all their youth, politically experienced; the stress of war had given them confidence. As friends, King's graduates, and veterans of the Moot, Jay, Livingston, and Morris had been associated for years; they disagreed with the freedom of old colleagues. They complained to and about each other because they were so used to each other. Jay and Livingston clucked so over Morris's absences because they counted on his contributions.

By venturing a revolution, Americans had swept their institutions aside and were in a position to start afresh—to consult first principles, as the eighteenth century put it. In fact, the example of the British system, and the authority of its most fashionable commentators, predisposed them to a tripartite structure of a governor, a two-house legislature, and a judiciary (Pennsylvania would experiment with a one-house legislature and no governor). But the work of any constitution was in the details.

Morris's relatives had been powerful colonial governors (they fought to limit only the power of governors they disliked), and Morris favored a strong executive. He proposed that the governor be able to veto legislation, and appoint state officials, but his colleagues were more cautious. Robert R. Livingston successfully argued that the veto rest with a Council of Revision, consisting of the governor, the members of the Supreme Court, and the chancellor, or chief judge of the court of equity. A similar dispute arose over the power of appointment: after a day of debating the appointment power, Jay and Morris met with Livingston in his room and agreed to a Council of Appointment, made up of four state senators, with the governor acting only as a tie-breaker. The first compromise enmeshed the governor with the judiciary, and the second bound him to the legislature. The members of the Convention had all the Morrises' bad memories of bad governors, without their experience of being good ones.

Morris fought unsuccessfully to keep voice-voting, instead of the secret ballot proposed by Jay. He succeeded with a proposal to require voters in assembly elections to own property worth £20, or $780. Morris wanted voters to declare a public choice, with all the pressures that entailed, and he wanted them to be men of some means, able to withstand pressure. His distrust of the reptiles had not diminished since 1774.

Neither had his support for rights. Morris fought a series of battles with Jay over the political status of Roman Catholics. Both men had Huguenot ancestors, but Jay's had been driven out of France more recently. His grandfather had fled a wave of Catholic oppression just ninety years ago, which was ninety years after the Gouverneurs moved to Holland; his ancestry was not a family linguistic tradition, but a living wound. In the *Federalist Papers,* Jay would boast that Americans were a "united people . . . professing one religion," by which he meant Protestantism, not Christianity.[2] In Kingston, he vowed "to erect a wall of brass around the country for the exclusion of Catholics."[3] His draft constitution granted "the free exercise of religious profession and worship . . . to all mankind." But on the floor of the Convention, he moved that Catholics be forbidden to own land or vote until they swore before the state Supreme Court that "no pope, priest, or foreign authority on earth" could absolve them of allegiance to the laws. This motion failed.

The next day, Jay offered a milder one, providing that liberty of conscience "shall not be construed to encourage licentiousness, nor be used in such a manner as to disturb or endanger the safety of the state." This passed; who could be in favor of endangering the safety of the state? Morris, however, offered and carried a small but significant amendment: that liberty of conscience not be construed so "as to excuse *acts* of licentiousness or justify *practices* inconsistent with the peace or safety of the state" (italics added).[4] Jay's motion could have been used to prosecute beliefs; Morris wished to be guarded only against bad actions.

Morris had no sympathy with Catholicism. His religious feelings, though earnest, were thoroughly deist: his God was all-powerful, beneficent, and otherwise unknowable. When Morris met large numbers of Catholics in Europe, he found the clergy corrupt—"The Cardinal is very devout," he wrote of one cleric. "He was once the lover of Madame's sister"[5]—the laymen superstitious and stupid, and their beliefs "absurd," "degrading to the Omnipotent, if indeed it were possible for men to honor or dishonor Him."[6] But he would let Catholics worship in New York as they wished. "It was always my opinion," he wrote Peter Van Schaak the following year, "that matters of conscience and faith, whether political or religious, are as much out of the province, as they are beyond the ken of human legislatures."[7]

Another contest of rights in Kingston joined Morris and Jay. Morris moved that the new constitution should urge "future legislatures" to abolish slavery, "so that in future ages, every human being who breathes the air of this state, shall enjoy the privileges of a freeman. . . . [T]he rights of human nature and the principles of our holy religion loudly call upon us to dispense the blessings of freedom to all mankind."[8] Slaves had worked at Morrisania for generations. New York was doubly bound to slavery: it had one of the largest slave populations of any northern state, and its colonial economy rested on a symbiotic relationship with the sugar islands of the Caribbean—the rich of New York City refined the sugar that West Indies slaves harvested, while the small farmers in the rural counties used their own slaves to grow produce for the sugar islands. Morris and Jay wanted to wean New York from this pernicious dependence, but New York was not ready to be weaned. Morris's motion failed, by a vote of thirty-one to five. Other northern states, notably Massachusetts and Pennsylvania, less attached to trade with the islands, soon abolished slavery; New York would not begin to follow them until 1799. Morris and Jay, themselves children of slave owners, were indignant. Until America accepted gradual abolition, Jay wrote, "her prayers to heaven for liberty will be impious."[9]

The first constitution Morris had a hand in writing was ratified on April 21. No one was entirely happy with it, but everyone knew that no one ever is. Jay, who had been called from Kingston by news of the death of his mother, wrote Morris and Livingston that, though "the birth" was "premature," since he didn't approve of the Spartan practice of destroying defective infants, "I shall nevertheless do all in my power to nurse and keep it alive."[10] "That there are faults in it is not to be wondered at," wrote Morris, "for it is the work of men perhaps not the best qualified for such undertakings." Morris, who did not commonly criticize himself, must have had his fellow delegates in mind. "God grant that it may work well for we must live under it."[11]

The three friends from the Moot had done well, pending the fortune of war; the case of another friend, Peter Van Schaak, was different. The political divisions that had sundered Morris's family split Van

Schaak's mind, and were ruining his life. The young lawyer was as shy as he was intelligent. "I never knew a man possessed of his acquirements," wrote one friend, "so modest and unassuming."[12] He had joined the first committees of protest, after the closing of the port of Boston in 1774. But he continued to hope that "some middle way should be found out," and he dreaded civil war—the condition toward which New York was drifting—as "the epitome of human wretchedness."[13] When patriot committees asked him to swear allegiance to the new government, he showed the stubbornness that the shy often have, and refused.

Van Schaek's private life was as battered as his public life. Six of his children died between 1771 and 1775, two of them within two days of each other. In 1776, he lost the sight in his right eye (in search of a middle way he had been reading too much Grotius, Pufendorf, and Locke). Caught in a wretched present, his thoughts turned to the past. "Those happy scenes of our clubs, our moots, our Broadway evenings," he wrote Jay, "fill me with pleasing melancholy reflections."[14] In 1778, Van Schaak's wife died of consumption, and he was banished as a loyalist to England. He took as his motto a line from the *Aeneid*, Virgil's epic of exile, *Susperanda fortuna ferendo* (We master fortune by accepting it).[15]

Morris wrote his old friend as soon as he heard that he was leaving America. "I am particularly afflicted, that you should be now obliged to relinquish your country, for opinions which are unfavorable to her rights." Morris considered the conduct of his fellow revolutionaries. "The infancy of the state must apologize for the defects of its legislature ... Adversity is the great school of moderation. If any of my countrymen are come thence unlearned, I will not blame, though I cannot commend." When they had suffered as much as Van Schaak—or, considering his withered arm, Morris—they might be less rigorous.

In public life, Morris went on, "it shall be my object to narrow as much as possible the circle of private wo." He called up the millennial vision of Revelation 21:4: "I would to God, that every tear could be wiped from every eye." But this was the world: " ... so long as there are men, so long it will and must happen that they will minister to the miseries of each other." He tactfully shared a hope with his suffering friend. "It is a delightful object in history, to see order, and peace, and happiness result from confusion, and war, and distress. It is a pleasing hope in life." And he concluded: "It is your misfortune to be one out of the many who have suffered. In your philosophy, in yourself, in the consciousness of acting as you think right, you are to seek consolation...."[16]

Fighting men often honor the courage of their enemies. In his letter to Van Schaak, Morris did something that may be harder: without abandoning or apologizing for his own principles, he consoled, and admired, a man whose principles were different.

In May 1777, the lawmakers in Kingston chose Morris to be one of New York's delegates to the Continental Congress in Philadelphia. But Morris was too busy to attend, for that summer the war came to the heart of New York.

The inner web of North American lakes and rivers had been noticed by white men as early as Samuel Champlain in the seventeenth century. The Hudson River, Lake George, and Lake Champlain formed an almost complete waterway between New York and Montreal, that looked especially seductive on a map. In the early eighteenth century, French and British armies fought terrific battles over obscure forest outposts that controlled key heights and portages. In these wars of empire France hoped to move south from Canada and split the enemy in two. After the Americans revolted, Britain, which by then owned Canada, hoped to do the same thing. A three-pronged operation was planned for the summer of 1777. Major General John Burgoyne was to march south from Canada, at the head of eight thousand British, Hessians, loyalists, and Indians. Lieutenant Colonel Barrimore St. Leger was to swing from the west, via Lake Ontario, the Oswego River, and the Mohawk Valley. General Sir William Howe was to push north from New York City. If all went well—and none doubted that it would—they would converge on Albany, the old Dutch upcountry hub, destroying the rebellion in New York and splitting New England from the middle states and the South. In the event, General Howe decided that more was to be gained by taking Philadelphia. But he left behind him in New York his second in command,

General Sir Henry Clinton, with seven thousand men and instructions to assist Burgoyne "if circumstances warranted." [17]

The plan had much to recommend it. The Mohawk Valley was sown with loyalist Indians, the fruit of years of cultivation by Sir William Johnson, an Irish adventurer who had an Indian mistress and a country gentleman's house smack in the middle of the wilderness. Burgoyne began well. Setting out from Canada in mid-June 1777, he sailed down Lake Champlain and captured Fort Ticonderoga, the northern key to Lake George, by the bold but simple expedient of hauling artillery to a mountaintop that the Americans wrongly thought was inaccessible. With the fort, the Gibraltar of North America, in his hands, Burgoyne's confidence soared. "None but stupid mortals can dislike a lively camp, good weather, good claret, good musick, and the enemy near," wrote one of his aides. "A little fusillade during dinner does not discompose the nerves of even our ladies." [18] Burgoyne expected to enjoy Christmas dinner in Albany.

Political power in Kingston had passed to an interim group, the Council of Safety, meant to bridge the gap between the Fourth Provincial Congress and the officeholders to be elected under the new Constitution. The Council now sent Morris to Fort Edward, on the southern end of Lake George, to investigate the fall of Fort Ticonderoga. "Having no powers," Morris wrote the Council, "I shall do what I think best." [19]

The American commander at Fort Edward was General Philip Schuyler, a hardheaded Dutch landowner whose estate lay near the village of Saratoga, twenty-five miles north of Albany. As a young man he had fought in several frontier battles against the French. Morris found that he had less than five thousand men, almost half of them militia, and only two old iron field-pieces, and that most of his officers, as Morris wrote the Council of Safety, were not "worth a crown." [20] Morris sized up the situation and proposed radical but hopeful measures. "Break up all the settlements upon our northern frontier . . . drive off the cattle, secure or destroy the forage." The gaps between the lakes and the Hudson River looked small on paper, but the terrain in them was wet, wooded, and steep. "If we lay it down as a maxim, never to contend for ground but in the last necessity, to leave nothing but a wilderness to the enemy, their progress must be impeded by obstacles which it is not in human nature to surmount."[21] This was the strategy that Washington, observing from afar, had hit upon: Burgoyne's success, he wrote Schuyler, "will precipitate his ruin."[22] It was the strategy that Schuyler was in fact following, ordering his men to fell trees, dam streams, and do everything possible to slow Burgoyne's advance.

The Council of Safety, however, wanted information that could prevent the public (and perhaps themselves) from panicking. To civilian eyes, the fall of Fort Ticonderoga was a disaster, and Burgoyne an irresistible force. "We could wish," wrote Jay, "that your letters might contain paragraphs for the public ... the people suspect the worst because we say nothing." Morris replied sharply that he had not known he was to "write the news," whereupon the Council called him home.[23]

The Council had found Morris's letter "disrespectful and unsatisfactory,"[24] but when Morris returned to Kingston at the end of July, he made a report that was vivid and alarming. Whatever Schuyler's strategic possibilities, he was outnumbered by nearly two to one. The loyalist-leaning counties of upstate New York could not send him more militia, while half of the militia he had were New Englanders, who disliked him for a disciplinarian and yearned to serve at home. The only source of reinforcements was the main American army under George Washington, and though a rumor on the Livingston family grapevine described Morris as "hopeless,"[25] the Council sent him and Jay to ask for help.

The commander in chief was marching to Philadelphia, which Howe evidently planned to attack, having sailed from New York with 160 ships and 18,000 men. Washington told the New Yorkers he had no men to spare. They rode on to Philadelphia, where they warned Congress that "the poor remains" of their state "must inevitably fall into the hand of the enemy."[26] Congress directed Washington to send five hundred riflemen to New York, and Morris and Jay returned to Kingston in late August.

Congress had made Schuyler the scapegoat for the fall of Fort

Ticonderoga, and replaced him with General Horatio Gates, a British army veteran with New England friends. Morris was "exceedingly distressed" at the New Yorker's removal, but hoped that the reinforcements would enable Gates "to act with éclat, if he has spirit and understanding sufficient for that purpose."[27] Better than spirit or understanding, Gates had the luck of good timing, for now the British began to suffer reverses, and as Morris, Schuyler, and Washington had predicted, the difficult terrain and their exposed situation made their reverses fatal. St. Leger had already turned back after bloody fighting in the west, and a reconnaissance party of Burgoyne's Hessians and loyalists had been whipped on the Vermont border. Burgoyne himself was moving south through the wilderness at a rate of one mile per day; he had to build forty bridges to cross the aquatic obstacles in his path. Militia flowed in to Gates as the tide turned, and on September 19 and October 6 he and Burgoyne fought two sharp battles near Saratoga.

One hundred fifty miles away, in occupied New York, Sir Henry Clinton finally decided, on October 5, to push north. In three days he cleared all the American positions between him and Albany, and wrote Burgoyne that help was on the way. The message never arrived—the bearer was captured, he swallowed it, and the Americans administered an emetic to retrieve it—but it would have done no good in any case, for Burgoyne's casualties were so heavy and his supplies so low that he had decided to limp back to Canada in retreat.

The government of New York sat in Kingston, like a spider in the center of a web of events, though without a spider's power. Jay had "gone to fetch his wife," Morris wrote Schuyler jauntily. Livingston was "solacing himself with his wife, his farm, and his imagination. Our Senate is doing I know not what. In Assembly we wrangle long to little purpose. . . . I tremble for the consequences, but I smile, and shall continue to do so, if possible."[28] Morris's temperament was tested when it became clear that the British heading up the Hudson from New York were burning patriot dwellings for spite as they went. On October 13, Kingston was evacuated. "The alarm in the town," Morris wrote Livingston, "exhibited more of the drolerie than the pathos of distress. The good dominie [a Dutch Reformed clergyman] and his yefrow [wife] . . . blowing between resolution and pallid fear load about half a ton upon my wagon and then eight of them, children included, were dragged only slowly. Before they went, Willy squealed, Sally bawled, Adam played tricks, and the yefrow [cried] like Hecuba at the taking of Troy."[29]

The lawmakers, driven from New York to White Plains to Fishkill to Kingston, moved once more, to the tiny village of Marble Town. After they left, the marauding British reduced Kingston to "a rubbish of ashes."[30] They were too late to save Burgoyne, however, who, on October 16, too weakened even to retreat further, surrendered to Gates. Morris had balked at supplying the Council of Safety with mere news, but he did not mind sending it to one of the lovely Livingston girls, now married, and to a loyalist no less, but still his correspondent.

> *With politics and nonsense*
> *I've lost my rhyming talents long since . . .*
> *In such a case I needs must choose*
> *(A Hobson's choice) to write the news.*
> *Know then, the great Burgoyne's surrounded,*
> *His arms magnanimously grounded.*[31]

The fighting along the Montreal–New York corridor was temporarily over, with the British in Canada and New York City, and the rebels holding the crucial center. The action would now mainly be elsewhere. Finally New York could spare Morris as a delegate to the Continental Congress. In October 1777 he left for Philadelphia, not to return to his home state, except for visits, for twenty-one years.

CHAPTER FOUR

Running a War

WHILE GENERAL BURGOYNE had been fighting and failing in upstate New York, General Howe, who should have been supporting him, had sailed into Chesapeake Bay, landed his army on the Maryland shore, and attacked Philadelphia from the south. Congress fled before him, in a confusion of "horses galloping, women running, children crying [and] delegates flying,"[1] and settled finally in the town of York, almost ninety miles to the west, across the Susquehanna River. After a visit with the Ogdens in New Jersey, Morris arrived at his new post on January 20, 1778.

The emergency seat of the national government was scarcely bigger than Kingston. Delegates complained of their setting: "Believe me," wrote one, "it is the most inhospitable scandalous place I ever was in."[2] Morris complained of the delegates: "Stuffed in a corner of America and brooding over their situation, they have become utter disagreeables."[3] Many of the glittering members of the early days of the Continental Congress had left, drawn to state politics, or other assignments: Patrick Henry and Thomas Jefferson, the greatest tongue and the greatest pen of the Revolution, had gone home to Virginia; Benjamin Franklin and John Adams, the international celebrity and the hardheaded Yankee firebrand, were serving as diplomats in Europe; George Washington was serving in the army. The loss of tone, together with the country's grim prospects, and the fact that states voted as units, not congressmen as individuals, encouraged absenteeism. There were seldom as many as twenty delegates on the floor at any time, and they fit easily into their meeting place, the courthouse on the town square.

Morris, going on twenty-six, was one of the youngest members of Congress. His enemies would hold that against him: one called him "the Tall Boy."[4] They would also come to resent his self-assurance: "for brass," wrote another, he was "equal to any I am acquainted with."[5] Morris's reputation for a lightness of pivot had accompanied him to Pennsylvania. Among his fellow New Yorkers, he bore the family reputation for impulsiveness and oddity, and his new peers took up the theme. Henry Laurens of South Carolina found Morris "guardless and incautious";[6] Robert Morris of Pennsylvania (no relation) expected him to be "immensely useful if he pursues his objects steadily (for I have been told his only blemish is being a little too whimsical)."[7] Morris himself pleaded guilty to being hopeful: "[I am] by nature a little sanguine and never look upon the dark side of objects unnecessarily."[8]

On his first day in York, Morris was given an assignment that would require him to study a very dark object indeed; he was put on a committee to visit Washington at his winter encampment, and to report on the condition of the army. Washington and his troops had lost Philadelphia to Howe in two autumn battles, but they had not fought badly, particularly in the second engagement at Germantown, a near-run thing, in which the American attack failed in part because the battlefield had been shrouded in fog. After their worthy losses, the army had marched into winter quarters in the rolling countryside of Valley Forge, eighteen miles northwest of Philadelphia, in December. Here their condition was grim, not from ice and snow, for the winter of 1778 was mild enough, but from disease, and lack of supplies and pay. Thanks to resignation and illness, the army had no general officer in charge of food or equipment. What they had instead, according to a doctor in the Connecticut line, was "fatigue—nasty clothes—nasty cookery . . . There comes a bowl of beef soup—full of burnt leaves and dirt, sickish enough to make a Hector spew."[9] The army suffered less from British mauling than from American disorganization and incompetence. When Morris and his fellow committee members arrived at Valley Forge, they were shocked by what Washington told them, and by what they saw. "Our troops," Morris wrote Jay, "*Heu miseros!*

[Alas for the wretches!] The skeleton of an army presents itself to our eyes in a naked, starving condition, out of health, out of spirits."[10]

Morris threw himself into the work of reviving this dejected force. The orderly, mathematical side of his mind rose to the challenge of re-organization and supply. The army needed structural changes—larger cavalry regiments, a corps of engineers—while the states, which were ultimately responsible for supplying it, required precise summaries of its needs. Morris drew up elaborate charts and tables for both pur-poses; his facts and figures, by making plain how badly off the army was, were polemical as well as practical. Valley Forge also stirred his passions. He "loved" the army, he wrote, "from acquaintance with some individuals and for the sufferings which as a body they had bravely and patiently endured."[11] Bravest and most patient in Morris's eyes was Washington; the bond they had formed in New York was strengthened by the work they did together at Valley Forge, and bur-nished by the letters they exchanged after Morris returned to Con-gress. "I was in your debt," Morris began one, meaning he owed Washington a letter. "But, believe me, my heart owes nothing."[12]

At Valley Forge, Morris met the marquis de Lafayette. Lafayette, whose father had died in battle when he was two, had been raised in the mountainous Auvergne in central France. When he made his debut at the court of Versailles—a ritual initiation required of all no-blemen—he struck his peers as uncouth and naive: he could not dance, and he loved his wife (a rich heiress to whom he had been married at age fourteen). The American Revolution gave him a reason for being. In the spring of 1777, as a nineteen-year-old captain of the muske-teers, he outfitted a ship, the *Victoire,* at his own expense and sailed to the United States. He was going, he wrote his wife, "to offer my ser-vices to the most interesting of Republics, bringing to the service only my candor and goodwill without ambition or ulterior motive."[13] The marquis partly deceived himself, for he was consumed with ambition. But he was also candid and good-willed.

He had arrived at Washington's headquarters in August, a bad time for foreign volunteers. Eager to recruit professionals to the cause, America's agent in Europe had been freely offering commissions in the American army, and a swarm of officers, both idealists and soldiers of fortune, had crossed the Atlantic to take up their promised ranks. American officers who had been fighting for two years resented the newcomers; many of the Europeans disdained the skills of the rustics they were coming to help. Wearied by the hard feelings that had been stirred up, Washington did not know what to expect when yet another European appeared before him. "We are rather embarrassed," he told the young marquis, "to show ourselves to an officer who has just left the army of France." Lafayette gave the perfect response: "I am here, sir, to learn and not to teach."[14] The fatherless young man and the childless commander in chief became a devoted pair. Their mutual admiration, so far from shutting Morris out, helped draw him and Lafayette together when they met in January 1778. From the height of his years, Morris declared that he was "deeply surprised at the mature judgment and solid understanding of this young man."[15]

Morris returned to York on April 15, and took up another cause dear to the army's interest—the payment of officers. When the Continental Congress appointed Washington commander in chief, he had stipulated that he would serve without pay; only his expenses should be covered. But this example of Roman virtue, however appropriate to the Father of his Country, could not serve for his officers. Since pay was erratic, and the paper money in which it occasionally came verged on worthless, officers needed the hope of future reward. Washington wanted them to have pensions of half-pay for life. "I do most religiously believe the salvation of the cause depends on it," he wrote Congress; "and, without it, your officers will moulder to nothing, or be composed of low and illiterate men, void of capacity for this or any other business."[16] Many in Congress, however, were leery of committing their states to a peacetime obligation, particularly for the benefit of an army; was not the standing army the traditional tool of despots?

After weeks of wrangling, the enemies of half-pay offered to support it so long as the measure was referred to the states for approval. This shirked responsibility, and would surely doom the proposal. The poisoned compromise split the state delegations evenly, with Pennsylvania "in a mighty flimsy situation," as Morris wrote Washington, who was following events from Valley Forge.[17] The two delegates from Pennsylvania who were in York were themselves split on the issue; Robert Morris, who supported half-pay, was at his country house in Manheim, twenty-five miles away. "Think one moment, and come the next," Gouverneur Morris urged him.[18] Robert Morris came, and the motion to submit half-pay to the states was defeated, with Pennsylvania's opposition, in the middle of May. Congress then passed a genuine compromise of half-pay for seven years. This was only a stopgap, but it was something.

While Morris was in York, he wrote a letter to his mother. In it, he speaks of having written often and receiving no replies; perhaps other letters went astray in crossing enemy lines. But it is the second of two long wartime letters to her that survive. Sarah Morris was not happy. She was over seventy years old; her family was split; her loyalist in-laws had suffered, and the soldiers of the king she obeyed were filching the books and cutting the trees of her estate. Her son tried to console her. "There is enough of sorrow in this world, without looking into futurity for it. Hope the best. If it happens, well; if not, it will then be time enough to be afflicted, and at any rate the intermediate space will be well filled."[19] He offered to comfort her in person. "[T]he early possession of power [has] taught me how little it deserves to be prized. Whenever the present storm subsides, I shall rush with eagerness into the bosom of private life." But, like Augustine praying to be pure, Morris did not wish for private life yet. Another maternal figure claimed him: " . . . while [the storm] continues, and while my country calls . . . I hold it my indispensable duty to give myself to her."[20] He wrote more bluntly and more beautifully to Robert R. Livingston. "This is the seed time of glory as of freedom."[21] Morris had moved in less than four years from local to state to national politics. York might be as grim a place as Kingston, and both were much less grand than New York, but the destinies of a nation were being decided in York, and in Valley Forge. Everyone touched by the liberal enlightenment professed to disdain power; Morris truly meant it. But he quickened to the presence of glory, in suffering soldiers or in great comrades.

Morris showed his spirit in York, yet he also showed his high spirits, which ignited two quarrels with long fuses. On his way to Valley Forge in January, he and another congressman had stayed at an inn in Lancaster. There they had become judges in a dispute between a British convoy that was supplying, with Washington's permission, enemy prisoners in American custody, and the laws of Pennsylvania. The British, who had stopped at the same inn, were settling their bill; because they carried hard currency, the innkeeper offered them a sizable discount. An American officer who was escorting them then insisted they should pay at the official local exchange rate, and the British, unwilling to be gouged, appealed to the two congressmen who happened to be handy. Morris, never shy, pronounced that the British, so long as they were proceeding under military safe-conduct, were subject to the law of nations, not to the laws of Pennsylvania. For good measure, he wrote a lecturing letter to the Pennsylvania state government. When he arrived in Valley Forge, Joseph Reed, a Pennsylvania congressman, warned him that he "would not do it if it was to do again."[22]

In March, Morris became involved in a clash of personalities. Jonathan Sergeant, Attorney General of Pennsylvania, had brought a complaint against the deputy quartermaster general of the army, one Robert Hooper, Jr., for using army wagons for private business. Hooper, who was a big man, hunted out Sergeant, who was a small one, and thrashed him, then wrote a letter to Morris declaring that, "as he had horsewhipped the Attorney General, he proposed to go through" the entire state government.[23] Morris thought the letter was rich, and showed it to his friends at Valley Forge, from Washington on down. Reed, offended for his state, wanted the letter as evidence against Hooper; but Morris, who had been happy to share it, now refused to surrender it, on the grounds that it was a private communication. Morris was arguably right about the inn bill, and guilty in the Hooper affair of nothing more than a good time (he later helped to prosecute Hooper, who was indeed guilty of misusing public property). But he had managed in a matter of months twice to offend the government of the state in which Congress sat. "You know, he is like the elephant in war," one New York delegate wrote Robert R. Livingston, ". . . more destructive to his friends than to his antagonists." [24] He would hear of both offenses again.

In the middle of June 1778, Morris made yet another move—this one, unlike all his previous movements as a legislator, not in flight from an advancing enemy but in the wake of a retreating one. The British decided to consolidate their forces, and evacuated Philadelphia for New York.

The city was bruised by its nine months' occupation. The State House, where the Declaration of Independence was signed, had been used as a hospital, and stank from the garbage and corpses that the British had dumped in a pit outside. British officers had lifted books and a portrait from Benjamin Franklin's library. The citywide bill for property damage and theft amounted to £187,000 (over $6 million today). The underfed inhabitants had a meager look. Robert Morris the Pennsylvania congressman predicted, however, that "they will fatten fast." [25] His confidence was based on the city's fundamental centrality and wealth. Boston was slipping, and New York was still growing. Philadelphia, with a population of 38,000, was clearly the largest and richest city on the continent. It is "to the United States," wrote Robert Morris, "what the heart is to the human body in circulating the blood." [26] Foreigners could be condescending about Philadelphian sophistication. One Frenchman wrote that the ladies "although very well shaped . . . lack grace and make very bad curtsies." Worse, "they pride themselves on a scrupulous fidelity towards their husbands." [27] But American visitors were agog. "To be placed on an elegant sofa alongside one of them, when they are displaying both the artillery of their tongues and eyes," wrote one colonel, was "almost too much for a healthy, vigorous young soldier to bear. . . ." [28]

Morris made a ferocious suggestion to Washington that he fine the city £100,000 for collaborating with the enemy. "Your idea," Washington wrote back gravely, ". . . widely differs from mine." [29] Not for the last time, Morris's quick, sharp mind outran his mild temper. He was more tolerant of principled pacifists. He reported to Robert Livingston that the Moravian Brethren, a German pacifist sect, were being harassed by local patriots. Although they were "averse to bearing

arms and taking baths," they were "good husbandmen and mechanicks."[30] Could New York find some way to woo them? Morris thought
no better of the Brethren's practices than he did of the beliefs of
Catholics, but he was willing to let them, and the state, profit by their
labor.

Morris and Congress returned to Philadelphia at the beginning of
summer. The "minutia are infinite," he wrote, and the heat "pestifer-
ous."[31] The rank eastern seaboard was responsible for the heat; the
minutia proliferated along with congressional committees. Every item
of official business, from the long-running responsibilities of government to the most fleeting problems, was handled by a committee, and
the labor of the committees fell on their chairmen. "You must not
imagine," Morris wrote years later, "that the members of these committees took any charge or burden of the affairs. Necessity, preserving
the democratical forms, assumed the monarchical substance of business. The chairman received and answered all letters and other appli-
cations, took every step which he deemed essential, prepared reports,
gave orders . . . and merely took the members of a committee into a
chamber, and for the form's sake made the needful communications,
and received their approbation. . . ."[32] Morris was one of these movers
and shakers. "I have no exercise," he complained in one letter, "unless
to walk . . . fifty yards to Congress and to return."[33]

His first significant action beyond the blizzard of daily business was
to join his fellow New Yorkers in signing the second new constitution
of his acquaintance, the Articles of Confederation. Congress had been
considering a form of government for two years. John Dickinson of
Pennsylvania had drawn up a draft in July 1776, a week after the Declaration of Independence, but "every inch" of it had been haggled
over.[34] By November 1777, one delegate wrote, "the child Congress
has been big with" was "at last brought forth," though he feared it
would "be thought a little deformed."[35] The Articles declared a "firm
league of friendship"[36] among the thirteen states, and gave Congress
power over foreign policy and warmaking (there was no executive, or
national judiciary). Other powers of government, such as raising revenue, depended on the approval of the states. State delegations voted

as units; nine states had to approve a law, all thirteen would have to approve a change in the Articles themselves. The new government was more than an ad hoc wartime alliance (the Union was declared to be "perpetual"), but not much.[37] By the end of July 1778, ten states had signed the Articles.

Morris also took up two great issues of long-range importance. Sometime in mid-1778, perhaps as early as his return from Valley Forge, he prepared an oration on financial and political reform, not for delivery—neither the journal of Congress nor the letters of the delegates mention it—but to organize his thoughts. The problems of the army that Morris had been grappling with were symptoms of larger problems—feeble credit and feeble government—and he outlined an ambitious plan to address them. The United States needed a foreign loan—but how to raise it? One potential asset the government could call on was land. Many states had colonial-era claims to land beyond the Alleghanies. Morris wanted these assigned to Congress, which could carve a new state for veterans out of them, and pledge the remainder as collateral. Meanwhile, Congress needed permanent sources of revenue. Morris suggested postal charges, a tariff, and a head tax of one dollar per person. Congress had to establish its preeminence by ending state currencies, and demonstrate confidence in its own currency by lifting price controls and publishing a record of its debts.

Morris, fresh from signing the Articles of Confederation, also sketched political reforms of the system he had just approved. "Every gentleman acquainted with our public affairs," he wrote, must know "that a body such as the Congress is inadequate to the purposes of execution." The business of managing financial and military affairs should be removed from congressional committees and given to boards of expert commissioners. Over them there should be a national executive—"either a Committee of three or a single officer such as [a] Chief of the States"—who would superintend their doings, and present their reports to Congress.[38] The grandson and nephew of governors envisioned one for the United States.

By August 1778, Morris began offering his ideas to Congress. In a report on the Board of Treasury, he proposed three permanent officials: a treasurer, a comptroller, and an auditor. Congress agreed, provided they were reconfirmed annually. The following month Morris presented a report on money and finance, in which he offered his other proposals (except for a national executive, which even he sensed was too radical to be considered). The reforms he was offering were radical enough. Morris asked the same body that had balked at paying officers' pensions to assume a host of other duties and powers. Congress printed only sixty copies of his report, and enjoined the printer and the delegates "not to communicate [it] or any part of it, without leave of the house." [39] After a month of secret debate, Elbridge Gerry, a delegate from Massachusetts, was asked to revise Morris's handiwork. He threw out the head tax, the tariff, and the plan for western lands, and focused on calling in old, depreciated congressional money, hoping thereby to bolster the value of newer issues. But "every adept in financiering," as one congressman put it,[40] went to work on Gerry's report, and in the end, Congress failed even to do that.

Other Americans besides Morris were grappling with the country's financial problems. One was Philip Schuyler, the New York general and grandee, who, when he became a congressman the following year, complained that not one of his colleagues was "adequate to the important business of finance." [41] Another was Alexander Hamilton, now a colonel on Washington's staff, shortly to be Schuyler's son-in-law, who was scribbling economic data and ideas in his army pay book. But their time was not yet. If Congress was a potential national government, then it would have to get a handle on its financial and structural problems; if it spoke only for an alliance of semiautonomous states, then it could keep scraping along.

Morris spent more time on issues of foreign policy, which were unavoidable, and which, for the first time during the war, seemed promising. Since the beginning of the Revolution, the United States hoped that the enemies of its enemy might become its friends. France, which had fought Britain four times in the last hundred years, watched the rebellion with interest, while officially maintaining its neutrality (Lafayette had left the country and his regiment without permission). But after Washington's two game battles outside Philadelphia, and

Gates's great victory at Saratoga, Versailles was willing to commit itself. Rumors of the Franco-American treaty, which had been signed in
Paris in early February, reached York in April. If they were true, Morris wrote Jay in one of his winged phrases, then "a spark hath fallen
upon the train which is to fire the world." [42]

Britain knew of the treaty before America did. Howe's return to
New York was a strategic retrenchment, in preparation for a world war.
London also hoped to stifle the Franco-American alliance by offering
the rebels generous terms. Parliament surrendered the right to tax the
colonies, and sent a three-man peace commission to America, headed
by the Earl of Carlisle, a thirty-year-old socialite. Over the spring,
summer, and fall, the twenty-six-year-old Morris wrote several official
responses to the commission, and a number of essays in the Pennsylvania newspapers, signed "An American," which took a stern view of its
offers.

"[T]he principles of your opponents are republican, some indeed
aristocratic; the greater part democratic," he lectured, "but all [are] opposed to Kings." He exhorted these opponents to a final effort. "Arise
then! To your tents! And gird you for the battle! It is time to turn the
headlong current of vengeance upon the head of the destroyer."
Britain could be attacked by American agents and raiding parties. "A
small sum of money would wrap [London] in flames . . . and the
dreaded scalping-knife itself may, in the hands of our riflemen, spread
horror through the . . . island." In peace, the United States would rise
to greatness. "The portals of the temple we have raised to freedom,
shall be thrown wide, as an asylum to mankind. America shall receive
to her bosom and comfort and cheer the oppressed, the miserable and
the poor of every nation and of every clime." [43]

John Jay wrote, of one of these performances, that it was "strikingly
marked with Morris." [44] This was true, and not entirely to his credit.
The style that could be so swift and sure in private letters had a ten-
dency to climb on stilts for public performances. Too often, Morris's
polemics are high-flying—the temple of freedom—or bombastic—
the summons to the tents. Only occasionally does a phrase like "comfort and cheer the oppressed . . . of every clime" express both his

imperial vision and his best personal qualities. His bluster about scalp-
ing knives showed the bloodthirstiness of a civilian (it is impossible to
imagine Washington, who had seen men scalped, writing such stuff).
The analysis of American political opinion showed where Morris
himself stood: the people are included, but republicans and aristocrats
lead the way. Despite his stylistic peculiarities, Morris was the best
Congress then had. "I have drawn and expect to draw," he wrote Livingston in August, "almost if not all the publications of Congress of
any importance." [45]

While Morris flayed the Carlisle commission, he helped plan Con-
gress's official reception of France's first minister, Conrad-Alexandre
Gérard, who arrived in Philadelphia in the flagship of a French fleet in
July. Gérard was received at the cleaned and aerated State House on
August 6, after which Congress and guest repaired to the City Tavern
for twenty-one toasts and a dinner costing $1,424 ($18,000 today).

The benefits of a French alliance were obvious—supplies, money,
troops, and diverting Britain's energy to other theaters. France could
also engage the sympathy of Spain, whose monarch, Charles III, belonged to the same family (the House of Bourbon) as His Most Christian Majesty, Louis XVI. But neither country would help the United
States out of the goodness of its heart. What were their war aims? Did
they match America's? Spain had lost Florida to Britain in the last
round of European conflict; she wanted it back. Spain had gained
Louisiana, the heart of the continent, from France, and intended to
keep it; the arrival of American settlers at Natchez, on the east bank of
the Mississippi, alarmed her. France had lost Canada to Britain. In the
early days of the Franco-American alliance, France proposed a joint
invasion, with an American force attacking Montreal from the south
while a French expedition sailed down the St. Lawrence to besiege
Quebec. Washington vetoed the plan, in a secret letter to Congress,
out of fear that it would succeed all too well: Canada was "attached to
[France] by all the ties of blood, habits, manners, religion and former
connexion of government. I fear this would be too great a temptation,
to be resisted by any power actuated by the common maxims of na-

tional policy."[46] But that still left much else for the new allies to settle among themselves.

Morris discussed America's goals in a private conversation with Gérard in October, and wrote a draft of American war aims for Congress in February 1779. His minimum demands were that an independent United States should stretch from Maine to Georgia on the Atlantic coast, and west to the Mississippi. But beyond these borders he left important American desires unsettled. Frontiersmen depended on navigating the Mississippi, whose spigot, New Orleans, belonged to Spain, while New Englanders counted on fishing the Grand Banks off Newfoundland, the richest waters of the North Atlantic. But Morris let both demands be conditional on trade-offs: to sail the Mississippi, the United States would have to help Spain conquer Florida; to fish the Grand Banks, it would have to waive claims to Nova Scotia. Morris wanted a relatively contained country, which was just what France and Spain wanted. Don Juan de Miralles, who pretended to be a shipwrecked slavetrader but was in fact Spain's unofficial agent in Philadelphia, called Morris "one of the most enlightened voters in Congress and very attached to the cause of the alliance. . . ."[47]

Morris's francophilia was not a legacy of his French heritage (Gérard thought he was Dutch). He wanted the United States to stay compact for its own good. Years later, he admitted that he had been "alarmed" over the vastness of the "Western wilderness, and expressed the wish that some other nation might people it, and by the pressure of foreign force, restrain our domestic feuds."[48] At the time, Gérard wrote home that Morris feared to extend the country westward, lest the frontier be encouraged to stand on its own. "[T]he poverty and vigor of the north were the best safeguards of the republic."[49] Morris's pro-French policy was wrong: the United States would get more out of the alliance by standing up for itself. But his fears of internal animosity were not groundless, as his career would show.

Morris's February 1779 draft of war aims inflamed New England, which tied up Congress for six months debating the status of the fisheries. In the end, Congress decided that while fishing the Grand

Banks was of "the utmost importance," it would not make the right to do so a diplomatic "ultimatum," when the time came to negotiate a peace treaty.[50]

In 1778 and 1779, foreign policy became entangled, as it often does, in domestic squabbles. The bitterest plunged Morris and Congress into a fight between Silas Deane, a diplomat, and Thomas Paine, secretary for the foreign relations committee.

Deane was a Connecticut lawyer who had been a delegate to the First and Second Continental Congresses. He was a man of "plausible readiness and volubility,"[51] as John Adams put it, and Congress sent him to France in 1776 to open undercover negotiations for supplies, even though he did not speak the language. The French government told him to deal with the baron de Beaumarchais, a watchmaker, spy, and playwright who was writing *The Marriage of Figaro* at the time. Beaumarchais ran a dummy company, Rodrigue Hortalez & Company, capitalized by France and Spain, which began funneling muskets and gunpowder to America. Deane stayed in Paris until 1778, when he returned to Philadelphia in the same fleet that brought Gérard.

If Deane expected congratulations for a job well done, he was disappointed. He had won the enmity of Arthur Lee, another American agent in Paris, who happened to be the brother of a congressman. Worse, he and Beaumarchais had drawn commissions on sales of supplies that, Lee charged, were meant to be gifts. As soon as Deane appeared, Congress began to investigate him behind closed doors.

Morris was one of his defenders. Deane, Morris wrote John Jay, "has rendered most essential services." Commissions were an inescapable feature of military procurement in the eighteenth century, and they often shaded into graft. But "many persons" in Congress "are very liberal of illiberality. . . . The storm increases, and I think some of the tall trees must be torn up by the roots."[52]

Deane went public with a self-defense in December 1778. This provoked a public attack at the end of the month by Thomas Paine. Paine's journey through life had been even stranger than Deane's. Born in the bleak and puritanical east of England, Paine had made corsets, cruised on a privateer, preached Methodism, and collected taxes. In 1774, he came to Philadelphia, at age thirty-seven, where he took up a new profession, journalism, and discovered that he was a genius. Paine's pamphlet *Common Sense* (1775), urging the colonies to declare their independence, found 150,000 purchasers in a population of less than 3 million—the equivalent today of a sale of 14 million. *The American Crisis,* a pamphlet written in the grim winter of 1776, achieved immortality:

> These are the times that try men's souls: the summer soldier and the sunshine patriot will, in this crisis, shrink from the service of his country; but he that stands it NOW, deserves the love and thanks of man and woman. Tyranny, like hell, is not easily conquered; yet we have this consolation with us, that the harder the conflict, the more glorious the triumph. What we obtain too cheap, we esteem too lightly:—'Tis dearness only that gives every thing its value. Heaven knows how to set a proper price upon its goods; and it would be strange indeed, if so celestial an article as FREEDOM should not be highly rated.[53]

This was as strong and singing as Morris and Thomas Jefferson at their best, or as Patrick Henry at his most eloquent. The closest parallel to this passage is the speech that Shakespeare gave Henry V on the eve of the Battle of Agincourt—"We few, we happy few, we band of brothers"—except that *The American Crisis* was not written by a playwright two centuries after the fact, but by a journalist on deadline, to be read to cold, desperate soldiers, many of whom would shortly be dead indeed.

Paine had the gifts of a great journalist, and the flaws of a mediocre one. He was slovenly, conceited, and feckless. He quarreled with everyone (though he did not easily hold grudges). He gave all the profits of *The American Crisis* to buy mittens for soldiers, then spent the rest of his life scrambling for pensions and appointments. At the time of his attack on Deane, he was serving as the secretary of the Committee on Foreign Relations.

Writing under his pen name "Common Sense," Paine declared that the French supplies on which Deane had taken commissions were in fact gifts, and he added that he had documents in his office "in hand-writing which Mr. Deane is well acquainted with" (i.e., Deane's own) to prove it.[54] Paine had raised the ante: he had publicly revealed that France had helped the United States on the sly, and by offering to pro-duce documents held by the Committee on Foreign Relations, he put the authority of the government behind the revelation. Great powers did many things on the sly, but they wished to keep their doings hid-den. Gérard demanded that Congress repudiate Paine.

The quarrel had spiraled beyond the question of Deane's crooked-ness, to the trustworthiness of the United States as an ally. In the en-suing debate, Morris handled Paine roughly. "And what would be the idea of a gentleman in Europe of this Mr. Paine?" he asked Congress. "Would he not suppose him to be a man of the most affluent fortune, born in this country of a respectable family, with wide and great con-nexions, and endued with the nicest sense of honor? . . . But, alas, what would he think, should he accidentally be informed, that this, our Secretary of Foreign Affairs, was a mere adventurer *from England*, without fortune, without family or connexions, ignorant even of grammar? . . . And if assured of the fact, and if possessed of common sense"—here Morris mocked Paine's pen name—"would he not think that we were devoid of it?"[55] Morris's efforts to have Paine fired failed, but Paine resigned under his own power.

Historians sometimes treat the fight over Deane as the seed time of American political parties, the conservative revolutionaries defending Deane, the radical ones attacking him.[56] "It gave me great pain," Mor-ris himself said during the debates, "to hear . . . the word *party* made use of. This is a word that can do no good, but which may produce much evil."[57] But the tendencies had been there all along, evident in the different rates at which Americans approached revolutionary ac-tion. Morris had seen the tendencies in New York, when he had ar-gued with the Liberty Boys over the British retiring with their armaments, or over the fate of James Rivington, the loyalist printer.

Morris and Paine would have many more dealings, not all of them (surprisingly enough, after that bad start) hostile. This fight had scarcely died down when Morris was drawn into the whirlpool of Pennsylvania politics. The state constitution had established a one-house legislature and a weak executive, in the hope of giving the people a pure and direct voice; Morris called it an "unwieldy mass, badly jointed." [58] Conservatives, such as Robert Morris and James Wilson, a young Scottish-born lawyer, wanted a system more like those of other states, with checks and balances. "Constitutionalists" and "Republicans," as they called themselves, feuded with each other. Meanwhile, inflation impoverished laborers, who accused the Philadelphia rich of being gougers and loyalists. The year 1779 was marked with riots, culminating in a battle in front of James Wilson's house that left five men dead. The Deane/Paine fight had been a culmination of earlier quarrels, but because of the state's size and centrality, the emerging party system in Pennsylvania would anticipate American politics for the next twenty years.

Morris tried to keep out of local broils, yet his flamboyant personality made him an attractive target. Joseph Reed, the Pennsylvania congressman he had met at Valley Forge, now in the state government, raked up his behavior at the inn at Lancaster, and his refusal to surrender the letter of Robert Hooper, the bullying deputy quartermaster, as symbols of congressional arrogance. Morris managed to soothe Reed privately ("[I cannot] appear on the public stage against every one who shall amuse himself with defamation"). [59] But while he was protecting this flank, he became vulnerable on another: his efforts, as chairman of the Commissary Committee, to supply the French navy with flour, led local radicals to accuse him of draining off the state's supply. Morris's enemies, finally, accused him of keeping company with loyalists. If that meant writing his family, he was clearly guilty.

What ended Morris's congressional career, however, was not fights in the nation's capital but his own position on a fight at home. For decades, the colonies of New York and New Hampshire had wrangled over the mountainous land between Lake Champlain and the Connecticut River. In time, the inhabitants asserted their own claim to it, calling it Vermont. One of the first victories of the Revolution had come when Ethan Allen and a party of Green Mountain Boys surprised the sleeping enemy garrison at Fort Ticonderoga. But Allen and his followers were as hostile to the domination of their neighbors as they were to that of Britain. New York State, spurred by rich land speculators, urged Congress to ratify its claim to Vermont. Morris dutifully made the case, but in private he was doubtful. "Vermont is yet Vermont," he wrote Jay, "and I think no wise man will pretend to say when it will cease to be so . . . [T]here are in it some ardent spirits"—the Green Mountain Boys—"whose termigant quality has been too little attended to. Strange that men, in the very act of revolting [i.e., New Yorkers and Congress] should so little consider the temper of revolters [the Green Mountain Boys]. But this is eternally the case."[60]

Morris opposed mobs when they bullied others, but he was reluctant to resist a claim to independence in dubious circumstances. This realism did not endear him to the New York legislature, which met in Poughkeepsie in October 1779 to reelect the state's congressional delegation. Morris was replaced by a politician with the sturdy Huguenot name of Ezra L'Hommedieu.

The arcs of Morris's careers in New York and in Congress reversed each other. At home, he had passed from petty squabbles to writing a constitution. In York and Philadelphia, he had passed from saving a gallant army to petty squabbles. For the moment, he was content to leave public life alone. He was, he wrote Robert Livingston, "no longer that wretched creature, a statesman."[61] Retired at twenty-seven, he settled in Philadelphia, intending to make money and to enjoy himself.

CHAPTER FIVE

Pain and Love

*M*ORRIS HAD BEEN dismissed by his constituents. John Jay had been sent to Madrid as America's minister to Spain, whence he wrote, in early 1780, a letter full of solicitude for his friend. "Where is Morris?" he asked New York's governor George Clinton (no relation to Sir Henry). "Keep him up. It is a pity that one so capable of serving his country should be unemployed, but there are men who fear and envy his talents and take ungenerous advantage of his foibles."[1] But Morris was keeping himself up, giving rein to both his talents and his foibles.

Philadelphia lawyers were already proverbial for their skill; Morris's grandfather had engaged one to defend John Peter Zenger. Now Morris was one. He had taken cases while he was a congressman, arguing that his salary alone did not cover his expenses or allow him to put anything by. One case had involved a disputed Pennsylvania election—yet another reason why the local politicians disliked him. Now he could litigate without the burden of congressional work. Then, as now, clients were attracted to a counsel with congressional expertise. Morris also took on Admiralty cases, a family specialty. "[I work] with a view to eat and drink," he wrote, "without burthening society."[2]

Morris allowed himself the distraction of a social life. In addition to the parties, dinners, and balls that Philadelphia threw in such profusion, Morris could pay attention to his women friends.

When Morris was a young man, he had courted Kitty Livingston, and in 1772, when he was twenty, he had told his mentor, William Smith, in the letter in which he sought advice on whether to visit England, that he had "naturally a taste for pleasure."[3] In that same year, his cousin, Robert Hunter Morris, wrote him in the following vein: "What in the devil's name is the matter with you? What mistress has jilted you? What whore poxed you?"[4] Talk like his cousin's is the cheap and universal coin of male bragging. It is impossible to tell, from this alone, whether Morris was a profligate or a virgin.

But as he moved through his twenties, the evidence accumulated that he was not the latter. Morris's exchanges of letters with his friends Livingston and Jay, and their letters to each other, assume that Morris is a ladies' man. In February 1778, after Morris arrived in York, he wrote Livingston that there were "no fine women" there.[5] That fall, from Philadelphia, Morris wrote him again: "You say that I have my *Soulagements* [consolations] and I thank you for your wish. I have experienced much pain during my short life," he added, a little tartly, "from being thought to be happier than I was."[6] In the spring of 1779, Jay the Huguenot, in a letter to Livingston, was quite blunt: "Gouverneur is daily employed in making oblations to Venus."[7] That summer, in a letter to Livingston, Morris protested once more, perhaps too much. He was at army headquarters in Middlebrook, in north-central New Jersey, "a dirty village," he pointed out, "where no society can be maintained. . . . The Graces abhor an abode where there is not one Venus to entertain them."[8] There is some teasing in this correspondence, and perhaps, on the part of both the grandee Livingston and the dour Jay, some envy. But the common assumption of all three men is that Morris requires female companionship, and that, given a decent opportunity, he can secure it.

A drawing done of Morris at about this time—the earliest of him that survives—suggests his inclinations, even as it helps explain his success. It is a profile by a Swiss artist, Pierre Eugène du Simitière. It shows a young man with a slightly receding hairline, a sloping forehead, and a large, long nose. He is not classically handsome, but the eye and the mouth redeem all. The eye is large and deepset, and the lashes are very long. The lips are full, especially the lower one. Together, they make an expression that is both lively and dreamy. Morris looks like a man to whom someone is talking, but who is thinking his own thoughts, probably pleasant ones. Women of the twenty-first century who see the picture say they would like to meet the subject.

1780 DISCLOSED the name of a woman Morris loved. She was connected with one of the great catastrophes of his life.

Early in May, Morris planned a visit to the country with Colonel and Mrs. George Plater, a Maryland congressman and his wife. Either in mounting his phaeton, a light, four-wheeled carriage drawn by a pair of horses, or in driving it through the streets, Morris was thrown, and caught his left leg in the spokes of a wheel. The ankle was dislocated and several bones broken. The physicians who attended him (his own was out of town) advised that the leg be amputated. "[W]ith that firmness of mind that accompanies him on all occasions," wrote one acquaintance, he consented "instantly."[9] Perhaps he was too quick. When Morris's doctor returned to Philadelphia, he offered his opinion that the leg could have been saved.

Morris bore the loss, and the possibility that it was unnecessary, "with becoming fortitude," as Robert Livingston put it.[10] Stories began to crystallize around the disaster. One friend, hoping to buck Morris up, drew the silver lining of losing a leg in such bright colors that Morris supposedly told him, "I am almost tempted to part with the other."[11] This sounds like the punch line of a story, very likely told by Morris on himself. The leg was also woven into sexual jokes. When John Jay, off in Madrid, heard about the accident in the fall, he wrote Robert Morris that he wished his friend "had lost *something* else."[12] Later, Jay wrote Gouverneur Morris himself, "I have learned that a certain married woman after much use of your legs had occasioned your losing one." All Morris said in answer to this was that the account was "facetious. Let it pass. The leg is gone, and there is an end of the matter."[13]

But perhaps Morris himself took up Jay's theme. Eleven years later, on another continent, a traveling Englishman, Henry Temple, Viscount Palmerston (father of the prime minister), recorded in his diary that he breakfasted in Paris with "Mr. Morris . . . an American, a gentlemanlike sensible man," who lost a leg "in consequence of jumping from a window in an affair of gallantry."[14] This was the only time Morris and Palmerston met. How had the Englishman learned this version of the story? Almost certainly from his French acquaintants. But who told them? Gossiping Americans, like Jay; or possibly Morris himself, fashioning another punch line. In later years Morris did link his leg with "something else." After flirting with one Frenchwoman, he wondered, in his dairy, if she would consider making an "experiment" with a "native of a New World who has left one of his legs behind him."[15]

In Philadelphia, in 1780, Morris took several months to recover. He spent them in the Philadelphia home of the Platers. George Plater III was a quiet, conventional Maryland planter, active in local politics; two years in the Continental Congress, from 1778 to 1780, were his only service out of state. His wife, Elizabeth Rousby Plater, was delighted to be in the nation's capital—or so it seemed to one French visitor. "Should any stern philosopher be disposed to censor French manners I would not advise him to do so in the presence of Mrs. P***. . . . [H]er taste is as delicate as her health; an enthusiast to excess for all French fashions, she is only waiting for the end of this little revolution to effect a still greater one in the manners of her country."[16] Colonel Plater was then forty-six years old; his wife was twenty-nine, a year older than Morris.

When Morris almost lost his arm as a boy, he would have been cared for by his mother, helped perhaps by the sisters of whom he was so fond. Now he was recovering in the home of this ardent, sensitive woman. Morris needed her attentions. For the second time in his life he had been maimed. In letters, or in front of visitors, he might armor himself in pleasantries; but his amputation, unlike his burned arm, was a wound he would be unable to conceal. Elizabeth Plater's sympathetic attention must have assured him that the world of women would remain open to him.

The Platers returned to Maryland after the colonel's time in Congress ended; Morris and Mrs. Plater corresponded. His attentions to her seem to have become excessive. In a letter to him of 1782, she speaks of his "sentiments" being what she "would wish them to be,"[17] which suggests that they may have been otherwise. Morris's friends knew of his attachment. In a 1783 letter to Morris, Robert Livingston mentioned a rumor about Colonel Plater, asking him if "your friend P——" was "really dead," or if he had "revived in pity to you? [The rumor was false; Plater would go on to be governor of Maryland.] He must certainly know that his death by lessening the sin would lessen your pleasure in loving" Mrs. P——.[18] Morris's friends were not a delicate lot, but Livingston's crack about the nature of Morris's love was a shrewd hit. Morris was grateful for womanly kindness; doubly grateful for the kindness of married women. The love of women pleased and flattered him, as it does every man. But after 1780, whenever a married woman loved him, she proved thereby that he was better than some other man, even a man who was physically whole. Elizabeth Plater was the first in a series of proofs.

In May 1790, almost ten years to the day after his accident, Morris heard another tale of death, this time a true one. He was having dinner in London with an English couple, Mr. and Mrs. Beckford, the latter of whom, in a previous marriage, had lived in Annapolis, Maryland. As Morris was leaving, his hostess told him that Elizabeth Plater had died. "I get away as soon as possible," he wrote in his diary, "that I may not discover emotions which I cannot conceal. Poor Eliza! My lovely friend; thou art then at peace and I shall behold thee no more. Never. Never. Never."[19] This is what Lear says when he holds dead Cordelia in his arms. Morris never wrote like this, or admitted to emotions that he could not conceal. Only Elizabeth Plater had stirred this in him.

Morris had himself fitted with an oaken peg, and though he would later experiment with false legs of copper and cork, he stuck with wood for the rest of his life. Except for an occasional slip in the mud or on stairs, or a tingling in his stump, he was not slowed down, physically or socially. He walked, danced, rode, climbed church steeples, and shot river rapids on his peg. It added to his chic—the fancier the surroundings, the greater the chic. "[D]omestics know not what to make of me, a thing which frequently happens at my first approach, because the simplicity of my dress and equipage, my wooden leg and tone of republican equality, seem totally misplaced at [a] levee. . ."[20] Misplaced maybe, but so cool. The line of the peg would have made Morris, a tall man, seem even taller, especially since he carried himself well. "Few men ever equaled his commanding bearing," wrote a doctor who knew him late in life. "[H]is superb physical organization enlisted attention." [21] He made the most of what he had, and what he had, even minus a leg, was impressive.

Once, Morris recalled his wound with a twinge. Peeling off his stocking one night after dinner in Vienna, he found that he had been wearing it inside out. "I remember to have heard, when young, that this portended good luck, and I remember also that, having gone out one morning early I broke my shin before I got back, and in taking down the stocking to look at it found it was wrong side outward. I bear the mark of that misfortune to this hour, a memento not to believe in such sayings." [22]

By the fall of 1780, Morris could report to Livingston that he had returned "to the beau monde." There followed the obligatory jest: "little then have the beau monde to rejoice," for they were acquiring "a wooden member." [23] Morris poor-mouthed himself, for they were acquiring a source of life. The same Frenchman who had noticed Mrs. Plater found Morris "a young man full of wit and vivacity." [24] Another Frenchman, the marquis de Barbé-Marbois, a diplomat, described Morris in action at a picnic in Chester, in the countryside outside Philadelphia. "We laughed, we drank champagne . . . in a word, this party was like all those of its kind, and I should not speak of it to you but for a little incident which amused me. . . . Governor [sic] Morris, whom the champagne had apparently made pretty drunk, got into a little sulky," a two-wheeled, one-man carriage. But "Mrs. Bingham, a young and pretty woman, took it into her head to get in with him." Anne Willing had been sixteen years old in 1780, when she married William Bingham, twenty-eight. Mr. Bingham had made a fortune in the Caribbean; Mrs. Bingham was as determined as Mrs. Plater to be a social success, and as a lively, rich young Philadelphian was even better placed to do so. "You must know," the marquis went on, "that Govérnér [sic] Morris had once lost a leg in driving a gig, and that that fact was not calculated to reassure Mr. Bingham." There were other facts about Morris that were not calculated to reassure Mr. Bingham. Too drunk to follow them himself, he "begged the fastest of the group to run after his wife and to tell her to get down out of the carriage.... The messenger succeeded in stopping the sulky in which Mrs. Bingham was, and he requested her to get out. She refused. 'Madam, it is your husband's command.' ... Mrs. Bingham called and waved good-bye, whipped up the horse, and continued the journey...."[25]

The marquis de Barbé-Marbois must have liked what he saw of American women, for he married one. The June wedding was celebrated by three days of dinners, at which Morris shone again. Peggy Chew, one of the bridesmaids, wrote a girlfriend that "Govr. Morris kept us in a continual smile (I dare not say laughter for all the world [outright laughing was considered indecorous behavior in young ladies, almost as bad as riding off in a sulky] but you may admit it in the back room)." Morris would bring many smiles to dinners, carriages, and back rooms.

CHAPTER SIX

Convulsion Deferred

W HEN MORRIS was in Congress, he had concerned himself with what the United States and France hoped to get out of their war. Before they could get anything, though, they had to win, and for years nothing went well. In 1779, a French fleet and an American army tried to drive the British from Newport, Rhode Island, and failed. The following year saw Arnold's treason, and the enemy's sudden conquest of everything south of Virginia. Congress, powerless to do much else, reorganized itself by establishing extracongressional offices for War, Foreign Relations, and Finance.

Morris made notes to himself, in his retirement, describing the ideal occupants of such posts. The minister of foreign affairs should be a man of solid "circumstances and connexions"—no more Deanes on the take. This was a description of Morris's friend, Robert Livingston, who got the job, though Morris also injected a good deal of himself in the portrait: "a genius quick, lively, penetrating"; a temper "festive, insinuating"; able to "write on all occasions with clearness and perspicuity."[1] The ideal minister of finances was easier to draw: "a regular bred merchant," who was also "practically acquainted with our political affairs."[2] That described only one man in America, and he was Morris's, and everyone's choice for the job: Robert Morris.

Robert Morris had come to America in 1747, at the age of thirteen, from Liverpool, and was apprenticed to a small Philadelphia merchant house run by the Willing family. By 1775, he was the senior partner, and the firm was doing business in London, Lisbon, Madrid, and the

West Indies. Like Gouverneur Morris, he came around to the cause of independence by deliberate stages; when he did, he expressed his convictions in a businessman's phrase: "I am content to run all hazards."[3] After the war began, he replaced his English business with French, and branched out into tobacco, indigo, privateering, and speculation. A large, friendly, fat man, he believed in living well for its own sake, and as a form of self-advertisement; his claret was "of a quality rarely to be met with in America" and his Philadelphia mansion a "temple . . . erected to hospitality."[4] From 1775 to 1778, he served in the Continental Congress, where he specialized in finance and procurement. His business and the nation's were often commingled—to his profit, his enemies alleged. The commingling also benefited the nation: on the eve of the Battle of Trenton, a desperate Washington asked Morris for funds. Morris, out of his own pocket, sent $50,000 (paper) for the troops, and a bag of gold for spies.

Gouverneur and Robert Morris were well suited to be partners. Thinkers who pride themselves on their realism often admire successful businessmen; men of business appreciate industry and intelligence, especially when they are sweetened by good humor and made unthreatening by youth. Their relationship was captured, in a joint portrait, by the Philadelphia artist Charles Willson Peale. Robert Morris stands beside a table, to the right and slightly in front of his partner, as befits his seniority and his wealth. His eyes, which look directly at the viewer, are bright and shrewd; his ample waistcoat conveys solidity. Gouverneur Morris, who sits beside him, is leaning slightly, at an angle of one o'clock. He looks out into the space beyond the right edge of the painting, and smiles. The bottom of his cravat lies carelessly over his waistcoat (Robert Morris's is smoothly tucked down). Gouverneur Morris is the confident, possibly wayward assistant; Robert Morris is the rock. In later years, Gouverneur would prove to be superior in judgment and dependability, as Robert fell by the wayside; but now they made a potent team, with Robert in the lead. When Robert Morris took office as superintendent of finance in May 1781, Gouverneur accepted his offer to be his assistant with a prediction that Robert would save America's finances. "[C]onsequently, malice will blacken

and envy traduce you. I will freely share in this bitter portion of eminence."⁵

The grim state of American finances in 1781 had been years in the
making. A modern economic historian, Clarence Ver Steeg, has laid out
the facts.⁶ The United States had raised $1.6 million in foreign loans and
$4 million by requisitions, the feeble substitute for taxation. (Congress
had no power to tax the states; it could only make requisitions on them,
which they paid as they were able, or willing.) Domestic loans—bonds
and IOUs—had raised $20 million; $37 million—almost three fifths of
the whole—had been raised by bills of credit, or paper money. The
United States had financed a war with printing presses, and inflation
was the inevitable result. In March 1780, Congress tried to yank the
reins by issuing new bills of credit, each dollar of which was worth forty
old dollars. But the new dollars, unbacked by any resources, began to in-
flate away in turn. Since most Americans were farmers, who could
tighten their belts and provide for themselves, they did not suffer as
badly as these figures might suggest. But the credit of Congress was ex-
hausted, and with it, its ability to wage war. Looking at the red ink, even
America's French allies hesitated to offer further loans.

"If you see the doctor," Gouverneur Morris wrote his new boss
gratefully, "tell him that fatiguing from four in the morning till eight in
the evening, and sleeping only from eleven till three agrees with me
much better than all the prescriptions in . . . the world."⁷ The Morrises
had much work to do. Their first step was to found a national bank.
"Money is of too subtle and spiritual a nature," Gouverneur Morris
wrote, "to be caught by the rude hand of the law."⁸ Efforts to create it
out of thin air, by printing it, or to fix its value, by price controls, would
backfire. The Morrises proposed a Bank of North America, capitalized at $400,000 ($5.2 million today), to encourage economic activity.
The bank would issue its own notes, which would then become a us-
able currency. Congress approved the plan in May, and a timely loan of
a quarter of a million dollars of French silver in the fall helped make up
the capital. When the Bank opened, it employed every means to win
investor confidence. Bank employees paraded containers full of silver
coins from the vaults to the cashiers to show how well funded the

Bank was. At the same time, Robert Morris set himself up as a bank, signing notes issued by the Office of Finance in $20, $50, and $80 denominations. Robert Morris's name carried such clout that the "Morris notes" circulated as cash. Finally, in the manner of all desperate enterprises, the Finance Office shifted its debts among its creditors like peas in a shell game. William Graham Sumner, the nineteenth-century economist and a great admirer of Robert Morris's, called it "the most vulgar kind of bill-kiting."[9] There were "many contrivances to rescue our finances from ruin," Gouverneur Morris admitted years later.[10]

As the summer of 1781 ended, the Morrises heard a rumor, and received a distress call. A French fleet was sailing to American waters, for a joint operation (the target was evidently Virginia, where the British army in the south was now fighting), but if Washington's troops did not get a month's pay, they would quit. The Morrises learned that the approaching French fleet had currency aboard; could they borrow it? The French navy needed the approval of the French army; the relevant official was in Maryland. The Morrises rode south to find him (Gouverneur would act as translator, since Robert knew no French), but on their way they were caught by a messenger who told them that the fleet had landed, and the loan was approved. The Morrises turned north, to go back to Philadelphia, and found the road blocked by French troops marching in the opposite direction, to Yorktown.

Seven weeks later, word reached Philadelphia of Cornwallis's surrender. On November 3, the Morrises joined the French minister at a *Te Deum* to celebrate the victory. As they left, they saw the British colors being paraded to Independence Hall. The occasion was "solemn and awful," as the official diary of the Finance Office (probably written by Gouverneur) put it. In unusual words for a Treasury document, the diarist offered a prayer to "thee, Oh Lord God, who hath vouchsafed to rescue from slavery and from death these thy servants."[11]

The war in North America was almost certainly over (fighting continued in the West Indies). But until a peace treaty was negotiated, the United States would need to keep its army in the field, watching the

British, who still occupied New York. Thanks to hard work, luck, and sleight of hand, the Morrises had financed the Yorktown campaign. But now the larder was truly bare.

The Morrises tried new contrivances. They angled for a loan from Spain; John Jay warned them that Madrid had "little money, less wisdom" and "no credit."[12] They hoped that the war would drag on—not on American soil, but in the Caribbean, where France and Spain were seeking spoils and might pay for American help. In December 1781, they began holding Monday night meetings with Livingston; Benjamin Lincoln, the minister of war; George Washington, the commander in chief; and Charles Thomson, the secretary of Congress, for the purpose of "consulting and concerting measures to promote the . . . public good."[13] This informal "cabinet" sought to give the government some executive cohesion, but it was also interested in lobbying for political and financial reform. For this purpose, Robert Morris turned to Gouverneur Morris's old target, Thomas Paine, who was as broke as the government and eager to be of help. Paine met with both Morrises; Gouverneur, he wrote, "hopped round upon one leg."[14] For $800 a year (about $10,000 today), Paine agreed to write articles "informing the people and rousing them into action."[15] His stipend was kept secret, for, as Gouverneur Morris delicately put it, "a salary publickly and avowedly given . . . would injure the effect of Mr. Paine's publications."[16]

One project that consumed much of Morris's time and ingenuity, though it had little effect, was his plan for a new currency. America's was chaotic. English tokens and Spanish and Portuguese coins all circulated, and each state had different rates of exchange. When he sat down to address this problem, he made two preliminary decisions: the United States should have a decimal system; and its basic unit should be of small value, to convert all the competing currencies into each other without remainders. The basic unit he picked—1/4 of a grain of silver (1/1,750 of an ounce)—was so tiny, however, that values expressed in it seemed huge. The Spanish dollar or piece of eight, the most common coin in the New World, was worth 1,440 of Morris's "quarters." Morris's mathematical skill had led him astray; in the pursuit of precision, his system had become too complex. A few years later, Congress adopted a different decimal system, proposed by Thomas Jefferson, dividing the American dollar (roughly equal to the Spanish one) into 100 cents. Americans would use fractions of dollars and small Spanish coins for decades, as they tried to assign the proper value to items in Jefferson's simpler but cruder scheme. An eighth of a dollar was a bit, which survives in the phrase "two bits"; a sixteenth of a dollar was a picayune, which survives in the name of the *New Orleans Times-Picayune*. But the rough and ready system finally took hold.[17]

In July 1782, the Finance Office issued a report, written by Gouverneur Morris, that was far more important. The Morrises proposed that the United States go to the market once again, with a new issue of loan certificates for investors. These bonds would pay 6 percent interest. They would be backed, not by requisitions on the states or by foreign loans, but by revenues (some of them adopted from Gouverneur Morris's reports to Congress in 1778): a 5 percent tariff on imports; a land tax of one dollar per 100 acres; a head tax of one dollar; and an excise tax of 12 1/2 cents (one bit) per gallon of liquor.

"With money," Morris wrote Jay, "we can do every thing."[18] Some of what he wanted to do was obvious: pay the army; pay the interest on the national debt; establish the credit of the United States. Every responsible person shared these goals. But Morris also envisioned a goal that few shared: a national government, based on the finance system. Congress's "ministers," he wrote, "have the arduous task before them, to govern without power, nay, more, to obtain the power necessary to govern."[19] A funded debt, with taxes and tax collectors, would create that power.

High hopes gave way to desperation, however, as 1782 wound down. Though Morris's report was approved by a congressional committee, Congress as a whole would not enact it. First Rhode Island, then Virginia vetoed the proposal for a 5 percent tariff (such a radical change to the Articles of Confederation required the unanimous approval of all thirteen states). The most Congress would do was ask the states for $1.2 million, to scrape by with interest payments. Jay reported to Congress that all they could expect from Spain was "delay, chicane and slight."[20] "[O]nly . . . a continuance of the war," Morris wrote, would "convince the people of the necessity of obedience to common counsels for general purposes."[21] But France had lost a major naval battle in the West Indies, and Britain wanted to settle. Clearly, the war was drawing to a close.

At the end of the year Washington's army went into winter quarters at Newburgh, New York, fifty miles up the Hudson from New York City. Now a new fear began to possess the officers—that when peace arrived, they would be sent home without pay, and only the flimsiest of IOUs. On December 29, a delegation of three officers, including Colonel Matthias Ogden, one of Morris's New Jersey in-laws, appeared in Philadelphia to make their case to Congress. The army's unhappiness filled the Morrises with hope. If the army joined the call for reform, something might be done.

"The army have swords in their hands," Morris wrote Jay on New Year's Day, 1783. "You know enough of the history of mankind to know much more than I have said, and possibly much more than they themselves yet think of." In other words, if the army were rebuffed, it could march; if it was not "yet" considering such an option, helpful friends might suggest it. ". . . I am glad to see things in their present train. Depend on it, good will arise from the situation to which we are hastening. And this you may rely on, that my efforts will not be wanting . . . [A]lthough I think it probable, that much of convulsion will ensue, yet it must terminate in giving to government that power, without which government is but a name."[22]

The army did not see it that way. In February, Morris wrote to Henry Knox, Washington's artillery commander, at Newburgh, and to Nathanael Greene, who was commanding the army of the south in South Carolina. "[A]fter a peace," he wrote Knox, Congress "will see you starve rather than pay you a six-penny tax."[23] "[W]ith the due exception of miracles," he wrote Greene, "there is no probability that the states" would ever pay the army, "unless the army be united and determined in the pursuit of it."[24] Knox asked the obvious question: if "the present constitution is so defective, why do not you great men call the people together and tell them so?"[25] The military man was telling the politician: Don't ask the army to do your work for you. Greene gave the obvious warning: "When soldiers advance without authority, who can halt them?"[26]

In early March, the political problem came to the attention of another officer, General Horatio Gates, once the hero of Saratoga, but now disgraced by defeat in the South. The young officers on his staff at Newburgh, where he was posted, saw an opportunity to help both their chief and the army, and they circulated an anonymous call to action. "If this, then, be your treatment while the swords you wear are necessary for the defense of America, what have you to expect from peace . . . [w]hen those very swords . . . shall be taken from your sides?"[27] It is now agreed that the author of the Newburgh appeal was Major John Armstrong, Jr., an aide of Gates's, though Morris had been so associated with stirring the army up that he was long suspected. It took all the authority, the dramatic presence, and the melancholy humanity of George Washington—for it was in Newburgh at a meeting of the sullen officers that, as he read them an appeal to do their duty, he paused and said, "Gentlemen, you will permit me to put on my spectacles, for I have not only grown gray but almost blind in the service of my country"[28]—to turn the army aside from its course.

Morris's actions in the early months of 1783 were folly that (no thanks to him) only just fell short of disaster, and his January 1 letter to Jay is among the worst things he ever wrote. How could such an admirer of George Washington have behaved so unlike him? Surely his civilian's ignorance is implicated in his airy talk of convulsion and swords, though there were also veterans of the battlefield who were willing to play with these materials. Another explanation—it cannot be an excuse—is that Morris's work, from 4:00 A.M. to 8:00 P.M. at the Finance Office, was not only fatiguing but mentally narrowing. For a year and a half he had been studying public life through the prism of America's financial problems. These were crippling, and potentially fatal. But solving them would require a better grasp of military and political affairs than either Gouverneur or Robert Morris, for all their knowledge of the world, showed. There is something, finally, in Morris's conduct in the run-up to Newburgh that is not unlike his proposal to base the currency on a quarter grain of silver. He could fall in love with his ideas, and he could carry them too far. This was a vice of his fertile mind, his social station, and his family background: the lords of Morrisania, who built boats in the woods and wore loon-skin caps, were not always the best models for a statesman.

In justice to the plotters, they did not continue to scheme and murmur. They had not intended to establish a military dictatorship, they had only chosen one of the worst possible ways to reform a republic. Also to their credit is the fact that they were right about Congress. Congress agreed to replace all previous pension plans with an offer of five years' full pay, but since the national government had no dependable source of revenue, the pledge was a sham.

In justice to Morris, when only a few months had passed, he showed a mellow hopefulness. "True it is," he wrote John Jay, who was then in Paris, "that the general government wants energy, and equally true it is, that this want will eventually be supplied. A national spirit is the natural result of national existence. . . . [T]his generation will die away and give place to a race of Americans."[29] Morris always wrote well; he had turned from poisonous phrases back to wise and generous ones.

In JUNE 1783, Morris saw Morrisania and his mother for the first time in seven years. Sarah Morris was ailing; his sister Isabella and her husband, Isaac Wilkins, were preparing, along with many other loyalists, to move to Nova Scotia. The estate, which was still behind British lines, was in a sad condition. British soldiers had taken cattle and cleared timber, and a loyalist regiment commanded by Colonel Oliver DeLancey (hereditary rival of the Morrises) had camped on the property for two years. Morris added up the damage and presented a bill to Sir Guy Carleton, the British commander in New York, for £8,000 (about $300,000 today). Carleton approved the charges, and it was sent to General Staats Long Morris in England to collect. (He ultimately got £1,341, or about $50,000.) Happily, the British had not touched the wine. "[W]e drank your health in Cape wine," Morris wrote the superintendent of finance, "which has stood on a shelf in this house twenty years to my knowledge, and how much longer I know not."[30]

As peace approached, he resumed contact with his long-suffering friend Peter Van Schaak. The cautious and thorough Van Schaak had been living in exile in Britain, where he had profited from the virtues of his vices. This moderate man who could not believe that British policies, however arbitrary or damaging, were the result of willful indifference or a design to oppress, had—by attending debates in Parliament and following arguments in the press—become convinced that Britain and its leaders were indeed willful and oppressive. His thoughts turned to his home. Morris welcomed him back: "My own heart, worn by the succession of objects which have invaded it, looks back with more than female fondness towards the connections of earlier days."[31] Van Schaak returned to New York in 1785. After so many harrowing years, he resumed his practice as a lawyer, remarried and had a second family, and, like the restored Job, lived out the rest of a long life in peace.

Morris's heart may have been stirred by memories, and by the sight of his old home. But the sorry condition of the estate, and the even worse condition of New York City—haggard, partly burned, its population shaken by the alternating flight and influx of patriots and loyalists as the fortunes of war shifted—determined him to stay in Philadelphia. He needed to make money, and that was the city where it could be made.

Morris gave up his job in the Finance Office, and went to work for Robert Morris as a private junior partner. Gouverneur Morris began to play the great American sport of land speculation, buying 2,800 acres in Pennsylvania, and, with Robert Morris's help, a slice of a 100,000-acre tract in upstate New York. When Robert Morris contracted with the French government to supply it with Virginia tobacco, Gouverneur Morris went to Virginia as his lawyer to untangle the legal problems (a "tedious disagreeable business").[32] Robert Morris bought him a share in a partnership with the merchant William Constable, son of an Irish surgeon in the British army, who had been educated in Dublin and Schenectady, New York; spent most of the war doing business in British-occupied cities; then discovered patriotism just in time to escape reprisal for having been a loyalist. Some of Morris's new business contacts would fail, and some had been scoundrels; they were all trying to figure out how to make money in the post-revolutionary world, and Morris would wheel and deal alongside them for years.

He did not abandon all interest in politics. In 1785 the Constitutionalists, the radical party in Pennsylvania politics, launched an attack on the Bank of North America, drawing on rural resentment of Philadelphia, and populist resentment of rich men, though many rich men, who wished to set up a second bank, aided in the assault. Those old enemies, Morris and Paine, leaped to the Bank's defense, each employing his characteristic tone of voice. Paine's pieces in the newspapers were clear and intense polemics, propelled by simple, striking images. "The proceedings on this business are a stain to the national reputation of the state. They exhibit a train of little and envious thinking, a scene of passion, of arbitrary principles and unconstitutional conduct. . . . As blood, tho' taken from the arm, is nevertheless taken from the whole body, so the attempt to destroy the bank [would] distress the farmer as well as the merchant."[33] Morris delivered a 10,000-word oration before the Philadelphia Assembly, which managed to make economics amusing:

> A grievous complaint is made of the want of money, and yet as grievous a complaint of the only means to obtain any. We have it not at home, and we must not receive it from abroad [that is, by encouraging foreign investors]. Do these gentlemen believe it will rain money now, as it did manna of old? And because they have the same perverseness with the children of Israel, do they expect the same miracles? To experience a want of public credit is, they say, terrible; but to destroy the only means of supporting public credit is, they say, desirable.[34]

The fight over the Bank sputtered on for several years.

In January 1786, Sarah Morris died, age seventy-two. The war had been a strain on her estate and her family, and the much older breach between herself and her stepchildren had never entirely closed. Two months before her death, Richard Morris sued her over her management of the estate. But she had held on to her home and her opinions through everything.

The heir of Sarah's portion of Morrisania was her husband's second oldest son, Staats Long Morris. But he was firmly ensconced in England, a lieutenant general in the British army and a member of Parliament. He would come back to America to dispose of his affairs, but he had no intention of transplanting himself. Richard Morris was interested in money, not land. Lewis Morris, the manor lord, had already inherited his portion of the estate, and was content with it. That left Gouverneur. After long delays, occasioned by Staats's slow progress—he did not arrive in New York until September—and by Richard's stubbornness in maintaining his suit, the Morrises finally came to terms in April 1787. Gouverneur bought the estate from Staats and paid off Staats's obligations, as heir, to Richard and the daughters. These transactions cost him £10,000 ($390,000 today). He could pay a quarter of that out of his own inheritance from his mother. But the remainder had been loaned him by William Constable and his new Philadelphia associates. Morris was not lord of a manor, but he had 1,400 acres, with river views. To keep it, and to keep himself in Cape wine, he would have to continue working at his many ventures.

CHAPTER SEVEN

Secure the Blessings

A BIT OF PUBLIC business lay on Morris's schedule, however. Without asking for it, he had been elected a delegate to the Constitutional Convention.

The Pennsylvania Assembly had chosen him for the state's delegation while he was out of town, celebrating the New Year in Trenton, New Jersey. Morris had been living in Pennsylvania for not quite nine years, and some complained that he had "no stake in their hedge."[1] The criticism of his rootlessness rang false, since Pennsylvania had a tradition of being kind to outlanders; of the original seven-man delegation, four besides Morris were from somewhere else: England (Robert Morris), Scotland (James Wilson), Ireland (Thomas Fitzsimons), and Connecticut (Jared Ingersoll). In the spring, the Assembly added an eighth delegate, the greatest of all transplants, Benjamin Franklin of Boston.

Morris had to know that large political forces were afoot. George Washington was calling for interstate cooperation on canal building, to develop the trans-Appalachian west; Henry Knox had been sounding the alarm over Shays's Rebellion, an uprising of hard-pressed farmers in western Massachusetts; Alexander Hamilton had drafted the call for a Constitutional Convention at a 1786 meeting in Annapolis. But Morris had not involved himself in any of these projects or controversies. He had made his best effort for reform in the Finance Office; the denouement of Newburgh represented a rejection of his efforts. But now he was called upon to try again. "The appointment was the most unexpected thing that ever happened to me," he wrote Knox. "Had the object been any other than it is I would have declined."[2]

Pennsylvania, the host state, chose a large and distinguished delegation. Franklin was a world celebrity; Robert Morris was the money man
of the continent; James Wilson had established a reputation as a political thinker. William Pierce, a delegate from Georgia who wrote vivid
and generally accurate sketches of all his colleagues (he commonly mis-
reported their ages), wrote this panegyric: "Government seems to have
been [Wilson's] peculiar study, all the political institutions of the world
he knows in detail, and can trace the causes and effects of every revolution from the earliest stages of the Grecian commonwealth down to the
present time."[3] The only delegation that matched Pennsylvania's in lus-
ter and depth was the seven-man team from Virginia, led by the young
governor, Edmund Randolph; two senior theorists, George Mason and
Thomas Jefferson's teacher, George Wythe; and one young and even
more brilliant theorist, James Madison. Madison, a year older than
Morris, was small, sober, and driven; at first blush he could seem prig-
gish. He sped through the college of New Jersey at Princeton in two
years, then suffered a nervous collapse, and he lost his first race for the
Virginia House of Burgesses when he would not treat the voters to
drinks. In a committee setting, however, his energy, his thoroughness,
and his immense learning made him a compelling force. After hours,
he revealed a taste for off-color stories. Greatest of the Virginians was
the greatest man in America, George Washington. In the Convention
as a whole there were eight signers of the Declaration of Independence,
including Robert Morris, Franklin, Wilson, and Wythe. Some famous
Americans, notably Samuel Adams and Patrick Henry, stayed home,
while others were otherwise occupied (John Adams was minister to
Great Britain, and Jefferson was minister to France). But the Convention had many ornaments, much solidity, and only a few ciphers.

Judged by his record alone, Morris ranked with the solid rather than
the glittering. At thirty-five, he was among the younger delegates, al-
though he was not, as he had been at Kingston, one of the youngest.
The junior member in Philadelphia was twenty-seven-year-old
Jonathan Dayton of New Jersey (twenty-nine-year-old Charles
Pinckney of South Carolina told everyone that he was twenty-four).
Morris had been selected because the resurgent Republican Party in

Pennsylvania appreciated his talents; even so, he had won only a bare majority of votes in the state Assembly (Franklin and Robert Morris had been elected unanimously). If Gouverneur Morris was to shine in Philadelphia, it would have to be through a special display of his talents on the spot.

Happily, one of his talents was public speaking. Morris was both an orator and an arguer; he could paint a glowing picture, or jab a rival in the gut. These gifts, augmented by his stature and his intelligence, made him a formidable force. William Pierce's portrait of him repeats what had by now become the traditional criticism—"he is fickle and inconstant, never pursuing one train of thinking, nor ever regular"—but wraps it in high, if somewhat alarmed, praise. "He winds through all the mazes of rhetoric, and throws around him such a glare that he charms, captivates, and leads away the senses of all who hear him. With an infinite stretch of fancy he brings to view things when he is engaged in deep argumentation that render all the labor of reasoning easy and pleasing." A good teacher, or a serpent in the garden? Pierce didn't seem to be quite sure. "No man," he concluded, "has more wit, nor can any one engage the attention more than Mr. Morris."[4] James Madison, who took the most complete notes of any delegate, and who posted himself in front of the presiding officer's chair the better to listen, wrote more soberly that "the correctness of [Morris's] language and the distinctness of his enunciation were particularly favorable to a reporter."[5]

The states had answered the call for a Convention, out of the same sense of urgency that had dogged Morris when he went to work for the Finance Office in 1781, or when he took his seat in Congress in 1778: the urgency arising from the United States's failure to cope with its debts. Urgency had become almost routine. The war had been won on loans and luck; a mutiny had been averted with an IOU; but still the government had no dependable source of revenue. Many of the state governments were as badly off: the farmers of Massachusetts had been driven to rebellion by property taxes levied to pay the state's crushing debt. On the bourses of Antwerp and Amsterdam, the money men of Europe traded American securities at a third to a quarter of their face value. The Thirteen Colonies were the first in the world to win independence, but the United States, despite its resources and the industry of some its citizens, was in a fair way to becoming the first Third World nation. The Convention offered itself as a last chance for reform. "[T]he fate of America," as Morris later put it, "was suspended by a hair."[6]

Morris got off to a false start. The Convention, which had been called to meet in mid-May, had a quorum by May 25. Franklin planned to nominate Washington to chair the proceedings, maintaining the symbiosis of their celebrity, but rain kept the eighty-one-year-old man at home, and Robert Morris made the motion in his place, which passed unanimously. Six days later, Gouverneur Morris left town. Business drew him away from the nation's business. A new estate manager at Morrisania required instructions, and one of William Constable's agents had arrived in New York from Europe with the news that their partner Robert Morris's bills were being protested (in effect, his checks were bouncing). America might be hanging by a hair, but Gouverneur Morris spent all of June tending to these matters. Morris was not the only absentee. Delegates came late, left early, or went away for weeks at a time, to nurse illnesses, tend their personal affairs (Pierce, who called Morris inconstant, himself left at the end of June in an effort to stave off bankruptcy), or register their disapproval of the goings-on. Alexander Hamilton of New York stayed away for two months because he despaired of real change; Robert Yates and John Lansing, Jr., the other delegates from New York, left for good in July because they believed the changes that had been approved were too drastic. Morris was back in his seat by July 2, however, ready for work.

He returned at a moment of drama, for the Convention, as Roger Sherman of Connecticut said, was "at a full stop."[7] The issue in its path was the ongoing power and influence of the states. Nearly all of the delegates wanted a government with greater powers, independent of the states, which over the years had withheld requisitions and vetoed the most modest taxes. But how was a stronger national government to be chosen? How would the states be represented in it? Wilson and Madison, the most aggressive minds of Pennsylvania and Virginia, wanted a Congress based on proportional representation, which would shrink the voice of the small states almost to nothing (Virginia and Pennsylvania, the largest, were nine times as populous as Delaware, the smallest). The small states pushed back, insisting that at least one house of Congress be organized as Congress was under the Articles of Confederation, with all states voting as equal units. Two days before Morris returned, Gunning Bedford, Jr., of Delaware, a young, angry fat man—"a bold and nervous speaker," wrote Pierce, "warm and impetuous in his temper"[8]—warned that if the large states changed the principle of representation, "the small ones will find some foreign ally of more honor and good faith." Bedford's threat, delivered on a Saturday, must have been the talk of the delegates all the following week; but Morris, who had tangled with everyone from his dearest friends to Thomas Paine, was not intimidated. "This country must be united," he observed on Thursday, July 5. "If persuasion does not unite it, the sword will."[9] Four of the next five speakers grappled with Morris's sword, either trying to draw it or to twist it deeper.

This sally displayed a quality of Morris's that the delegates would become accustomed to over the next two and a half months: his ability to provoke, and his delight in doing so, whenever anyone showed an arrogance equal to his own. At the end of August, the Convention examined another sore spot, the slave trade. The Carolinas and Georgia, where mortality was higher than it was along the Chesapeake, depended on the traffic to refresh their slave labor force. Most of the delegates, though, northerners and southerners alike, were too humane to proclaim what they permitting, and so the relevant clause then on the floor was wrapped in cotton wool: the "importation of such persons as the several states . . . shall think proper to admit, shall not be prohibited."[10] Morris offered an amendment: the "importation of slaves into North Carolina, South Carolina, and Georgia shall not be prohibited. . . ." This little change, he said, "would be most fair and would avoid the ambiguity. . . . He wished it to be known also that this part of the Constitution was a compliance with those states." With offensive tact, he added that if his language "should be objected to . . . he should not urge it."[11] After two piqued southerners and two anxious northerners shushed him, Morris withdrew his motion.

The Convention tolerated such a man because he was as amusing as he was annoying. He may never have slapped Washington on the back, but he was not afraid to poke fun at Franklin. During a discussion of term limits for the executive, the sage, in a pious mood, declared that "[I]n free governments the rulers are the servants, and the people their superiors. . . . For the former therefore to return among the latter was not to *degrade* but to *promote* them." To which Morris only remarked that "he had no doubt our executive" would be modest enough "to decline the promotion."[12] On another occasion, Elbridge Gerry of Massachusetts, earnest and crotchety, warned against letting the vice president preside over the Senate. "The close intimacy that must subsist between the president and vice-president makes it absolutely improper." "The vice president then will be the first heir apparent that ever loved his father," said Morris.[13]

These were sly hits at republican cant, and human nature. Sometimes he indulged in broad comedy. Early in August, Morris proposed that foreign-born Americans be citizens for fourteen years before they could serve in the Senate. A lively argument followed, with Wilson, the Scot, opposing such a long residency requirement, while Pierce Butler of South Carolina, an Irishman, supported it. Morris spoke up again, in the name, he said, of "prudence. It is said that some tribes of Indians carried their hospitality so far as to offer to strangers their wives and daughters. Was this a proper model for us? He would admit [immigrants] to his house, he would invite them to his table, [he] would provide for them comfortable lodgings; but would not carry complaisance so far as to bed them with his wife."[14] The delegates' accounts of the Constitutional Convention are interesting, but they are not light reading; most of what lightness there is comes from Morris.

Madison, the careful reporter, occasionally checked his notes of long and controversial speeches with their speakers. One such effort was a "very extravagant" speech of Morris's, probably one of his tangles with Bedford over representation. "It displayed," wrote Madison, "his usual fondness for saying things and advancing doctrines that no one else would. . . . [W]hen the thing *stared him in the face* (this was Mr. Morris's exact expression) . . . he laughed and said, 'Yes, it is all right.'"[15]

Morris spoke 173 times at the Convention, more often than any other member, despite the fact that he missed all of June. Wilson, who spoke 168 times, and Madison, who spoke 161, placed and showed, even though they attended every session. What things, peculiar to himself, did Morris say?

Morris was a passionate nationalist. He had come "as a representative of America";[16] to "form a compact for the good of America."[17] "Among the many provisions which had been urged, he had seen none for supporting the dignity and splendor of the American empire."[18] There were other nationalists at the Convention: Madison; Wilson; Hamilton, when he chose to speak; Washington, though he hardly spoke at all. None were as rhapsodic as Morris. He attacked every centrifugal or sectional force, assailing the states—"What if all the charters and constitutions of the states were thrown into the fire, and all their demagogues into the ocean? What would it be to the happiness of America?";[19] assailing entire regions—the west could not furnish "enlightened" lawmakers, for "the busy haunts of men, not the remote wilderness, were the proper school of political talents";[20] if "the southern gentlemen" persisted in angling for power, "let us at once take a friendly leave of each other."[21] Morris's attacks on the west and the South goaded the sober Madison into saying that he "determined the human character by the points of the compass."[22]

Morris spoke out against democracy in every branch of government. This was not an unusual position at the Convention: "The evils we experience flow from the excess of democracy," Elbridge Gerry said roundly during the Convention's first week.[23] But Morris added a twist of his own. A broad franchise across the board would empower the rich, who would control poor or fickle voters. "[T]he people never act from reason alone. The rich will take advantage of their passions and make these the instrument for oppressing them."[24] "Give the votes to people who have no property, and they will sell them to the rich who will be able to buy them."[25] Morris had had these concerns since 1774, when he smiled at the bellwethers leading the sheep at Fraunces Tavern; such concerns were a hereditary privilege of the Morrises, who had done their share of herding over the years. Morris's solution was to segregate rich and poor each in their own branch of Congress, so that their pride would encourage mutual distrust. "[O]ne interest must be opposed to another interest. Vices . . . must be turned against each other."[26]

Morris attacked slavery more strongly than he had at Kingston. His great philippic came in the course of a discussion of how slaves should be counted in the rule of representation. By August, it was clear that one house of Congress would be apportioned on the basis of population; Delaware would have the fewest representatives, Virginia and Pennsylvania the most. This would also be true of the Electoral College, when that strange system was finally rigged. In both bodies, the southern states wanted slaves to be counted equally with freemen; this would boost the power of their masters, without conferring any benefit upon the slaves, since of course slaves could not vote. Some northerners—notably Rufus King of Massachusetts—asked why slaves should be counted at all? On August 8, Morris rose to ask the same question. Slavery, he began, "was the curse of heaven on the states where it prevailed. . . . Travel through the whole continent, and you behold the prospect continually varying with the appearance and disappearance of slavery. The moment you leave the [New England] states and enter New York, the effects of the institution become visible; passing through [New Jersey] and entering Pennsylvania, every criterion of superior improvement witnesses the change. Proceed southwardly, and every step you take through the great region of slaves presents a desert increasing with the increasing proportion of these wretched beings." But he was just warming up. "Upon what principle is it that the slaves shall be computed in the representation? Are they men? Then make them citizens and let them vote. Are they property? Why then is no other property included? The houses in [Philadelphia] are worth more than all the wretched slaves which cover the rice swamps of South Carolina." Finally, a masterly sentence, long, dense, and relentless. "The admission of slaves into the representation when fairly explained comes to this: that the inhabitant of Georgia and South Carolina who goes to the coast of Africa and, in defiance of the most sacred laws of humanity, tears away his fellow creatures from their dearest connections and damns them to the most cruel bondages, shall have more votes in a government instituted for the protection of the rights of mankind than the citizen of Pennsylvania or New Jersey who views with a laudable horror so nefarious a practice."[27]

The picture of trans-Atlantic woe and hypocrisy that follows the colon is folded like a Chinese screen. At either end stand Americans. Moving inward, the laws of humanity are defied, and the protection of rights is mocked. At the center, a monstrous irony: the act of enslavement is rewarded by votes. In Morris's sentence, the laudable horror of the Pennsylvanian accomplishes nothing. Neither did his speech. Roger Sherman of Connecticut spoke for the majority: "the admission of the Negroes into the ratio of representation" was not "liable to such insuperable objections."[28] The Convention compromised, counting each slave as three fifths of a person.

The nature of the executive was one of the trickiest questions the Convention addressed, not settled until the home stretch. No one knew how long his term should be, how many he should have, or how he should be picked. Franklin favored a plural executive, a committee of three; Gerry feared the executive would be picked by the Society of the Cincinnati, the veterans' group of Revolutionary War officers. Brooding over the entire discussion was the silent presence of Washington, who had in effect been the nation's executive as commander in chief, and had set a very high bar (too high?) for trustworthiness. Morris was a leading spokesman for the executive, repelling assaults on him, and seeking to extend his powers. "We are acting a very strange part," he complained in August. "We first form a strong man to protect us, and at the same time wish to tie his hands behind him."[29] Morris spoke up for his grandfather, his uncle, and the only man he idolized.

Morris's success as an advocate was mixed. His analysis of rich and poor voters was an interesting opinion merely, thrown out for the edification of the delegates, then put aside; he lost on slavery. Nationalism would be an open question for the rest of his life, and beyond. The office of the president that finally emerged was to his liking, but that had more to do with the tidal pull of Washington than anything he said. Morris didn't get everything he wanted, but then no one did. Hamilton had wanted a president for life; Madison thought the national government should be able to veto state laws; George Mason wanted it to be able to pass sumptuary laws, regulating foreign luxuries and conspicuous consumption. Morris took his defeats with better grace than many. For all his sharp words and strong opinions, he was disinclined to sulk. "[T]o the brilliancy of his genius," wrote Madison when he was an old man, "he added what is too rare . . . a readiness to aid in making the best of measures in which he had been overruled." [30]

Morris was an indefatigable speaker, but his greatest service was done as a writer. On July 26, the Convention adjourned for ten days so that all the resolutions that had been so far approved could be offered to a Committee of Detail, for presentation as a draft. In the interval, Washington and Morris went to Valley Forge to fish for trout; Washington looked at the ruined outworks where his men had suffered so. On August 6, the Committee of Detail presented its handiwork, which was followed by five weeks of further discussion.

On September 8, the Convention selected a five-man committee to "revise the stile" and "arrange the articles" of the Constitution. [31] The chairman was Dr. William Samuel Johnson of Connecticut, a sixty-year-old lawyer and classicist who had just been named president of King's College, now christened Columbia. But the energy on the committee would come from its younger members: Rufus King, Madison, Hamilton, and Morris. As with the committee assigned to write the Declaration of Independence eleven years earlier, here was a surfeit of talents. In 1776, John Adams wrote voluminously and Benjamin Franklin wrote well, but the assignment had gone to Thomas Jefferson. Madison, Hamilton, or King would have done a fine job, but they gave the task to Morris. Perhaps his blazing performance over the last two months, like a jockey making his move at the far turn, decided them. His draft was done in four days.

Unlike Jefferson in 1776, Morris was not writing out of his head. He was bound by the resolutions of the Convention. Yet time and again, he shaped and smoothed; and though he was a lawyer, he avoided as much as he could the legalistic repetitions that his profession loves. The effect of his changes is to make for clarity, simplicity, and speed.

Consider a passage from Article VI, based on Article VIII of the draft of the Committee of Detail (one of Morris's improvements was to compress the draft's twenty-three articles into seven). The Committee of Detail said:

> The Acts of the Legislature of the United States made in pursuance of this Constitution, and all treaties made under the authority of the United States shall be the supreme law of the several States, and of their citizens and inhabitants; and the judges in the several States shall be bound thereby in their decisions; any thing in the Constitutions or laws of the several States to the contrary notwithstanding.[32]

Morris made it this:

> This constitution, and the laws of the United States which shall be made in pursuance thereof; and all treaties made, or which shall be made, under the authority of the United States, shall be the supreme law of the land; and the judges in every state shall be bound thereby, any thing in the constitution of any state to the contrary notwithstanding.[33]

Morris's rewrite is not poetry, but it is cleaner. Three clanking "the several States" become "the land," "every state," and "any state." "[T]he acts of the Legislature" become "the laws." Two bits of lint are removed: "and of their citizens and inhabitants" (who else do laws apply to?); "in their decisions" (how else are judges bound?). One seeming bit of lint is added: "or which shall be made," but it actually makes an important point. Morris wanted the states to be bound both by future treaties and by those already in force. Even so, he managed to chip eight words out of a passage that was only seventy words long to start with.

Or consider how Morris cleaned up the prohibition on state armies and navies. The analogous passage in the Articles of Confederation (the old and the new Constitution agreed on this point) had been a lazy bumble:

> No state shall engage in any war without the consent of the united states in congress assembled, unless such state be actually invaded

by enemies, or shall have received certain advice of a resolution being formed by some nation of Indians to invade such state, and the danger is so imminent as not to admit of a delay, till the united states in congress assembled can be consulted: nor shall any state grant commissions to any ships or vessels of war . . . unless such state be infested by pirates, in which case vessels of war may be fitted out for that occasion, and kept so long as the danger shall continue, or until the united states in congress assembled shall determine otherwise.[34]

The Indians and pirates impart an unexpected flavor of a boys' book, but as constitution writing, this simply fails.

Article XIII in the draft of the Committee of Detail had cleaned things up to this:

No State, without the consent of the Legislature of the United States, shall . . . keep troops or ships of war in time of peace . . . nor engage in any war, unless it shall be actually invaded by enemies, or the danger of invasion be so imminent, as not to admit of a delay, until the Legislature of the United States can be consulted.[35]

Morris, in Article I Section 10, wrote this:

No State shall, without the consent of Congress . . . keep Troops, or Ships of War in time of Peace . . . or engage in War, unless actually invaded, or in such imminent Danger as will not admit of delay.[36]

He cuts sixty-one words down to thirty-six, making danger more imminent by describing it more rapidly. Morris the stylist would not admit the delay of inelegant verbiage.

Sometimes Morris saved time by showing instead of explaining. Article II of the draft of the Committee of Detail declared that "The Government shall consist of supreme legislative, executive; and judicial powers."[37] Morris eliminated this entirely, and simply began his first three articles by announcing that "all legislative powers," "the executive power," and "the judicial power" shall be vested in a Congress, a president, and the courts.[38]

Madison described Morris's trimming and polishing best. "The finish given to the style and arrangement of the Constitution fairly belongs to [his] pen . . . A better choice could not have been made, as the performance of the task proved."[39]

Did the careful scribe try to smuggle in an argument for nationalism? Eleven years later, Albert Gallatin, a Pennsylvania congressman who had not been at the Convention, claimed on the floor of the House that Morris had played with the punctuation of Article I Section 8. The section begins:

> The Congress shall have Power To lay and collect Taxes, Duties, Imposts and Excises, to pay the Debts and provide for the common Defence and general Welfare of the United States . . . [40]

Clearly, everything after "Excises" explains what the taxes, duties, imposts, and excises are for. But, said Gallatin, Morris had put a semicolon after "Excises," which made providing for the common defense and the general welfare "distinct power[s]" of Congress. Roger Sherman of Connecticut, however, had spotted the "trick," and a comma was substituted, thereby ratcheting the powers of Congress back to their proper level.[41] At the time the charge was made, Sherman was dead, and Morris was out of the country, Morris was not above sleight of hand, but he made his convictions explicit elsewhere.

The Preamble was the one part of the Constitution that Morris wrote from scratch, and here he showed creativity, and condensed thought. The version of the Committee of Detail was as plain as paint. "We the people of the States of New Hampshire, Massachusetts" and so on through all the states to Georgia, "do ordain, declare, and establish the following Constitution for the Government of Ourselves and our Posterity."[42] This was a roll call, and an announcement. But what the ends of government might be, the Committee of Detail refused to say. The proposed constitutions offered by delegates at various times during the Convention had been more forthcoming. Madison had come to Philadelphia with a plan in his pocket, which defined the "objects ... of Confederation" as "common defence, security of liberty, and general welfare"—phrases borrowed from the Articles of Confederation.[43] Charles Pinckney's plan quaintly defined the purposes of government as the "common Benefit" of the states, and "their Defense and Security against all Designs and Leagues that may be injurious to their Interests and against all Force and Attacks offered to or made upon them or any of them."[44] Robert Patterson of New Jersey looked to "the exigencies of Government" and "the preservation of the Union."[45]

Morris wrote a grave little essay, as quiet as it is comprehensive.

> We, the people of the United States, in order to form a more perfect union, to establish justice, insure domestic tranquility, provide for the common defence, promote the general welfare, and secure the blessings of liberty to ourselves and our posterity, do ordain and establish this Constitution for the United States of America.[46]

The last of Morris's six goals are Madison's three, rearranged so that "liberty," now prized for its "blessings," opens out to the future. Two inconspicuous rhymes—*insure/secure* and *tranquility/liberty/posterity*—and one strong alliteration—*provide/promote*—bind the paragraph together. In the final version, someone—the printer?—made a tiny improvement, canceling the second, redundant "to."

Morris's Preamble names "the people," rather than the thirteen states, as the source of legitimacy and power. This, not any sly semicolon, was his last statement of nationalism. Later historians dispute whether he intended anything so meaningful: Morris's version, they say, was a verbal maneuver to finesse the fact that some states—Rhode Island had sent no delegates to Philadelphia—might stay out of the Union for years. At the time, critics of the Constitution were not so indifferent. Patrick Henry, who had refused to attend the Convention, identified "that poor little thing—the expression, 'We the *people*; instead of the *states*,'" as a momentous shift.[47]

Truly, it was momentous. Washington had united Americans in war and now—as the hands-down favorite for the new country's first executive—in peace. The delegates to the Constitutional Convention had created a federal government that was far more finished and practical than its predecessor. Yet many Americans still held their states to be semiautonomous. It would be no accident that southern secession in 1861 would proceed under the slogan of "states' rights." When Gouverneur Morris changed "We the people of the states" into "We the people," he created a phrase that would ring throughout American history, defining every American as part of a single whole. Those three words may be his greatest legacy.

As an old man, Madison warned against expending "so much constructive ingenuity"[48] on the phrases of the Preamble. The meat of the Constitution, he believed, was its careful machinery of provisions. The same objections might apply to the self-evident truths in the opening of the Declaration of Independence. The business of that document is the indictment of George III, and the assertion of sovereignty. Strictly speaking, Jefferson's little thoughts about man, nature, and God are superfluous. Anyone interested in such topics can read Locke, or ponder the Bible. Yet Jefferson in 1776 thought it was important to consider first principles, as did Morris eleven years later, and their colleagues, on both occasions, agreed.

After a few adjustments, the document was approved by all the state delegations in attendance on September 15, though Edmund Randolph, George Mason, and Elbridge Gerry announced that they would not sign it. To win them over, Morris thought of a trick, attested in Madison's notes, which Franklin agreed to propose to the delegates on the 17th, their last session: surely everyone could sign "in witness" to the fact that the vote of the states had been unanimous?[49] The trick didn't work, and the Constitution went out into the world with the signatures of thirty-nine framers, minus the holdouts. Morris's occupies the lower left-hand corner of the page.

In later years, Morris's attitude toward the Convention and his handiwork was appreciative without being worshipful. "In adopting a republican form of government," he would write in 1803, "I not only took it as a man does his wife, for better, for worse, but what few men do with their wives, I took it knowing all its bad qualities."[50] One of republican government's flaws was impermanence. The framers, he wrote in 1811, knew they were working with "crumbling materials. History, the parent of political science, had told them that it was almost as vain to expect permanency from democracy as to construct a palace on the surface of the sea. But it would have been foolish to fold their arms and sink into despondence because they could neither form nor establish the best of all possible systems. . . . As in war so in politics, much must be left to chance."[51]

The fight to ratify the Constitution had easy victories and sharp struggles, and it took nine months, until eleven states had ratified, including all the largest ones. Morris took no part in it. Alexander Hamilton asked him if he would contribute to a propaganda campaign that Hamilton had conceived, a series of essays for the New York newspapers, to be signed "Publius." Morris declined. William Duer, another friend of Hamilton's, offered his services, but Hamilton declined to accept them. Hamilton ended up working with Madison and John Jay; the *Federalist Papers* they wrote are clear, earnest, and intelligent, often ringing, but they have made their way without Morris's sparkle. In 1788, Morris went once more to Virginia, to attend to Robert Morris's tobacco business. He visited Washington at Mount Vernon, met local grandees like the Randolphs (Jefferson's cousins), and attended the state ratifying Convention in June. He sent Hamilton keen but lighthearted reports of the debates. "Be of good chear. My religion steps in where my understanding falters and I feel faith as I lose confidence. Things will yet go right, but when and how I dare not predicate. So much for this dull subject."[52]

Morris had disengaged himself once more from public affairs. Having been chosen, against to his will, to make an effort for which he then gave his all, he went back to his private business.

Part 2

The French Revolution

CHAPTER EIGHT

Death and Love

$\mathcal{R}$OBERT MORRIS, Gouverneur's mentor and senior partner, was stretched thin. In the language of modern business, he was highly exposed, juggling a number of ventures, whose prospects of success ranged from decent to dubious. Like many other businessmen in his situation, then and since, he tried to cover himself by pursuing yet more ventures.

As with almost every American of means, he had invested in land. Land speculation was the glimmering El Dorado of the founding period, the way to get rich quick. As early as 1775, he had bought a plantation on the Mississippi River hopefully called the Orange Grove Estate, even though not one orange seed had yet been planted there. Now he was loaded with hundreds of thousands of barren, promising acres along the St. Lawrence and Genesee rivers in upstate New York. If the United States needed a capital, perhaps Trenton, New Jersey, would be a likely site, and a good bet; as a senator in the newly created Congress, he could lobby for his hunch. In 1785, the French government had agreed to pay him 1 million livres ($1.5 million today) in return for supplying France with all its tobacco for three years; shipments from Virginia and Maryland had not come fast enough, however, so he was in arrears. The Penn family, the former proprietors of the colony of Pennsylvania, hoped that the British government would reimburse them for their lost feudal rights. Perhaps they would sell their claim at a discount. Most audaciously of all, Robert Morris hoped to buy the United States's $34 million debt (almost $450 million today) to France at 50 cents on the dollar. With that block of IOUs in hand, he would become at one stroke a major force in European banking.

All these plans and pipe dreams suggested the desirability of sending an intelligent and trustworthy associate to France. The French government, French speculators in American land (as eager as the natives), and Robert Morris's potential French partners on the American debt deal were best dealt with directly. In December 1788, Gouverneur Morris sailed from Philadelphia, arriving in France forty days later. Rival teams of speculators, who had their own designs on America's debt to France, treated him as an enemy agent, which indeed he was. "[B]e on your guard against G. Morris," wrote one to a partner.[1] He carried with him a cargo of solid value: letters of introduction from George Washington. Most such letters, he had written Washington, were "a kind of paper money," but the General's, he knew, would be good as gold.[2] In return, Washington wanted his younger friend to buy him a watch, not "trifling" or "finical," but large and flat, with "a *plain handsome* key."[3]

Gouverneur Morris needed to work and prosper in order to complete his purchase of Morrisania; Europe would offer him an even greater field than Philadelphia. But Morris was going for more than money. His trip would fulfill a fifteen-year-old desire to see the big world, to rub off his barbarisms among the "truly polite." When he had expressed that hope in his youthful letter to William Smith, he had thought of spending time in London, as his grandfather and his uncle had done. London, at just under 1 million souls, was an order of magnitude larger than any American city—a new world compared to New York and Philadelphia, to say nothing of York or Kingston. Paris, at 600,000 almost equally great and bustling, would be a shade more strange.

In the night memory of America lurked the image of France as a bogeyman. Throughout the colonial period, France had been the champion of the Pope and the patron of Indian marauders. Washington had fought Frenchmen on the frontier in his twenties; John Jay's grandfather had fled France as a refugee. Brave Wolfe's death before the walls of Quebec was still a subject for popular song. France represented sin as well as danger. The Frenchmen who visited America during the Revolution and noticed with amusement the fidelity of American wives, were noticed in their turn, for the rubes were as observant as the sophisticates. The twin prospect of threat and laxity could provoke the watchfulness of upright Americans or titillate the curiosity of adventurous ones. The experience of the Revolution, without quite obliterating these American reactions, had overlaid them with gratitude. After the Constitution had taken effect, the U.S. Senate hung a portrait of America's benefactor Louis XVI on its walls; George Washington displayed a similar portrait at Mount Vernon.

Every American emotion, positive and negative, was augmented by France's size, wealth, and power. At 26 million souls, France was six times as populous as the United States. Britain, with a population of only 15 million (one third of it in Ireland), might have a better navy, a larger colonial empire, and a more modern financial system. But travelers who had no national axes to grind routinely spoke of France as the greatest nation of Europe. If they criticized its shortcomings, it was in the course of marveling that such a nation could not do better. Indeed, though she was hemmed by enemies, France had fought her neighbors, sometimes single-handed, for more than a century, and while she had failed to impose her hegemony on the continent, neither had she ever been decisively beaten.

Three great Americans had spent time in France during the Revolution and its aftermath, and their reactions covered the gamut of American attitudes. Benjamin Franklin had joined Silas Deane in Paris at the end of 1776 and stayed, through the signing of the Treaty of Paris, until 1785. He had a high old time. The septuagenarian played the French like a pianoforte, and they delighted to be played by him. "The Spaniards," he wrote an American friend, "are by common opinion supposed to be cruel, the English proud, the Scotch violent, the Dutch avaricious, etc., but I think the French have no national vice ascribed to them."[4] Some ascribed a vice to them, however, and accused Franklin of sharing it. In another letter Franklin defended himself. "Somebody, it seems, gave it out that I loved ladies; and then everybody presented me their ladies (or the ladies presented themselves) to be embraced; that is, have their necks kissed. For as to the kissing of lips or cheeks it is not the mode here; the first is reckoned rude, and the other may rub off the paint. The French ladies have, however, a thousand other ways of rendering themselves agreeable, by their various attentions and civilities and their sensible conversation."[5]

John Adams, who joined Franklin as a diplomat in 1778, and lived in Paris on and off until 1785, had a more mixed reaction. His second night on French soil, a Frenchwoman, punning on his surname, asked him, as a descendant of Adam, "how the first couple found out the art of lying together?" "To me," Adams wrote, "whose acquaintance with women had been confined to America, where the manners of the ladies were universally characterized at that time by modesty, delicacy and dignity, this question was surprizing and shocking." He improvised some tale about magnetic attraction, then added, "[t]his is a decent story in comparison with many which I heard . . . concerning married ladies of fashion and reputation."[6] At the same time, he could not help being thrilled by the country. He called it "one great garden,"[7] filled with "[e]very thing that can sooth, charm and bewitch."[8] Art improved nature. "The richness, the magnificence, and splendor is beyond all description. This magnificence is not confined to public buildings . . . but extends to private houses, to furniture, equipage, dress and especially to entertainments." He worried that it had come at a cost—"the more elegance, the less virtue"—and he worried further that "even my own dear country" would yearn "to be elegant, soft and luxurious."[9] A part of him certainly heard the siren call.

Thomas Jefferson, who took Franklin's place as American minister to France in 1785, was the most censorious. His teenage daughter Patsy could write artlessly about all the beautiful "winders [of] died glass . . . that form all kinds of figures."[10] But her father knew what evil had reared the windows. Though France was blessed by "the finest soil upon earth" and "the finest climate under heaven," it was "loaded with misery, by kings, nobles, and priests, and by them alone."[11] It foreshadowed the hereafter, "where we are to see God and his angels in splendor, and crowds of the damned trampled under their feet." French morals were as bad as the French social system. "Conjugal love having no existence among them, domestic happiness, of which that is the basis, is utterly unknown." Jefferson's harsh reaction was based on the circumstances of his visit as well as ideological disposition. The late 1780s, his time in France, was a period of bad harvests and unusual rural suffering. One of his most affecting letters, a meditation on the unequal distribution of property addressed to James Madison, was prompted by an encounter with a wretched woman day laborer outside Fontainebleau, the site of the royal hunting lodge. Jefferson allowed that the French were temperate—"I have never yet seen a man drunk"—and musical—"[I]t is the only thing which from my heart I envy them, and which, in spite of all the authority of the Decalogue, I do covet." [12]

All three Americans agreed on one point: the disposition of the French to please. The French national character had not calcified into mere arrogance. Perhaps the French could afford to be other things besides arrogant, because they still had so much to be arrogant about. A wistful Franklin wrote, after he returned to Philadelphia, that he still dreamed of Paris, and of "the sweet society of a people . . . who, above all the nations of the world, have in the greatest perfection, the art of making themselves beloved by strangers." [13] Parisians "are the happiest people in the world, I believe," wrote John Adams, "and have the best disposition to make others so." [14] "[S]tern and hauty republican as I am, I cannot help loving these people, for their earnest desire and assiduity to please." [15] Even the begrudging Jefferson admitted that "a man might pass a life" in Paris "without encountering a single rudeness." [16]

Morris's quirky temperament would react upon all these social phenomena during the almost six years he lived in France (perhaps the one sentiment he did not feel, at least initially, was fear of French might, although that would change as France did). One of his first acts upon arriving on this great theater of civilization, power, and temptation was to buy a blank journal, bound in apple-green vellum, in which, on March 1, 1789, he began to keep a diary. He kept it faithfully, writing as much as five hundred words per day. By 1792, the pressure of events began to shorten his entries, and at the beginning of the following year, danger made him stop writing altogether. In the fall of 1794, when he prepared to leave France, he began writing again, which he continued to do for the rest of his life, though seldom with the thoroughness of his first Paris days. When an adult takes up the diarizing habit it can indicate some psychological turning point or need. Morris knew, early on, that Paris was a special place; he wished to observe it, to observe himself, and to observe himself in the reactions of others.

Some of Morris's early associates in Paris were fellow Americans. He overlapped eight months with Jefferson, who would leave in September 1789 to become the United States's first secretary of state. The two American aristocrats were alike in their palates. Jefferson, Morris noted, served a good dinner and "excellent" wines[17] (when Jefferson sailed for home, he took 288 bottles with him). They found, however, that they disagreed in their political views. The Virginian hoped that France might abolish the social distinctions whose oppressive effects he deplored. "How far such views may be right respecting mankind in general," Morris wrote in his diary, "is I think extremely problematical. But with respect to this nation I am sure it is wrong and cannot eventuate well."[18] They also differed in the freedom of their conversation; Morris's risqué expressions, a common friend recorded years later, made Jefferson "blush . . . to the temples."[19]

In late November 1789 appeared the adopted American, Thomas Paine. Paine had designed a single-arch iron suspension bridge, and since 1787 he had spent his time going back and forth between France and his native Britain hoping to build a prototype. Despite their recent collaboration in defense of the Bank of North America, Paine and Morris remained an odd couple. Paine was garrulous, earnest, and sometimes broke. Morris was fluent, witty, and provident. "Paine calls upon me," Morris wrote after one visit, "and talks a great deal upon subjects of little moment."[20] On another occasion, Morris loaned Paine some money, "telling him at the same time that he is a troublesome fellow."[21] Yet he also acknowledged that Paine's writing could be "splendid" and "novel."[22] The two acquaintances would hobble along, until their relations became very much worse.

Morris also saw again the Franco-American hero, the marquis de Lafayette. Lafayette's years in America had given him the most glorious career it was possible for a youth of his disposition to imagine. He had fought for a noble cause, and won the love of a nation. George Washington sent him admiring and heart-sore letters after the marquis returned to France; the state of Virginia presented a bust of him to the city of Paris; the island of Nantucket sent him a 500-pound cheese. Lafayette cherished the love he had earned overseas, and never let the French forget it. When his first two children were born, he named the boy George Washington and the girl Virginia. At his Paris household, his family spoke English, and his messenger was dressed as an American Indian. The young nobleman looked for new idealistic causes to serve. He proposed to settle liberated slaves at Cayenne in French Guiana (which caused Washington to praise "the benevolence of [his] heart");[23] he served in the Assembly of Notables, a 1787 meeting of the princes, dukes, marshals, and other lords of the realm, to discuss reform of the French tax system. The one flaw in him that his American friends began to notice as he entered his thirties was his love of the applause he had received. He would never consciously do a dishonorable thing to win more, but he had not learned the republican art of schooling his ambition. Jefferson thought that Lafayette had a "canine appetite for popularity and fame,"[24] while the marquis made Morris reflect that there were two kinds of ambition, "the one born of pride, the other of vanity, and his partakes most of the latter."[25]

The world of the international upper class that Morris now inhabited could be quite small. At one Paris dinner he saw John Paul Jones, the American naval hero, meet a Scottish nobleman whose seaside castle Jones had raided during the Revolution. After the raid Jones had sent back the family silver, and the young lord now thanked him for his "polite attention."[26] On a business trip to Amsterdam, Morris met General Baron Friedrich von Riedesel, the Hessian commander who had fought at Saratoga while Morris was fleeing to Marble Town; together, they criticized the tactics of General Burgoyne. During a jaunt to London, Morris did a favor for two cosmopolitan ladies. Mrs. Angelica Church, the American wife of an English businessman, had commissioned an allegorical design for the ceiling of a garden folly from Mrs. Maria Cosway, an Italian-born artist. Morris wrote an accompanying verse:

> *Here Friendship adorn'd by the Graces we see*
> *Maria, design'dby thy Art.*
> *Yet the Emblem was sure not invented by thee*
> *But found inAngelica's Heart.*[27]

The three had more in common than their interest in ornamental architecture, for Mrs. Church (the former Angelica Schuyler) was in love with her brother-in-law, Alexander Hamilton, while Mrs. Cosway had captivated another founding father in Paris, the widower Thomas Jefferson. Morris paid no gallant attentions to either woman.

Morris, who took rooms on the right bank in the rue de Richelieu, not far from the Louvre, typically spent his mornings meeting bankers and government officials, and writing his business correspondence, which sometimes included lengthy reports in French. If there were more still to be done, he would write late at night, however long he had stayed out and however much he would add to his diary. In the middle of the day he would make calls, and occasionally sightsee (he had pedestrian artistic tastes, admiring paintings for their subjects rather than their quality). Beginning in the early evening, he would socialize with his French friends.

He had come to France in time to see the sunset of the *salon*. These periodic teas and suppers, presided over by fashionable and intellectual ladies, where everything from love to philosophy might be discussed, so long as it was done cleverly, had begun to lose their aura of excitement and power. "You know, Madame," one politician told an arbitress, "the reign of women is over." "Yes, monsieur," she answered, "but not that of the impertinent."[28] Yet as late as 1789, duchesses of discourse still tried to maintain their sway over society. Mme de Necker, whose Swiss banker husband was a genius at self-promotion, and perhaps at finance, ruled one court of talk. The *salon* of her daughter, the twenty-two-year-old Germaine de Staël, already formidable as the author of a tract on Rousseau, shone with equal glory (Morris called Mme de Staël's gatherings "the upper region of wits and graces").[29] The household in which Morris came to spend the most time was that of the comte and Mme de Flahaut.

Alexandre-Sébastien de Flahaut de la Billarderie was a sixty-three-year-old veteran whose job, as Keeper of the King's Gardens, brought him a small salary, no work—assistants did it all—and two apartments in the Louvre. (Although the royal art collection was housed there, most of the palace was still residential.) His wife, Adelaide, was twenty-eight. The two had been married for ten years. She had already begun her first novel, *Adèle de Senanges,* a tale of romantic love that was clearly wish-fulfillment (Adèle is the short form of Adelaide). A later critic would call it "a pastel so pale as to be almost colorless."[30] "One only finds [her novels]," an even later critic would write, "in the backs of provincial bookcases, or the libraries of old chateaus . . . bound with pink or red leather . . . illustrated with old-fashioned engravings of young people in lace shirt fronts, tragically pledging eternal love in the moonlight. . . ."[31]

Her writing is safe from critics now, for it is no longer read at all. But when she first published her novels, they were widely admired—Pierre Bezuhov read her in St. Petersburg—and there would come a time in her life when they kept body and soul together. Mme de Staël, who did not like Mme de Flahaut, depicted her in one of her own novels as "flatter[ing] the vanity" of those around her "with great skill," while "screening from them what passed in her heart."[32] Another acquaintance, who was more charitable, told her that she knew how to keep her emotional balance. "Your good nature would be the death of more misfortunes than destiny could send your way."[33] Mme Vigée-Lebrun, the French portrait painter, testified that her large brown eyes were "the liveliest in the world."[34] When Morris first met her at a dinner at Versailles late in March, he found her "a pleasing woman. If I might judge from appearances, not a sworn enemy to intrigue."[35]

Her lover, and a frequent guest at her *salon,* was Charles-Maurice de Talleyrand-Périgord, bishop of Autun. Two years younger than Morris, the clergyman came from an ancient aristocratic family. In the ninth century, a count of Périgord quarreled with Hugh Capet, founder of the French royal family. "Who made thee count?" Capet asked. "Who made thee king?" the count shot back.[36] Over the next eight centuries, the family had distinguished itself by high-handedness and rapacity. Charles-Maurice added supple intelligence to the mix. He needed all his wiles to succeed in life, for when he was only months old he suffered a disastrous accident, falling from a chest of drawers on which his nurse had laid him, thus crippling his right foot. The shoe he was obliged to wear as an adult was round like the pad of an elephant; a metal rod ran up the inner side of his leg, to a leathern band which was wound below his knee. Since this disfigurement made a career in the military impossible, his family directed him to the Church, of whose doctrines he believed not a word, although he maintained the forms. He became Mme de Flahaut's lover, and her son Auguste-Charles-Joseph de Flahaut, born in 1785, was generally supposed to be his, rather than her husband's. After a busy and successful career as an ecclesiastical administrator, he was consecrated bishop in March 1789. Morris met him at the Flahauts' in April, though he did not take note of him until two months later, when he described him in his diary as "sly, cool, cunning and ambitious. . . . I know not why conclusions so disadvantageous to him are formed in my mind, but so it is. . . ."[37]

There was nothing like the cut and thrust of Parisian talk in the English-speaking world. Next to the conversation of eighteenth-century France, the poetry of Alexander Pope looks lush and elaborate, the quips of Samuel Johnson like lucky hits with a blunderbuss. For all his early education in the French language and his use of it in business correspondence, Morris frequently felt at sea, especially at first. His French women friends would gently mock his pronunciation. But in time he became adept at the higher badinage. "*Il me dit des méchancetés* (He's telling me naughty things)," one lady exclaimed over supper. "*Ah! Il est bien capable* (He's certainly capable of it)," a friend replied.[38] He could produce his own epigrams: "*[Il y a] deux espèces d'hommes. Les uns sont faits pour être pères de famille et les autres pour leur faire des enfants.*"—There are two kinds of men, one made to head families, the other to give them children.[39]

When the talk turned to politics, it could be learned as well as supple, for the French had read Locke as well as their own *philosophes,* but the third generation of political Morrises was less impressed with their erudition: ". . . none know how to govern, but those who have been used to it," he told one dinner companion, "and such men have rarely either time or inclination to write about it." Political books, therefore, "contain mere utopian ideas."[40] Significantly, he made this observation to another American in Paris; he wouldn't have wasted it on a Frenchman.

The dank underside of French talk was gossip, which flowed like a drainpipe under the bright surface. At various times Morris heard that Louis XVI tortured cats; that one nobleman was the incestuous offspring of Louis XV and his own daughter; that another nobleman lived with *his* own daughter. Such stories found a printed echo in *libelles,* pornographic satires published abroad and nominally illegal, but widely available. In a society where bishops took mistresses (not parading the fact, but certainly not denying it), some of these tales may even have been true. The French did not care whether they were true or not. Everyone was vile, and nothing had consequences. In one of his first letters to Washington from Paris, Morris observed that "when a man of high rank . . . laughs today at what he seriously asserted yesterday, it is considered as in the natural order of things."[41]

Both the virtues and the vices of the French circles in which Morris moved flourished in idleness. The French kings of the seventeenth and early eighteenth centuries had sought to curb a fractious aristocracy by making it spin around the sun of themselves. The nobles had retained many privileges and some responsibilities (chiefly military) but there was not sufficient outlet for their energies. When they could not talk, flirt, or gossip, they played. One day, Morris visited an estate in the country. After breakfast (which was served at noon), the party went to mass. In the gallery of the chapel, where the quality—including a bishop, an abbé, and a duchess—worshipped, "we are amused," Morris told his diary, "by a number of little tricks played . . . with a candle, which is put into the pockets of different gentlemen, the bishop among the rest, and lighted while they are otherwise engaged . . . to the

great merriment of the spectators. Immoderate laughter in consequence . . . This scene must be very edifying to the domestics who are
opposite to us, and the villagers who worship below." [42] Morris hardly
ever darkened a church door, but he knew better than to play games
when he did.

Morris had arrived in Paris at what seemed to be a hopeful political
moment. France was an absolute monarchy in which all power radi-
ated from the sovereign. But at the urging of Jacques Necker, the Swiss
financier, Louis XVI had called a meeting of the Estates-General, an
assembly of representatives of the clergy, the nobility, and the com-
mons, the traditional orders of the realm, which had not met since
1614. The reason the king revived this old forum was money. France's
foreign policy, particularly its support of the American Revolution,
had bankrupted the state. The government could not raise money because the nobility were exempted from paying many taxes. The 1787
Assembly of Notables, in which Lafayette served, had been unable to
propose workable reforms, so the king and Necker were turning to the
nation in an effort to engineer consensus. Superficially, France's situation resembled the United States's at the opening of the Constitutional Convention—war debt; a political system that blocked any
revenue stream; a call for change.

Morris attended the inaugural procession of the Estates at Versailles, the royal palace outside Paris, on May 4, 1789. The day was so
bright that he got a sunburn, and he spent a good part of the ceremony
talking about Robert Morris's tobacco contract with another specta-
tor. But he observed the elaborate ritual. The clergy wore robes of
black, white, gray or red. The nobles (among whom was Lafayette,
representing the Auvergne) wore black, with golden waistcoats and
sashes. The Third Estate, the commoners, were dressed in black. The
king wore a beaver hat with white plumes and a diamond pin. Morris
noticed that "[n]either the King nor Queen appear too well pleased." [43]
Louis XVI was cheered enthusiastically; his queen, Marie Antoinette,
was barely cheered at all.

Louis, mild, benevolent and young for his age at thirty-five, had, by
summoning the Estates, given himself the image of a liberal, patriotic

king. Marie Antoinette, two years younger, was popularly supposed, not without reason, to be against change and devoted to the interests of Austria (she was by birth a Hapsburg). Morris noticed the disparity in their receptions, and pitied the queen's humiliation. ". . . I see only the woman, and it seems unmanly to break a woman with unkindness." [44] The next day, when the session was formally opened, an old commoner in the Third Estate who came in farmer's clothes, instead of the prescribed black, received "a long and loud plaudit." [45] In a letter to America describing this mixture of imposing ceremony and unstable sentiments, Morris detected "the pang of greatness going off." [46]

Once convened, the Estates fell to quarreling over representation. The Third Estate, which was as numerous as the nobles and the clergy put together, wanted voting by head, rather than by Estate, which would boost its relative strength. The dispute consumed the attention of the *salons*. "[T]he conversation degenerates into politics," Morris complained one evening in May.[47] "States General chit chat," he complained again as the month ended.[48] As June wore on, the Third Estate began meeting separately, called itself the National Assembly, and accepted sympathetic clergy and noblemen as members.

The struggle between the Estates seemed to recall Morris's own experiences: the New York Provincial Congress replacing the colonial Assembly, then writing a state constitution; large and small states fighting in Philadelphia. Morris did not see the resemblance. The American state governments had grown out of colonial political experience, then worked together for twelve years before the Constitutional Convention. America did not take its institutions from a drawing board. The French, he wrote early in July, "want an American constitution . . . without reflecting that they have not American citizens to support" it.[49]

Louis XVI had been willing to inaugurate a reform movement that he could control, but when the Third Estate recreated itself as a national legislature with constitutional ambitions, he balked. He no longer had a free hand, however, for when in the second week of July he dismissed Necker, planning to replace him with a group of yesmen, the streets of Paris erupted. Morris went out in a carriage to see the commotion with Mme de Flahaut, and a hunchbacked abbé ("one of her favorites . . . far from an Adonis . . . it must therefore be a moral attachment").[50] They saw a troop of cavalry pelted with stones at the Place Louis Quinze (now the Place de la Concorde). The court at Versailles—a two-hour carriage ride away from Paris—assumed that the disturbances were minor. But on July 14, the fortress of the Bastille in the heart of the city was stormed by a mob, its commanding officer killed, and its prisoners and gunpowder liberated. "I presume," Morris wrote in his diary, "that this day's transactions will induce a conviction that all is not perfectly quiet."[51]

Morris observed these developments with a light heart—he found the abbé's fear during the riot "diverting"[52]—and indeed life went on: he wrote light verse for Mme de Flahaut, he wrangled over the tobacco contract. Yet only a week after the fall of the Bastille, he saw a different face of the mob. He had eaten dinner—in his diary, he noted the price—then waited for his carriage under the arcade of the Palais-Royal, a building next to the Louvre that housed clubs, shops, and cafés. "In this period the head and body of M. de Foulon"—a politician—"are introduced in triumph. The head on a pike, the body dragged naked on the earth. Afterwards this horrible exhibition is carried through the different streets."

Foulon was guilty of two offenses: he had been willing to help the king replace Necker (he would have been the number two man in charge of foreign affairs in the new ministry); and he was accused of keeping bread out of Paris, to starve it into submission. The first offense was real; the second was an urban legend—the reason there was so little bread in Paris was that hail, drought, and ice had impeded growing and milling for a year. After Morris saw the "horrible exhibition," it was shown to Foulon's son-in-law, who was himself "cut to pieces, the populace carrying about the mangled fragments with a savage joy. Gracious God what a People!"[53]

Morris had made his share of rash suggestions in his life as a revolutionary politician—fining the city of Philadelphia; egging on the Newburgh conspirators. But when confronted with instances of summary justice, he had always been sympathetic to its victims, from the

*M*orris at twenty-seven—the young heartbreaker.
[The Emmet Collection, Miriam and Ira D. Wallach Division of Art, Prints and Photographs, The New York Public Library, Astor, Lenox and Tilden Foundations.]

His daily companion after his accident in 1780.
[Collection of The New-York Historical Society, accession number 1954.148.]

Houdon's statue of Morris's hero, George Washington, for which Morris was the body model.

[Library of Virginia.]

Two Morrises: mercurial, relaxed Gouverneur; solid, steady Robert.

[Courtesy of the Pennsylvania Academy of the Fine Arts, Philadelphia. Bequest of Richard Ashhurst.]

The manor house of Morrisania in the early
twentieth century, a few years before it was torn down.

[Courtesy of the Bronx County Historical Society.]

Morris's summer house in Gouverneur, New York, which still stands.

[Photograph by Emily E. Johnstown. Courtesy of the Gouverneur Museum.]

Morris in 1789—an American in Paris.

[Published as a frontispiece in Anne C. Morris, ed., *Diary and Letters of Gouverneur Morris* (New York, 1888).]

The Constitution, Morris's handiwork.

[U.S. National Archives.]

Thomas Paine. "A troublesome fellow."
[By courtesy of the National Portrait Gallery, London.]

The Marquis de Lafayette. "He will be
unable to hold the helm."
[Courtesy, Winterthur Museum.]

Talleyrand. "Sly, cool, cunning and ambitious."

[From a print in the Bibliothèque Nationale.]

Adélaide de Flahaut. "Not a sworn enemy to intrigue."

[From a print in the Bibliothèque Nationale.]

Morris at fifty-eight,
married at last.

[Pastel by James Sharples, Courtesy
Frick Art Reference Library.]

Mrs. Gouverneur Morris. "If
the world were to live with
my wife, I should certainly
have consulted its taste."

[Pastel by James Sharples, Collection of Angus J. Menzies.]

The streets of New York—Morris's legacy to the city.

Morris's last resting place—St. Ann's, the South Bronx.

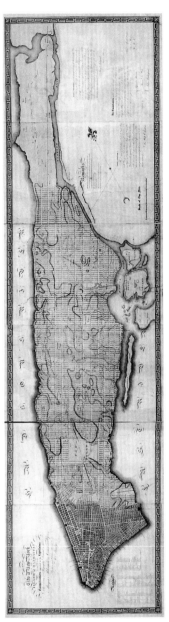

printer Rivington to his Tory in-laws to his friend Peter Van Schaak. In all the evacuations and arsons of the American Revolution, he had never seen anything like this. He had called "the mob" "poor reptiles," but when he had sarcastically predicted that they would soon "bite," he had meant that they would wield political power. Now here was a mob on the move, carrying its trophy. He had already decided that the French had no political experience; was this what they had instead?

During his time in Paris, Morris associated with the rich and well-born—people of his own class, and higher—so his accounts of violence can leave the impression, dear to revolutionary polemic, that only they suffered. But the mob could turn on commoners , too. Some months after the murder of Foulon, Morris learned of a baker who was beheaded and "carried in triumph through the streets. . . . His wife is said to have died with horror when they presented her husband's head stuck on a pole." Morris wrote of this with real wrath. "Providence" would not "leave such abominations unpunished. Paris is perhaps as wicked a spot as exists . . . yet this is the city which has stepped forward in the sacred cause of Liberty." [54]

Morris dined with Jefferson several evenings during the most turbulent July days; the Virginian had been advising Lafayette on a French bill of rights. In his letters, Jefferson described the summary executions but did not dwell on the gore or the tumult. To Paine, then in Britain, he praised the "coolness" of the National Assembly,[55] and to John Jay, he emphasized the virtue of the rioters. "There was a severity of honesty observed, of which no example has been known. Bags of money offered on various occasions through fear or guilt, have been uniformly refused. . . ." [56] Jefferson was hopeful. Many Frenchmen were grimly pleased. When Antoine Barnave, a leader of the Third Estate, was asked what he thought of the deaths of Foulon and his son-in-law, he answered with a question of his own: "What, then, is their blood so pure?" [57]

Less than a week after his encounter with Foulon's dismembered corpse, Morris made love for the first time to Adèle de Flahaut. Recording the event in his diary, he was unusually laconic, slipping behind the mask of three dots. Mme de Flahaut was to help him write a document. "We sit down with the best disposition imaginable but instead of a translation . . ." [58]

Morris had been plucking at the web of Parisian sexuality for months. He picked up a prostitute once in the Palais-Royal, when he was drunk, a deed he evidently considered a lapse, for it made him feel "the object of my own contempt and aversion." [59] Generally, he confined his attentions to the women of his own sphere. He noted pretty arms and eyes, and the willingness with which they were displayed; he conversed with his lady friends as they put on their dresses over their shifts, and as they bathed (such situations arose frequently between French acquaintances, and were not considered unseemly, or particularly erotic). He swatted up worldly conversation. Mme de Staël's husband, a Swedish diplomat, told him that Frenchwomen are "greater whores with their hearts and minds than with their persons." [60]

He and Mme de Flahaut had been actively interested in each other since early spring. After running into him in the gardens of the Tuileries, she invited him to view the statues in the Louvre. The day was not a success. The weather was rainy, and the courtyard muddy. Mousieur le comte came along, and retired with his wife after the sightseeing was done. Morris slipped getting into a carriage, called on another countess whose repartee left him tongue-tied, then scolded his waiter at dinner. "[He] must I think despise me for pretending to talk angrily before I can talk French." [61]

Both he and Adèle persisted, however. By late June, she asked him about his reputation as a ladies' man, which had followed him across the ocean. He first denied it, then, heedless of the contradiction, assured her that "I never lost my respect for those who consented to make me happy. . . . This idea," he added to himself in his diary, "will I know dwell on her mind, because the combination of tenderness and respect with ardency and vigor go far towards the female idea of perfection in a lover." [62]

After the fall of the Bastille, Morris made an explicit proposition: he told Adèle that he could not be "only a friend." He added that he did not mean to inspire a passion in her, that he did not want to feel a passion himself, and that he was timid. "[A] very strange conversation," he admitted, but he counted on the mixture of brass and diffidence, hot and cold, to capture her interest. ". . . I am much mistaken if it does not make an impression."[63] Three days later, she countered with a complication of her own, confessing a "marriage of the heart,"[64] without identifying her heart-husband [i.e., Talleyrand]. Morris knew anyway (no wonder he had drawn disadvantageous conclusions about the bishop). Five days later, in the early evening, between dinner with Jefferson and his daughters and a call on Lafayette, Morris was left alone with Adèle at her apartment in the Louvre, and did not complete his translation. "[V]ery sleepy," he wrote toward the end of that day's diary entry.[65]

As it began, so the affair continued. Morris's emotional reserve, Mme de Flahaut's devotion to other men (not including her husband), endless games of cat-and-mouse, intense and stolen bouts of lovemaking (Howard Swiggett, the first biographer to do the counting, concluded that the lovers never spent a whole night together) were the materials of their attraction. There was also love—braided, as the years passed, with the thickening rope of death.

CHAPTER NINE

Liberals in Power

HE POLITICAL EFFECT of July's violence was that the king recalled Necker, and put Lafayette at the head of the National Guard, a popular Parisian militia which had arisen to guard the National Assembly. Three months later, a crowd of Parisian women marched out to Versailles and demanded that the royal family come to the city, where they could be watched. There followed a long period of calm in which the new legislature and the newly limited monarch tested their relations with each other.

One of the busier legislators was Talleyrand. Morris attended an autumn session of the National Assembly, sitting behind Mme de Flahaut, and watched the bishop. He was not impressed with what he saw: "... there is a great deal of noisy debate on various subjects, if indeed such controversy can be dignified with the name of debate."[1] Talleyrand made his mark, not by speechifying, but by proposing a plan to nationalize the property of the Catholic Church, worth about 3 billion livres (or $9 billion today). The bishop argued that church property was not owned by individual churchmen, but served a social purpose—"enabl[ing] the clergy to carry out its functions"[2]—that justified the superintendence of the government. The windfall of confiscation would also help the Treasury balance its books.

The man of the hour was Lafayette. The hero of one revolution was once again leading troops in another. This time, however, he enjoyed a lonely eminence, for he was not under the guidance of a greater hero, nor was it clear what loyalty the National Guardsmen he commanded owed him. At a dinner *chez* Jefferson in mid-September—the last one Morris would attend before Jefferson left for home—Morris asked Lafayette if his troops would obey him. Lafayette answered that, although they would not do guard duty in the rain, they would follow him into action. "[H]e will have an opportunity," Morris thought to himself, "of making the experiment."³ The marquis, who had a dramatic temperament, made skillful use of symbols, inventing a tricolor cockade for the National Guard, with the red and blue colors of the coat of arms of Paris flanking the white of the House of Bourbon, the royal family; this became—and still is—the national color scheme. But he operated in a vacuum of authority, traditional institutions having crumbled and new ones not yet taken hold. The moment he faced a situation not amenable to his charisma, he might be lost. "He means ill to no one," wrote Morris in his diary, but "[i]f the sea runs high, he will be unable to hold the helm."⁴

Morris distilled his impressions in letters to the man both he and Lafayette adored, who since April had been president of the United States. Morris had been acting as Washington's personal shopper, buying not only the watch he had requested but ornaments for the presidential table (Morris's tastes ran to items that were solid and relatively inexpensive). He had also served as Washington's body model, posing for a statue by the French sculptor Jean-Antoine Houdon. Now he was Washington's eyes and ears. His judgments were not kind. Louis XVI he called "a small beer character," who "at the slightest shew of opposition . . . gives up every thing, and every person."⁵ Necker was "afloat upon the wide ocean of incidents"; his proposals were "feeble and ineptious."⁶ "The new order of things," he concluded, "cannot endure. . . . The present set [of leaders] must wear out in the course of the year."⁷

He backed his judgments with anecdotes. One concerned an evening at Mme de Staël's, when the duc de Clermont-Tonnerre rehearsed an oration he intended to give in the National Assembly. The duke (whose second surname meant "thunderclap") spoke on crime and punishment, an important topic in a country where the old regime had had the power to imprison people indefinitely. The duke argued that criminals should not only be freed at the end of stated terms, but freed from all social stigma as well, which struck Morris as utopian. The speech, Morris wrote, "was very fine, very sentimental, very pathetic, and the style har-

monious." It was greeted with "[s]houts of applause and full approbation. When this was pretty well over I told [the duke] that his speech
was extremely eloquent, but that his principles were not very good. Universal surprise. A very few remarks changed the face of things. The position was universally condemned, and he left the room."[8]

Morris was showing off for Washington—see how I herd this room-
ful of Frenchmen—but he was also making a serious point. Too many in
the French political elite spoke for effect; if the effect misfired, they were
too ready to change their minds. Americans called Morris fickle and inconstant, but Morris felt surrounded by people more fickle than he. The
penchant of the French for oratory was analogous to their fondness for
theory and for gossip. Neither words, nor ideas, nor rumors were
grounded in experience, and they could change in the blink of an eye.

Morris's counsel to his French friends was a mixture of the solid and
the inflammatory. The National Assembly expected the sale of national land, including church property, to float an issue of paper livres,
called *assignats*. Morris, the veteran of too many American financial
schemes, thought the revenues would not come in at the rate the
French expected, and the *assignats* would therefore degenerate into
unbacked paper. He was right. Four hundred million livres-*assignats*
were issued in December 1789. Six years and many issues later, 100
livres-*assignats* were worth only 1.4 livres in hard money.

Morris's other bit of advice, repeatedly offered to Lafayette, was
that he should wage war against Austria and Britain by invading Flanders (the present-day Belgium) and Holland. Austria owned Flanders,
and Britain would not tolerate a French power play so near its shores.
Morris thought such an invasion would be winnable, and the old
Francophile in him wanted to see a French victory. Besides, he explained, "[y]ou want something to turn men's attention from their present discontents."[9] Morris, blithely throwing armies about the map of
Europe, could never foresee the true costs of war. His advice, however,
had the merit of realism, for the nations of Europe were looking for
easy targets—Britain had its eyes on Spain; Prussia, Russia, and Austria had theirs on Poland—and even France, given its troubles, might
be another victim. Better for it to strike first.

One of the channels for his advice was Mme de Flahaut, who was still, despite her connection with him, Talleyrand's mistress. Morris and Adèle mingled their lovemaking with politics. At one midday tryst at the Louvre, Adèle said she hoped to exert a moderating influence on Marie Antoinette through the queen's physician, who was one of the regulars at the Flahaut *salon*. Morris thought that Adèle might well have a good effect. Since the queen was "weak, proud, but not ill-tempered . . . a superior mind would take that ascendancy which the feeble always submit to. . . ." "I would give her a man every night," Adèle answered pertly, "and a mass every morning." The two lovers also drew up a new ministry, in case Necker should fall. They naturally put Talleyrand in the financier's place as chief minister of the realm. *"Enfin, mon ami,"* Adele said, *"vous et moi nous gouvernerons la France"* (Then, my friend, you and I will govern France). "[T]he kingdom," wrote Morris in his diary that night, "is actually in much worse hands." [10]

They had each other whenever they could, wherever they were. In their intoxication they made love in her apartment at the Louvre; in his carriage; and in the visitors' waiting room of a convent in Chaillot where Adèle's old governess lived as a nun. Morris did not record their encounters in graphic detail, unlimbering instead the full battery of eighteenth-century euphemisms, reinforced with his own odd humor. They performed "the rites";[11] he conferred "the joy"; they did "the needful." [12] They "sacrificed to the Cyprian Queen [Venus]";[13] they "perform[ed] the first commandment given to Adam, [i.e., be fruitful and multiply] or at least we use the means." [14] Over and over, Morris boasted, like a teenager (or at least, like a teenager who knows Latin), that he was *suaviter in modo, fortiter in re*—gentle in manner, resolute in the deed.[15]

Adèle sought to impress Morris with her fidelity, promising to be true to him rather than Talleyrand. He sought to impress her with his independence. "I . . . insist that she shall pursue only the dictates of her own inclination and understanding. . . . She is hurt at my reasonableness." [16] Adèle nevertheless managed to make her rational American promise to give her a golden ring. "So I find I have a wife upon my hands indeed." [17] When she was not trying to overcome his coolness with ardor, she flirted with William Short, Jefferson's former secretary.

Morris, for his part, flirted with other Frenchwomen, including the wife of one of his French bankers, and Mme de Staël.

Their erotic solar system included two fixed planets. The lesser was her husband, who appears as the traditional cuckold of French and Italian comedy, Morris praising the excellent partridges he brought home, and on which Morris supped, Adèle hoping he might become the French minister to the United States (thus allowing her, as she explained, to follow Morris there). The greater planet was Talleyrand, who knew well what was going on, but chose to ignore Adèle's behavior while he pursued his own affairs, until January 1790, when he reproached her with betrayal. In a panic, she told Morris she must write him and try to patch things up. She gave "many reasons" for doing so, none of which Morris felt were sensible. "[H]owever I agree for one she does not give": "it is necessary to her peace" of mind.[18]

Notes of tenderness do come through the din of passion and calculation. One afternoon, after tea, Morris visited Adèle and found her suffering from an old ailment: an *accoucheur,* or male midwife, had injured her during the delivery of her child, "since which she has suffered much by pain in the side. . . ." Morris's intimate and unhappy experiences with doctors always made him treat illness with seriousness and compassion. He gave Adèle medical advice but did not "attempt to caress her"[19]—a considerate omission. Another time, after he had set her down at the Louvre and driven off to call on Lafayette, he realized with regret that he had "need . . . of her conversation."[20] Even in the cool and self-regarding pages of his diary, Adèle comes off as an intelligent and lively companion—not, indeed, unlike him.

$\mathcal{I}$N FEBRUARY 1790, Morris left Paris and Mme de Flahaut for an extended stay in London. Robert Morris's affairs, it was becoming clear, were shaking at their foundations. Robert Morris's fundamental problem was that he was operating in two divergent markets: he had plunged in land, and he hoped to plunge in government paper, or debt. But as the American government got its finances in order, land became a less attractive investment by comparison, while the value of the government paper he hoped to buy kept going up. As a U.S. senator,

Robert Morris's principles and his interest tugged in opposite directions. By supporting a strong and solvent federal government, he indirectly undermined his own prospects as a land speculator. More and more often, the richest man in America found that his bills were being protested in European cities.

Gouverneur Morris, meanwhile, was doing better than his patron. He got good tips from home. Alexander Hamilton, the new Treasury secretary, was a discreet man, but insiders tried to divine his intentions. After dining with Hamilton, Robert Morris's old associate, William Constable, wrote Gouverneur Morris breathlessly that the debts of the individual states would "undoubtedly" be paid by the federal government.[21] Constable guessed right. Meanwhile Gouverneur Morris's land investments, along the Genesee and St. Lawrence rivers in upstate New York, were more compact than his friend's unwieldly ventures.

Gouverneur Morris's main reason for going to Britain, however, was that he had an assignment from George Washington. The president wanted him to sound out British intentions on issues left over from the Revolutionary War. Britain had promised to vacate frontier forts on American soil, from upstate New York to Detroit, which controlled the fur trade, and to compensate American slave owners for liberated slaves. Neither of these things had been done. Britain had also neglected to send a minister to its former colonies, or to propose a new treaty regulating commercial relations with them. The former was a mark of disrespect; the latter left important economic interests in limbo. Washington directed Morris to use his "abilities, address and delicacy."[22]

Morris, with his restless mind and uninhibited tongue, was not an obvious choice for a diplomat. But Washington had clearly been impressed with his sprightly letters on French affairs. (If he had known of the bellicose advice Morris had been giving Lafayette, he might have thought better of the assignment.) The success of Morris's mission was foreshadowed on the day of his first call on the foreign secretary, the Duke of Leeds. Before being shown into the duke's office, Morris noticed, on the table of a meeting room, where it had evidently been a topic for discussion, a map of Poland. The neighbors of that unhappy country were carving it up, and Britain was watching what they did.

This was a more pressing matter at the moment than American commerce or forts in Detroit. When Britain's thoughts turned to the New World, it was only to wonder if the United States would allow a British army to march from Canada across American territory to attack Spanish possessions (the answer to that was an emphatic no). Morris was not the first, nor would he be the last, American diplomat in London to find that the United States was low on the list of British concerns. "These men," Morris wrote Washington after much fruitless talk, "do not yet know America. Perhaps America does not yet know itself. ... We are yet but in the seeding time of national prosperity...."[23]

For the rest, Morris visited with his half brother the general. He learned of the death of Mrs. Plater and wrote his little rhyme for Angelica Church and Maria Cosway. He saw quite a bit of Thomas Paine, who had appeared in Paris the previous autumn promoting his design for a bridge, and who was now doing the same in London. Morris and Paine consulted with Edmund Burke, the great liberal politician, about how best to help American sailors who had been impressed into the British navy, and Morris heard Burke perform in Parliament. "His speech contained [enough] matter to make a fine one, and to mar the best."[24]

Morris returned to Paris in November. In his nine months abroad, titles of nobility had been abolished, and Necker had resigned, unsuccessful and unlamented, though there had been no dramatic shifts of course. There was greater change *chez* Flahaut, for Morris found that Viscount Henry Wycombe, a twenty-five-year-old British nobleman, was Adèle's newest lover. The young man's father, a liberal British peer, had sent him to France to learn manners, and he had evidently done well. Morris called at the Louvre his first night back in Paris and found Lord Wycombe *"un peu enniché"* (somewhat settled in).[25] The next day, Mme de Flahaut would not receive her American friend.

Morris and Adèle began a new bout of emotional warfare. There were recriminations and ruptures, seductions and distractions. Morris imagined he had seen Adèle for the last time, and congratulated himself on getting out of a "sentimental scrape."[26] Then he vowed to "recover my empire over her,"[27] which he did by employing *fortiter in re.*

She offered not to see Lord Wycombe, but Morris refused her offer. Morris in turn distressed her by flirting with Lady Sutherland, the wife of the British minister to France, and with the marquise de Nadaillac, whom he described as "virtuous and coquette and romantic . . . [w]hat fine materials for seduction!"[28] One December evening, the comings and goings at the Louvre were so dense that he found himself with Adèle, Lord Wycombe, and Talleyrand (M. le comte was out). "She has just now much the advantage of me," Morris noted like a scorekeeper at a tennis match.[29]

Adèle de Flahaut was an ardent woman, and not prudent with her emotions. But she had good reason to seek out so many well-connected men. Her husband, now sixty-four, was a bad politician, a flamboyant reactionary royalist. Whichever way France went, it was not likely to go his. The salary for his no-show job had been cut by one third, and he had been publicly criticized as a parasite by a member of the National Assembly. Adèle was seeking security for herself and her son; she was willing to try the renegade bishop, the one-legged American, or the young *milord*.

Gouverneur Morris was true to his original intentions. He wanted intellectual and physical intimacy. He prized Adèle's mind as well as her touch. But he had no interest in marriage, or any definite relationship. His father had been a distant and depressed figure. He did not covet a union like Colonel Plater's, or Mr. Bingham's, or the comte de Flahaut's. Ultimately he valued his freedom more than Adèle's happiness. One weary afternoon at the Louvre, when Adèle was sick and heartsick both, she told him, *"Si jamais je vous ai fait de la peine, vous me l'avez bien rendu"*—If ever I hurt you, you have surely paid me back.[30]

In November 1790, France received an unexpected blow from across the English Channel. Edmund Burke published *Reflections on the Revolution in France.* The long pamphlet was a shock, as much for who said it as for what it said. Burke had not only helped American seamen; in a long career of liberalism, he had supported the American Revolution, Irish Catholics oppressed by their Protestant landlords, and Bengalis robbed by the East India Company. Now, however, he assailed the course of events in France. Burke saw the abolition of titles, the populist imagery invoked by Lafayette, and the enforced move of the king and queen to Paris as dangerous alterations of the social fabric. In "this new conquering empire of light and reason . . . [a]ll the decent drapery of life is to be rudely torn off. All the superadded ideas, furnished from the wardrobe of a moral imagination . . . to cover the defects of our naked shivering nature, and to raise it to dignity in our own estimation, are to be exploded. . . ." A nation stripped of custom and ritual, Burke warned, could maintain order only by calculation and force. "In the groves" of the Revolution "at the end of every vist[a], you see nothing but the gallows."[31]

Three months later, Burke was answered by Thomas Paine's *The Rights of Man*. Paine set his plain speech, by turns biting and matter-of-fact, against Burke's operatic eloquence. He scoffed at Burke's talk of drapery and wardrobes: "He pities the plumage, but forgets the dying bird."[32] The French Revolution had ended real injustices. "The older [governments] are, the less correspondence can they have with the present state of things. Time, and change of circumstances and opinions, have the same progressive effect in rendering modes of government obsolete, as they have upon customs and manners."[33] Burke's vision of the gallows struck Paine as delirious. "Whom has the National Assembly brought to the scaffold? None."[34] (This was literally true, since the mob was not the National Assembly, though Paine ought to have reflected what influence the former might have on the latter.) *Reflections on the Revolution in France* was an instant bestseller; *The Rights of Man* was an even greater one.

Morris read *The Rights of Man* in early April; Paine, who had come back to Paris, was telling him proudly how popular his pamphlet was. Morris found "good things" in both Burke and Paine.[35] Unlike Burke, he had no illusions about the old order. One night at Mme de Nadaillac's, he met the abbé Maury, a leader of the right wing in the National Assembly, and some "proud aristocrats" who were his supporters. They struck him as rotten and petty. Maury "looks like a downright ecclesiastical scoundrel, and the rest . . . have the word *Valet* written on their foreheads in large characters. Maury is formed to govern such men and such men are formed to obey him or anyone else."[36] But unlike

Paine, he had no faith in the apostles of the new order. "There is not a man among them fitted for the great tasks in which they are engaged," he wrote Washington, "and greater tasks are perhaps impending."[37]

Greater tasks or greater trials. On April 18, the Monday before Easter, the king and queen left the Tuileries Palace in Paris to spend Holy Week in the suburb of Saint-Cloud, halfway to Versailles. Louis was suffering from religious guilt. In addition to nationalizing church land, the government over which he presided had nationalized the Roman Catholic Church by requiring its priests to swear an oath of loyalty to the new regime. The Pope had condemned this requirement and those who obeyed it. Talleyrand, who had sworn the oath, had been excommunicated. Louis, torn between his office and his conscience, wished to celebrate Easter away from public scrutiny. His carriage was stopped at the palace gate, however, by an angry crowd, which was soon joined by the National Guard. For almost two hours, Lafayette vainly commanded his own soldiers to move aside; one Guardsman called the immobilized king a pig.[38] In the end, the carriage and its occupants stayed home. "[V]ery much of a riot at the Tuileries," wrote Morris in his diary. "I am a long time in expectation of a battle, but am at length told that the King submits."[39] Lafayette, humiliated, resigned; but then, Morris noted caustically, "found afterwards various reasons for not doing it. This is like him."[40]

The conclusion Louis XVI drew from the Tuileries riot was that he was a prisoner rather than a head of state, and he resolved to escape in earnest. In June, Morris was back in London, negotiating with the Penn family to buy their compensation. There, at the end of the month, he heard that the king and queen had fled Paris in disguise. Their goal was the Flanders border, two hundred miles to the northeast, where they could be free from their revolutionary overlords, and perhaps be helped by Marie Antoinette's royal Austrian relatives. "This," Morris realized, "will produce some considerable consequences. If they get off safe a war is inevitable." How could France live in peace with a rival power that was assisting its runaway king? But "if they are retaken it will probably suspend for some time all monarchical government in France."[41] How could the nation trust a sovereign who didn't trust it?

Just short of their goal, Louis and Marie Antoinette were stopped and recognized in the Argonne woods town of Varennes. Six thousand armed peasants and National Guardsmen escorted them back home.

When Morris himself returned to Paris at the beginning of July, he found Paine "inflated to the eyes and big with a litter of revolutions." Paine and the marquis de Condorcet, a mathematician friend of Jefferson's, had founded a republican club, calling for Louis to be deposed. Marie Antoinette's physician told Morris that the thirty-six-year-old queen's hair had turned gray from her ordeal. Morris called her husband a "miserable creature," [42] who would remain in place only because there was no alternative.

The flight to Varennes destroyed the mystique of royalty. The greatness Morris had felt going off at the opening of the Estates-General two years earlier vanished utterly in the stealthy escape and the enforced return. It also ended Lafayette's effectiveness. He had wished to keep the king safe, and to keep him wedded to the Revolution—to force him, in effect, to be a royal Washington. Clearly, he had failed. Before the king had been retrieved, Lafayette was threatened by a prim young lawyer in the legislature, Maximilien de Robespierre: "You, M. Lafayette, will answer to the Assembly on the fate of the King with your head." [43] When Morris called at Lafayette's his second night back, the general was out, and his wife was "half wild." [44] The liberal nobility who had begun the Revolution, and the erratically liberal king who had occasionally supported it, were spent forces.

Louis XVI and Lafayette nevertheless hung on in their posts for another year, while France was preoccupied with inflation, constitutional tinkering, and, at long last, the Austrian war that Morris had recommended. In this strange twilight period when the king had been stripped of power and respect, Morris chose to help him. The American republican, whose comments on Louis's political skills had been as cruel as they were funny, now became an informal adviser. Perhaps Morris was moved by Louis's distress, as he had been by the suffering of American troops at Valley Forge. Perhaps, disdaining all sides, he felt obliged to prop up the weakest, lest its equally unworthy enemies prevail.

For whatever reason, Morris wrote Louis helpful letters, and the draft of an address to be given to the National Assembly. He even learned, in November, that someone had suggested he become France's minister of foreign affairs ("I laugh at this," he commented in his diary).[45] His correspondence with Louis XVI sparkled with the wit he lavished on Washington. He advised the king not to bribe legislators, because they were not "worth corrupting." He suggested that Louis give bread to the poor as a grand gesture, observing that the French "seldom concern themselves with the good, but rhapsodize over the beautiful."[46] His proposed speech would have made Louis sound like Morris at the Constitutional Convention. Of the Declaration of the Rights of Man, Louis was supposed to say that since "such pronouncements hav[e] so far produced only metaphysical discussions, a King need not comment on them, as his functions demand a knowledge of Man as he is, rather than as he ought to be."[47] Louis never gave this speech.

Morris even drew up a constitution for France. His third effort at constitution writing was a very Anglo-American document. The king was the executive, with control over foreign policy, the military, the colonies, and commerce. He also had the power to veto laws and appoint administrators, down to the level of mayors. The legislature was to consist of a Senate, appointed to life terms by the king, and a National Assembly, elected for staggered eight-year terms by married men twenty-five or older. Only the National Assembly could propose taxes. Judges were also to be appointed by the king, but there was to be trial by jury. Apart from the fact that the executive was hereditary, Morris's framework was not unlike the most conservative ideas bruited in Philadelphia in 1787. True to his strictures on the Declaration of the Rights of Man, his Preamble (which he called "Principles") wasted no time enumerating human rights. Instead, he declared that "the position of a state, its climate, the extent of its territory and the habits and manners of its citizens, have an influence in determining the proper form of government."[48] Two revolutions in two countries had made Morris a comparative anthropologist: as men varied from place to place, so did their duties, rights, and opportunities. The one universal exception he recognized was religious liberty: "religion is the relation between God and man; therefore it is not within the reach of human authority."[49]

There was an obvious contradiction between Morris's view of the world and his handiwork: if men differed so, how could an American advise Frenchmen? While Morris was writing his constitution in December 1791, he was visited by a man, whose name he did not record in his diary, who had undertaken a similar project. His caller had sent "a constitution for America to Gen. Washington. He says that he has made such objects his study for above 50 years. That he knows America perfectly well though he has never seen it, and is convinced that the American Constitution is good for nothing. I get rid of him as soon as I can but yet"—here was the Morris touch—"I cannot help being struck with the similitude of a Frenchman who makes constitutions for America and an American who performs the same good office to France. Self love tells me that there is a great difference . . . but self love is a dangerous counsellor."[50]

He drew close, in sentiment at least, to the queen. Here the source of his attraction is easy to understand: he had written in 1789 that it was unmanly to break a woman with unkindness, and now the unkindnesses were coming thick and fast. One December afternoon he attended the Comédie Française, sitting in the balcony, and saw the queen in a seat below his. One of her attendants pointed out Morris to her, and their eyes met. "My air, if I can know it myself, was that of calm benevolence with a little sensibility."[51] In a crowded room and a hostile world, he wanted to show her support.

Here Morris's emotional and erotic life intersected with public events. Through the varied tapestry of his relations with women—the *méchancetés,* the Cyprian rites, the medical advice, the valued conversations—there ran a thread of affection. Morris liked women and he listened to them; that was why he was successful with so many of them, however warily he juggled his successes. But in the new France, love had a political resonance. Versailles had long been dominated by royal mistresses (only Louis XVI's uncharacteristic fidelity broke the pattern). More recently, the *salons* of the enlightened had taken their cue from bright liberal hostesses. As the Revolution approached and progressed, however, the omnipresence of women came to seem part and parcel of a decadent system. Rousseau, that strange intellectual scout, had set the critical tone in his *Letter to D'Alembert* decades earlier. "Follow the hints of Nature, consult the good of society, and we will find that the two sexes must meet occasionally, but live apart."[52] Now his prophetic discomfort with the power of women was widely shared. If virtue was manly, then vice was effeminate.

The most conspicuous victim of political misogyny was Marie Antoinette, who had been the subject of a flood of political pornography since the early 1780s, in which the kindest epithet bestowed on her was *l'Autrichienne*, the feminine form of Austrian, but also playing on *chienne* (bitch). She was depicted as a masturbating bisexual nymphomaniac, surrounded by lustful officers and lesbian aristocrats with whom she coupled insatiably. A 1790 print showed an awkward Lafayette kneeling before her and fondling her crotch; the primary butt was not him, but her boundless lust.[53] Adèle de Flahaut's suggestion that the queen be given a man each night was a mild echo of this filth.

Adèle herself with her cuckold husband and her international cast of lovers was closer to the image of an old regime whore than Marie Antoinette, but she was not very close. For the image was a fantasy—a projection of all the traits that the new masculine mood rejected. The elite was also reaping all the tales that their own libelous tongues had told; when gossip was popularized and politicized, it became lethal.

Without consulting any French pornography, Burke had intuited some of this in his *Reflections*. In the new "scheme of things," he had written, "a queen is but a woman; a woman is but an animal; and an animal not of the highest order."[54] But Burke was a royalist, who valued queens more than ordinary women. Morris respected the queen because she was a woman. At the end of the year he asked one of Marie Antoinette's friends if he might have a lock of her hair.

At the beginning of February 1792, he heard news from the United States which yanked him away from his constitutional daydreams and France's fantasy life: President Washington had appointed him minister to France.

CHAPTER TEN

Radicals in Power

ASHINGTON APPOINTED Morris, relying on their long friendship and on Morris's firsthand knowledge of the country. But when the nomination went to the Senate, there was a sharp debate.

Some of the senators had all the old objections. Roger Sherman of Connecticut, who knew Morris from the Continental Congress and the Constitutional Convention, credited him with a "sprightly mind" and a "ready apprehension," but warned that he was "an irreligious and profane man. . . . I am against such characters."[1] Sherman did not know about Mme de Flahaut, Mme de Staël, Mme de Nadaillac, and his other French friends, but he would have known of Morris's Philadelphia socializing.

Equally important, the French Revolution had become an issue in the emerging American party system. Distance had not dimmed Secretary of State Thomas Jefferson's hopes for the Revolution, and by a happy coincidence, the American politicians who were most skeptical of its success were those who disagreed with him on other matters, or who stood in the way of his ambition. By praising the French Revolution, Jefferson and his friends could attack them. Jefferson had already used what we should now call a blurb that he wrote for the Philadelphia edition of Paine's *Rights of Man* to pick a fight with Vice President John Adams (Jefferson hailed Paine's work as a corrective to "political heresies which have sprung up among us," meaning the opinions of John Adams).[2] When Paine learned in London of Morris's nomination, he wrote Jefferson that the appointment was "most unfortunate."[3] Jefferson didn't need to be told; he thought Morris had been poisoning the president's mind against the Revolution with his ironic letters.[4] During the debate in the Senate, Jefferson's ally James Monroe of Virginia attacked Morris as a "monarchy man . . . not suitable to be employed by this country, nor in France."[5] After more than two weeks of discussion, Morris was confirmed by a vote of 16 to 11.

The president sent a monitory letter to his successful nominee. Washington touched lightly on the political complexion of the vote —Morris would need no assistance divining that. He did feel it necessary, however, to read his no-longer-so-young friend a lecture (Washington was now almost sixty, Morris had just turned forty):

> [Y]ou were charged . . . with levity and imprudence of conversation and conduct. It was urged that your habits of expression indicated a hauteur disgusting to those, who happen to differ from you in sentiment. . . . [T]he promptitude, with which your lively and brilliant imagination is displayed, allows too little time for deliberation and correction; and is the primary cause of those sallies, which too often offend, and of that ridicule of characters, which begets enmity not easy to be forgotten, but which might easily be avoided, if it was under the control of more caution and prudence.[6]

Morris vowed to put away childish things. "*I now promise you,*" he wrote back, "that circumspection of conduct which has hitherto I acknowledge formed no part of my character."[7] Morris took a new house, on the rue de la Planche, on the left bank of the Seine, across the river from the Louvre and the Tuileries.

After the inevitable delays, the new minister was presented to the king and queen at the beginning of June 1792. It was the first time, despite all his observation and advice, that he had met the royal family face to face. The foreign minister had given Morris permission to forgo the traditional dress sword, since it would have hung unflatteringly alongside his wooden leg. The queen showed him her son, age seven, and remarked that he was not yet very big. "I hope, Madame," Morris replied, "he will be large and truly great."[8] He would be dead in three years.

Paine was back in France, driven there after having brought out a second part of *The Rights of Man* that was a frank call to world revolution. "[T]hough the vegetable sleep will continue longer on some trees and plants than on others, and though some of them may not *blossom* for two or three years, all will be in leaf in the summer, except those which are *rotten*."[9] He told Morris that he was "cock sure of bringing about a revolution in Great Britain."[10] Instead, the British government moved to prosecute him, and he fled their hostile attentions, never to return to his native country again.

On the surface, Morris honored the promise he had made to Washington to be circumspect. At his first meeting with the foreign minister, he admitted that, as a "private individual," he had offered constitutional suggestions to French politicians; but now that he was a "public man," it was his "duty not to meddle with their affairs."[11] His earliest letters to the secretary of state were models of vivid reporting. "The best picture I can give of the French nation is that of cattle before a thunderstorm. . . . [W]e stand on a vast volcano, we feel it tremble and we hear it roar but how and when and where it will burst and who may be destroyed by its eruptions it is beyond the ken of mortal foresight to discover."[12]

Below the surface of his official duties, however, Morris was laboring to save Louis XVI from destruction. In June, there was a second popular irruption into the Tuileries; Prussia, which had come into the war on Austria's side, now took up the king's safety as a cause and issued a threatening manifesto, which drove the radicals to desperation. Morris and Louis's advisers together plotted to bribe enough soldiers to guarantee another escape, or at least some safety in the event of another confrontation. The king gave Morris 1 million depreciated livres of his own money for safekeeping. Like a good banker, Morris informed him of the risks. His own house "did not strike him as any safer than the palace of the Tuileries," but "if his Majesty could find no other person to take charge of it he would consent . . . and put it to the use he would be good enough to indicate."[13] The only extenuation a diplomat might plead for such conduct is that Louis XVI was still nominally head of the state to which Morris was accredited, and could justly take steps to protect himself. Still, the American minister was meddling in French affairs.

The feared attack came on August 10. Across the river that morning, Morris heard "[t]he cannon begin, and musketry mingled with them announce a warm day."[14] The royal family was bundled to the National Assembly, and rebellious soldiers and citizens fought with loyalist troops, killing six hundred of them, and burning their stripped and mutilated corpses on bonfires. The weather was oppressively hot; the leaves were already falling, and later that week Morris noted that some perch, which were alive at six in the morning, were spoiled by midday. "So rapid a state of putrefaction I never yet saw."[15]

This was the second French Revolution. The king would be formally deposed in a matter of weeks; Morris gave the bulk of Louis's funds to a co-conspirator, and sent the rest of them to England. The National Assembly itself was a dead letter, to be replaced by a National Convention, which was supposed to begin work on yet another constitution (no one would be consulting Morris this time), though the power in the state had passed to the militias of Parisian neighborhoods (or *sections*) and the political clubs that rallied them.

As a diplomat, Morris lived in a bubble of immunity. But accidents always happen, especially in revolutions. His fellow diplomats, who asked for their passports as they were recalled by their governments, experienced delays and other forms of petty harassment. In a letter, Morris felt constrained to remind a colleague that "observations respecting the legality of a government should not be committed to post offices subject to its inspection."[16] Meanwhile, the French elite with which he had been wont to socialize was in hiding, or under arrest, or being executed. A guillotine went up outside the Tuileries at the end of August. "Another man is beheaded this evening for *Crime de lezé Nation*" (crimes against the state), Morris noted in his diary. "He published a newspaper against the Jacobins [a radical political club]. This is severe at least."[17] Foreign armies pushed in from the frontiers—a bombardment at Verdun over a hundred miles away was heard in the city—spurring the radicals to murder their enemies summarily in the city's prisons. There were times when the tension in the diplomatic community became extreme. "I laugh a little too much at the distresses of the Baron Grand Cour," Morris wrote one night, "and Lord Gower gets a little too much in a passion with Lord Stair."[18]

When he needed his nerves, they did not fail him. On the night of August 29, militia of the local *section* came to Morris's door. "[A] number of persons enter, upon an order to examine my house for arms said to be hidden in it. I tell them that they shall not examine—that there are no arms and that they must seize the informer [responsible for the false report] that I may bring him to punishment. I am obliged to be very peremptory and at length get rid of them." The next morning, their superior, the *Commissaire de Section*, called on Morris and made his government's apologies. Morris remarked that he "behaved very well."[19]

It was well that Morris's bluff had worked, for, though he was not hiding arms in his house, he was hiding aristocrats. Mme de Flahaut and her son had sought shelter there on August 10; the comte de Flahaut was hiding in another place, though he had visited them several times. Yet another refugee appeared at Morris's door shortly after the militia left. No one marked for death, however, could long trust his life to a Parisian bolt hole. Shortly thereafter, Adèle paid a morning call on the assistant secretary of the Commune of the Tenth of August, the new revolutionary regime of the city. Besides the zealots, both virtuous and bloodthirsty, that the Revolution had thrown up, were the scoundrels, taking advantage of their positions. Many governments consist of little else, but times of turmoil give scoundrels unusual power. Mme de Flahaut asked the assistant secretary, who was in his dressing gown having his hair done, for passports for herself and her husband. He refused, and withdrew to an inner room to complete his toilet. He had left a stack of passports on his desk, however, and she reached for them. Through the glass of his inner door, he saw her, and strolled back out to say that they were of course useless without his signature. She left with a signed passport, which she returned the next day, and blanks on which she forged his signature. Perhaps she had bribed him, with money or herself; perhaps the tableau of her need and his power had given him gratification enough. Adèle and her son crossed the Channel at the end of September; Morris would not see her again for three years.[20]

Talleyrand was able to make a less harried exit, with a passport that was his reward for writing the new government's justification for deposing the king. He shortly found himself in the English countryside, in Surrey, in a circle of exiles enjoying the hospitality of Mme de Staël. Fanny Burney, the unmarried English novelist, who came to know the exotic refugees, was charmed with them, not least with Talleyrand. "His powers of entertainment are astonishing, both in information and raillery."[21] But all was not well in Surrey. Fanny's father, Dr. Burney, learned from a friend that Mme de Staël was having an affair with one of her guests. "I do not wish our Fanny to have the smallest connection with such an adulterous demoniac...."[22] Fanny leaped to Mme de Staël's defense. It was, she wrote her father, "a gross calumny ... she loves him even tenderly, but so openly, so simply, so unaffectedly and with such utter freedom from all coquetry. ..."[23] They were, of course, having an affair.

After the degradation of his king, Lafayette concluded that the Revolution had betrayed itself, and at the end of August he rode away from his army with a party of officers, hoping to reach Holland. The Austrians captured him, however, and imprisoned him as a dangerous revolutionary. "[M]y cell," he wrote, "is three paces broad and five and a half long.... The wall next to the ditch is dripping with moisture.... I am often afflicted with fever; I have no exercise, and little sleep...."[24] "Thus," Morris wrote Jefferson, "his circle is completed. He ... is crushed by the wheel he put in motion. He lasted longer than I expected."[25] Morris directed the Dutch bankers who handled the United States's transactions to advance 10,000 livres on the credit of the nation for Lafayette's personal expenses in prison, and to tell the Austrians that America would hear with "great concern" if their hero "should be in want."[26] Some months later, he would loan Mme de Lafayette 100,000 livres of his own money.

Morris stayed at his post. He represented the United States, but to whom did he represent it? One government had collapsed, and its interim replacements might fall to revolutionary rivals, or invading enemies. The most pressing problem before him was monetary: the United States owed a payment of 6 million livres on its debt to France, and Morris had to decide whether it should be paid, and to whom. William Short, who was now minister to Holland, and thus responsible for dealing directly with the money men of Amsterdam, doubted that a debt contracted with Louis XVI could be collected by the men who had overthrown him. If "a bond given to A.," he wrote Morris, has been "robbed by B. . . . could you, knowing that, pay the money to B. and consider yourself honestly discharged from A.?"[27] Morris told Short to pay the money on schedule to the government *du jour.* He urged it from expedience. "[L]et who will be king or minister, those who bring money will be well received."[28] He also urged it as a matter of right. "The corner stone of our own Constitution is the right of the people to establish such governments as they think proper."[29] If the French wished to have a bad government, or many governments in succession, that was their affair. The American minister would meddle to save lives, but he would honor his country's obligations.

He would not, however, enter into new obligations, particularly if they carried a whiff of corruption. One way that the United States had agreed to pay down its debt was to give $800,000 to French agents in America, who needed it to buy supplies for the French colony of Santo Domingo—today Haiti and the Dominican Republic. (Sugar islands made huge profits, but they required high maintenance, since they produced few staples locally.) This was a particularly attractive arrangement for the United States, since the French would be spending their money in America. As France crashed, Morris was now approached by three officials—M. Monge, minister of the Marine, M. Le Brun, minister of foreign affairs, and M. Clavière, minister of public contributions—who wanted him to authorize payment of the $800,000 directly in France. M. Le Brun was both urgent and insulting, reminding the American minister that "[your] independence is our work . . . we do not say this to stir your gratitude but to excite your goodwill."[30] Morris put the ministers off, saying he could not act on his own responsibility. In fact, he divined their true motive: greed. If the $800,000 were paid in Europe, they could take nicks from it in the form of commissions, and other graft. If it were paid in the United States, the opportunity would be lost to them. Beautiful women in distress were not the only targets of revolutionary rascals.

In the whirl of events, Morris's distance from his capital, at a time when a trans-Atlantic crossing typically took a month or two, and could take much longer, was a source of perplexity to him. Morris wrote President Washington and gave him two options. "I need not tell you, Sir, how agreeable [it] would be to me . . . to have positive instructions." On the other hand, "[t]he United States may wish to temporize and see how things are like to end, and in such case, leav[e] me at large with the right reserved to avow or disavow me according to circumstances. . . ."[31] Morris was willing, if necessary, to be made a scapegoat; but the risk would be sweetened by the freedom, which he always relished, of acting on his own.

On September 20, French artillerymen turned back a charge of Prussian grenadiers at the Argonnes town of Valmy; an army of revolutionaries had stopped the premier professional soldiers of Europe. The poet Goethe, who had come on the campaign as a flunky of the Duke of Saxe-Weimar, told the beaten Germans that "from this place and this time forth commences a new era in world history and you can all say that you were present at its birth."[32] Through the fog of the war, Morris heard conflicting and inaccurate reports of what was happening at the front. Before him, in Paris, the new National Convention met and declared the end of the monarchy, and the inauguration of a new calendar—Year One of the Republic. One of the delegates was Thomas Paine. On the grounds that he had "sapped the foundations of tyranny, and prepared the road to liberty,"[33] Paine was given French citizenship, and elected as a member from Pas-de-Calais. He accepted the honors, even though he knew little French. But he knew enough to understand the cries of *"Vive Thomas Paine"*[34] that greeted him when he took his seat.

Pressed by cares, and anxious not to leave compromising records in case the militia revisited his house, Morris shrank his diary entries to brief notes of the weather and public events. More details are preserved in his letters. "Some days ago a man applied to the convention

for damages done to his quarry. . . . The damage done to him was by
the number of dead bodies thrown into his pit and which choked it up
so that he could not get men to work at it."[35] Early in January 1793, he
abandoned his diary altogether.

The National Convention was in the midst of trying Louis Capet,
as he was now called, having been stripped of his title. The mild and
indecisive young man was charged with a long list of crimes, from
killing his own subjects to plotting against the Revolution he had
sworn to uphold. There was much truth to the latter accusation. But
had he not been sufficiently punished for this by losing his throne?
Many of the delegates thought so, among them Paine. In a speech read
for him by a translator, he urged France, "the first of European nations
to abolish royalty," to be "the first to abolish the punishment of
death."[36] Perhaps the former monarch could be rehabilitated by being
exiled to the republican atmosphere of the United States. After the
Convention voted—narrowly—for execution, Paine pleaded to delay
the sentence. Jean-Paul Marat, a radical journalist, screamed that
Paine's translator must be mistaken. Louis was beheaded on January
21, on a morning of winter fog.

In his report to Jefferson, Morris wrote of the "solemnity" of the occasion—"I have seen grief such as for the untimely death of a beloved
parent"[37]—though other observers were struck by the indifference, or
even lightheartedness of the populace. Morris had sent Jefferson a
more balanced epitaph for Louis XVI back in August, when the
throne first fell. "The King . . . has an uncommon firmness in suffering
[but] not the talents for action."[38]

The former Keeper of the King's Gardens was arrested shortly
thereafter. One of the passports that Mme de Flahaut secured had
been for her husband, who had not yet used it, instead lying low in the
Channel port of Boulogne. There he was seized, then managed to escape by bribing his jailers. The authorities still had one way to control
him, however: his honor. They arrested his lawyer as an accomplice to
his escape, and the old man, even more gallant at the end of his life
than he had formerly been comical, turned himself in, took full responsibility, and was executed.[39]

Throughout the spring of 1793 Morris was subject to searches and arrests. After one incident, he was obliged to complain to his friend Le Brun. "I beg, Sir, that you will have the goodness to secure me against similar accidents, troublesome in themselves, and scandalous from their publicity."[40]

To avoid difficulties, he bought twenty acres and a house in the village of Seine-Port, twenty-seven miles down the river from Paris, and spent as much time there as possible. "My little territory," he wrote, had "a pretty little garden and some green trees, and more grass than my neighbors. . . . The river is about the size of the Schuylkill at Tweed's ford, but deeper. . . . My prospect is rural and extensive." In one direction he could see "the ruins of baths which once belonged to the fair Gabrielle, favorite mistress to Henry the Fourth." In the other stood "the magnificent pavilion built by Bouret," a financier. "He expended on that building and its gardens about half a million sterling, and after squandering" two million more, "he put himself to death because he had nothing to live on. . . . [T]he objects just mentioned are well calculated to show the vanity of human pursuits and possessions. My time is spent in reading and writing. . . ."[41]

Much of his official correspondence was devoted to helping American ship captains whose vessels had been captured by French privateers for the offense of carrying British goods. (France had declared war on Britain in February.) The efforts of the two belligerent superpowers to harass and control American shipping would be a cause of complaint for the next twenty years. Morris also provoked the French government by continuing to shelter aristocrats. He let the comtesse de Damas stay at Seine-Port, then refused to let her be arrested there. As Le Brun wrote a colleague, the deed "shows only too well Morris's natural disposition to cover with the mantle of impunity persons suspected of aristocracy."[42] Morris denied the charge. "It never entered my mind . . . to interfere with the carrying out of the law of France. My opposition was founded only on the circumstance of an arrest in my house; I explained in a very clear manner to your commissaries that I would have given up the person if I had been asked, instead of [being shown] an order to *take* her."[43] As proof of his goodwill, he offered to bring the "citizenness" into Paris himself. The countess survived this imbroglio; in the caprice of despotism, sometimes a spirited delaying action was enough to spare a life.

When he could, Morris enjoyed himself. At one dinner in Paris, Morris's host offered his guests two bottles of Greek wine, then as now, cheap stuff. But by mistake, the second bottle actually contained Tokay, or fine Hungarian dessert wine—"some of the best," wrote Morris, "I ever tasted. I drink the greater part of it, praising always his Greek wine, till his brother-in-law, astonished at my choice, tastes it and all is discovered."[44] Morris bought, for a few sous a bottle, some Tokay sealed with the Hapsburg double eagle, which had found its way to a Paris grocery store. It had been part of the empress Maria Theresa's wedding present to her daughter, Marie Antoinette.

The widow Capet was tried in October 1793. Like Louis, she was accused of some things that she had actually done, such as corresponding with her Austrian relatives on the eve of the war. The prosecutors focused their energy, however, on her fantasy crimes, most notably the charge that she and her sister had molested her son. The "fucking tart," as one editor called her,[45] was guillotined on October 16. Despite royalist fantasies that he had somehow escaped, the son would die in prison, of tuberculosis, in 1795.

Paine gave no speeches in defense of the former queen's life, for by this time he himself was falling victim to the shifts of revolutionary politics. Morris described him in one letter as "besotted from morning till night," and added, "he would be punished if he were not despised."[46] Despised or not, punishment was coming. Paine had allied himself with a faction of the National Convention called the Girondins, named after the Gironde, a region of France from which several of them came. In the last days of the monarchy, they had been radicals, pushing for a republic. Once in power, they advocated a policy of world revolution. Paine agreed with both views, though his primary link to the faction was that many of the Girondins spoke English. As the situation of the country worsened, however—with depreciating currency, an ever-widening coalition of foreign enemies, and rebellions in several provinces—another faction, the Jacobins (who took their name from the former convent which was their meeting place), came to the fore. They were not more ruthless than the Girondins, but they were more focused, and they were better politicians. The leading Girondins were purged from the Convention in the summer, and executed along with Marie Antoinette in the fall. Achieving immortality through honesty, the Convention declared that "Terror is the order of the day." Parliamentary immunity protected Paine for a while, but he was arrested on Christmas morning.

"Thomas Paine is in prison," Morris wrote Jefferson in January 1794, "where he amuses himself by publishing a pamphlet against Jesus Christ."[47] Morris was referring to Part I of *The Age of Reason*, an attack on organized religions, particularly Christianity, which the former Methodist preacher had first published in French. The book does all that humor and literalism can do to undermine Christian dogma. "[I]t appears that Thomas [the disciple] did not believe the resurrection; and, as they say, would not believe, without having ocular and manual demonstration himself. *So neither will I;* and the reason is equally as good for me and for every other person, as for Thomas."[48] Paine was not an atheist but a deist. In substance, his beliefs were not far from Morris's, though his aggressive polemics were worlds away. After talking with one superstitious old Catholic, Morris wrote that he would be unlikely, at his age, to find a better faith. "[T]herefore it is best to leave him in possession of his present property."[49] Meanwhile, Paine petitioned for release as an American citizen. The French responded that, by serving in the Convention, he had forfeited that status. "[I]f he is quiet in prison," Morris told Jefferson, "he may have the good luck to be forgotten. Whereas, should he be brought much into notice, the long suspended axe might fall on him."[50] Paine never forgave Morris for his tactical inattention; it marked the end of their long and curious relationship.

Morris's own fate was being decided by the interplay of French and American politics. In April 1793, before the Girondins fell, they had dispatched as their minister to the United States Edmond-Charles Edouard Genet, a charming and enthusiastic thirty-year-old. Morris, who dined with him before he left, thought he had "the manner and look of an upstart."[51] Genet's missions were to ask for a speedier repayment of the American debt; to arm French privateers in American ports; to encourage private invasions of Spanish Louisiana from American soil; and generally to promote fraternal comradeship between the two republics. Jefferson, the secretary of state, was not opposed to any of this; he gave one of Genet's agents an introduction to the governor of Kentucky. American partisanship had grown sharper since his own passage of words with Vice President Adams in 1791. Jefferson's supporters, who called themselves Republicans, and a party led by Treasury Secretary Alexander Hamilton, who called themselves Federalists, disputed a range of issues from finance to foreign policy to constitutional interpretation. The Republicans held banquets in Citizen Genet's honor, seeing him as a celebrity foreign well-wisher. "It is beyond the power of figures or words to express the hugs and kisses [they] lavished on him," wrote a Federalist journalist. ". . . very few parts, if any, of the Citizen's body, escaped a salute."[52]

Very soon, however, it became apparent that Genet's welcome had gone to his head. He openly challenged the Washington administration to be friendlier with France, and he fancied he could appeal to the people over the president's head. Jefferson had his own doubts about Washington's instincts, but he knew that crossing the Father of his Country in public was madness. Genet "will sink the republican interest if [we] do not abandon him," Jefferson wrote Monroe.[53] By August the Washington administration, Federalists and Republicans alike, asked France to recall its bumptious minister.

By then the Jacobins were happy to purge Girondin diplomats. They found Genet guilty of "giddiness" and "vanity,"[54] and of needlessly offending a friendly nation, and they summoned him home, undoubtedly to be executed. (Genet prudently stayed put, and married the daughter of Governor George Clinton of New York.) The United States's request to recall Genet, however, gave France the opportunity to request the recall of Morris. The Jacobins could thus get rid of two obnoxious men in one swoop.

Morris knew that the French government had asked for his recall, but months passed before the machinery of the American government

produced a replacement. It turned out to be the earnest Virginia Francophile, James Monroe, who arrived in Paris in August 1794. French
parties meanwhile had come and gone "like the shadows of a magic
lantern," as Morris put it.[55] Robespierre and the Jacobins had ruled,
and in their turn been guillotined. Morris, relieved to be free from the
"torment of attention" to business,[56] shut up his houses in Paris and
Seine-Port and left France in mid-October for Switzerland. By the
end of the month, he was dining on the shores of Lake Geneva with
Jacques Necker, the man who had summoned the Estates-General to
deal with the French debt, and with Mme de Staël, who had come
home from Surrey.

WHILE MORRIS was still at his post, he had gotten a letter from
N. J. Hugon de Basseville, who was secretary of the French ambas-
sador to the court of Naples, and who, in an earlier incarnation, had
tutored Robert Morris's children. "I do not ask you, sir," wrote Basseville, "if you have not more than once regretted the tranquil banks of
the Delaware; it is enough for a philosopher to have seen a revolution
in his own country." Then, he asked, "why has ours not resembled
yours in every way?"[57]

Why should the two revolutions have resembled each other in any
way, given the different circumstances of the two countries? Yet the
closeness in time, the appearance of key actors in both, and the similarity of some ideals, led many to expect a similarity of outcomes. Even
the skeptical Morris thought he was competent to give his French
friends advice; he certainly believed he was competent enough to
meddle. So Basseville's question was a good one.

As a man who had helped write two constitutions, Morris thought
that France's revolutionary constitutions had been undone by the
overwhelming power of a one-house legislature, which was itself "at
the mercy of such men as could influence the mob."[58] The legislature
bullied and finally overthrew the king, and the political clubs and their
riotous supporters bullied the legislature. This view accurately described the course of the Revolution during the time he was in France.
The forces that should have checked the runaway legislatures were in-

competent to their task. We know Morris's low opinion of the king; he had an equally low opinion of his supporters, who busied themselves with "little paltry intrigue[s] unworthy of anything above the rank of footmen and chambermaids."[59]

But these were only political problems. The constitution maker did not think constitutions by themselves could make or unmake a nation's happiness. Morris believed that France's problems were more fundamental.

Partly they were a matter of national temperament. "The French will all tell you," Morris wrote an American colleague early in his stay, "that their countrymen have *des têtes exaltés*" (inflamed imaginations). "A Frenchman loves his King as he loves his mistress—to madness—because he thinks it great and noble to be mad. He then abandons both the one and the other most ignobly because he cannot bear the continued action of the sentiment he has persuaded himself to feel."[60] This erotic simile confuses as much as it explains: was Talleyrand madly in love with Adèle de Flahaut? Was Morris calm? The sudden shift from worship to execration does describe the course of Louis XVI from the opening of the Estates-General, when he was cheered, to the return from Varennes, when he was doomed. But bolder leaders had managed to command the passionate devotion of the French for years at a stretch; another such was in the offing as Morris wrote.

A problem easier to be analyzed was education. The French, Morris believed, were not properly trained to live in freedom. This was true of both the leaders and the led. It was an opinion he formed early, and held stubbornly. "[A] nation not yet fitted by education and habit for the enjoyment of freedom," he wrote John Jay two weeks before the Bastille fell, " . . . will greatly overshoot their mark."[61] "[S]upposing that they should even adopt a good [constitution]," he wrote Washington, a year after he left France, " . . . they will not be easy under it, for they never appeared to me to have the needful education . . . for free government."[62]

But how was a lack of that magnitude to be made up? In the constitution he wrote for France, Morris included an article (Article VII) on "Education and Worship." He proposed that 30 percent of the

Catholic Church's tithes be devoted to public education, and that one tenth of that be reserved for a National Academy.[63] Morris's interest in education was typically American; Washington wanted the United States to have a national university, and he and Jefferson hoped to lure the faculty of the University of Geneva to staff it.

It was too late, however, for such measures to help France—or Europe. Morris would spend the next four years touring a war-torn continent.

CHAPTER ELEVEN

Europe at War

I FLOAT, DEAR lady, like all light substances on the stream
of time, too indolent to row, too ignorant to steer. . . ."[1]
So Morris wrote, as he journeyed, to one of his friends from
his Paris days. In a life of light letters, this was only one more, even
as, in a life of ever-changing residences, he was only extending the
series.

But Morris had a special reason for being in motion at this time of
his life. The pressures of the last five years—of what he had done and
seen—required release. At the end of December 1794, he wrote
Washington a summary of his experiences in Paris, as balanced and
somber as an inscription on a tomb. "I saw misery and affliction every
day and all around me without power to mitigate or means to relieve,
and I felt myself degraded by communications I was forced into with
the worst of mankind. . . ."[2] A man who valued his ability to bring relief, both to himself for his own injuries and to his friends in their
grief, had been impotent; a man who did not suffer fools had been
obliged to treat with fools, thieves, and murderers. Morris had feasted
on horrors, and though in the Europe of the 1790s they could not be
put out of mind, he could put some distance between himself and
them.

The twin engines of his travels were love and politics. After leaving
Switzerland in November, he went north, and arrived in Hamburg
early the next month. Hamburg lies on the right bank of the Elbe, fifty
miles inland from the North Sea. It had ben an independent commercial city since the Middle Ages, and a major port for American goods

since independence. This was reason enough for Morris to visit there, but in March 1795, Hamburg acquired another attraction.

After escaping from France, Adèle de Flahaut had lived in London, evidently supported by her old friend Lord Wycombe. Talleyrand was a frequent visitor, though indigence did not make her attractive in his eyes. If the letters of his that survive can be trusted (they may not be authentic), he seems to have behaved rather coldly toward the mother of his son. She worked at her novels, too poor to hire a copyist—"I was a real writing machine," she remembered years later.[3] When writing did not bring in enough money—and when did it?—she made women's bonnets. In time, she left London for the continent. Morris arranged for her lodgings in the Hamburg suburb of Altona.

In the second week of April he picked her a violet "on the south side of a steep hill," the first of the season.[4] He gave it to her, with a little poem.

> Reçois les prémices que je viens de cueillir;
>   Depuis longtemps tu sais qu'elles te sont consacrées—
> Mes travaux et mes soins, mes jeux et mon loisir,
>   Les fleurs du printemps et les fruits de l'été.
>
> Voilà l'hiver qui vient, et d'un pas de géant,
>   Où le jour est si triste et la nuit est si bonne;
> Jouissons au plus vite, jouissons, chère enfant,
>   Car déjà je me sens au milieu de l'automne.[5]
>
> Take the first fruits I have just picked;
>   You know that they are all for you—
> My work and my cares, my jests and my leisure,
>   The flowers of spring and the fruits of summer.
>
> See winter come, with a giant's step,
>   When the day is so sad and the night is so good;
> Then let us celebrate, my dear child,
>   Because already I'm in the midst of fall.

Morris's original is much better than this translation, for it rhymes and almost scans. Although his verses are never quite good enough to be good, they are charming. The wonder is that they are not awful.

Adèle no doubt appreciated the flower; what did she think of the poem? The theme is an ancient one: nature speeds through its cycles, from birth to death and back, but our lives do not come round again. Our night ends all, so seize the day. But what poetic convention allowed Morris to say that his work and his jests had been all for her (literally, consecrated to her)? They had done much for, and to, each other, but he had always withheld the pledges she had sought. After the execution of her husband, she was free to take another. But Morris had assured her, when he was thirty-seven, that he would not marry her. Now that he was forty-three, though he was feeling intimations of mortality, he was still not ready to commit himself.

Twice that spring, Adèle was "taken with a bleeding from the breast"[6]—a possible sign of a tumor, and reason for her to provide her son with stepfather, in case he should lose his mother.

In June 1795, Morris left Adèle and Hamburg for England. While he was living in Paris, he had taken an extended trip of nine months there; now that he had no fixed abode, he would take twelve. Love and verse occupied his thoughts. In a poem written for his sister-in-law, the wife of General Morris, he asked himself the question, could he still be attractive at a dance? Nature's answer was no; but the author chose to ignore it. "In nature's spite, / To Cupid I devote the night." When he rewrote the poem in French on a rainy day, it ended more anxiously. *Je puis aimer toujours, mais comment puis-je plaire?*—I can always love, but how can I please?[7]

Most of Morris's time, however, was taken with politics. He was presented to George III, and had one of those bland conversations, punctuated with interjections—"Oh, aye," "Ah, what!"—that everyone who met the monarch had.[8] He met a figure of the American future, the twenty-eight-year-old John Quincy Adams, son of Vice President John Adams; Morris found him "tinctured with suspicion"[9]—a judgment that would ring down the decades. He met William Pitt, the prime minister and son of a prime minister. Given his family, Morris moved comfortably in a world where elections had not quite untangled themselves from hereditary succession.

He renewed an acquaintance, made on a previous visit, with William, Lord Grenville, Pitt's cousin and foreign minister. He and Grenville consulted about European affairs, and Morris promised, when he resumed his travels on the continent, to write Grenville reports of the state of opinion in the courts of central Europe. Morris was not a mere medium of news, but freely offered his suggestions. The main problem, from Grenville's point of view, was that Prussia, wearied with fruitless exertions, had dropped out of the anti-French coalition. To woo it back, and thereby reestablish the European balance of power, Morris proposed a grand territorial swap, like a game of musical chairs. The heart of the deal was that Prussia would acquire Hanover, in north-central Germany, the homeland of the British royal family, while Britain would pick up Flanders. Holland and Austria would be compensated in various ways, and Morris even offered rewards for France—in one version, the territory of Alsace on her eastern border, in another, her former Caribbean and Indian colonies, now British prizes of war. Morris's reason for giving France overseas possessions showed his perverse intelligence—the more she had to lose, the more fearful she would be.[10]

When Morris finally returned to America, his political enemies would accuse him of having been on Grenville's payroll. This was absurd; he didn't need the money. The pleasure of hearing himself talk and reading himself write was compensation enough. Five years earlier, Morris had given similarly ambitious advice to Lafayette. Now that France had changed, he was offering his advice to the other side. At all times, Morris enjoyed playing with maps.

One thing he saw in the British Isles made him think of home. On a trip to Scotland, he inspected a newly opened canal, that bisected the country at the bottleneck between the Firth of Forth on the North Sea coast and the Clyde River, on the west. He admired the locks, the stonework, and the vessels using it. "When I see this," he wrote in his diary, "my mind opens to a view for the interior of America which hitherto I had rather conjectured than seen."[11]

In May 1796, he heard news of Adèle from a French émigré in London. Her health had not turned for the worse, but their intimacy had, for Adèle was said to be engaged to the Portuguese minister to Denmark (the Danish border was then a few miles north of Hamburg). Morris left for Hamburg in June. He did not question his old lover about her plans immediately upon his arrival, but one night, when he had taken her for a drive in his carriage after dinner, she told him along the way (*"chemin faisant"*) "whereabouts she is with her Portuguese lover."[12] Jose Maria de Souza-Botelho Mourao e Vasconcellos was thirty-seven, seven years younger than Morris, two years older than Mme de Flahaut. He had read *Adèle de Senanges,* her first novel, and conceived a desire to meet its author. Morris's diary says no more about him, or Adèle's connection to him, at this point. In their games of cat-and-mouse, there had been both scenes and silences. The laconic diary could be a facade, masking a frank conversation; it could be the true record of things unsaid. Morris left Hamburg at the beginning of July.

Over the next eight months, he visited the major cities of central Europe, and several of the lesser ones. He was by now an accomplished traveler, who had learned that "the art of living consists . . . in some considerable degree in knowing how to be cheated."[13] His account of life on the road in the Holy Roman Empire glitters with the comedy of discomfort—bores, vermin, astonishing food—which English travel writers would raise to the level of art. At one dinner, he was exposed to a "Saxon delicacy"—candied beetles. "These animals resemble in some respects what in America they call the locust, but are not so large, and have, besides, the hard cover of a bug to their wings, which cover is a bright brick-colored brown. How it should enter into people's head to eat them, unless driven to it by famine, one could hardly conceive, and the making them into sweetmeats is utterly inconceivable."[14]

Both the petty states and the major powers belonged to a dying world. Berlin, the capital of Prussia, was "a great unpeopled town," a stage set. "The immense appearances, I think, want solidity." All that remained of the power amassed by Frederick the Great was the brutal manners of realpolitik; negotiating with Prussians was easy, Morris explained to Grenville, "for it is not necessary to clothe propositions in honest and decent forms."[15]

Vienna made him rediscover his American priggishness. "A great number of women of the town are here," he wrote of midnight mass three days before Christmas. "The principal object of a great part of the congregation" was making assignations. " . . . I own that this mode of employing an edifice dedicated to sacred purposes does not accord with my feeling."[16] New Year's Day made him more thoughtful. The Prince Esterhazy, captain of the Hungarian guard, came to court in a scarlet uniform embroidered with pearls—"four hundred and seventy large pearls and many thousands of inferior size." Esterhazy was "the richest subject in Europe." Yet he lived in such a style that his estate was mortgaged to creditors, who paid him an allowance, which he regularly exceeded. "Here is the history of the feudal system in its decline. . . . [T]he government rejoices at the consequent humiliation of a haughty nobility, without considering . . . the power which is to spring up in its stead."[17] Once the nobles fell, would the local Neckers and their successors be any better?

The sinking star of feudalism still shed light. General Moszyn'ski, a Polish nobleman in Vienna, wore epaulettes set with huge diamonds. "But a finer thing than his jewels . . . was the conduct of his servant, who, when his master was made prisoner during the late troubles in that miserable country, possessed himself of his valuables and whispered to him, 'If you escape, you will find me at Leipsic [Leipzig].'"[18] The master escaped, and the servant was true to his trust.

The old order could not survive without leaders as competent as its servants were loyal. The revolutionary who was pushing old rulers over like ninepins as Morris moved about Europe was Napoleon Bonaparte, a Corsican artillerist who had survived the Jacobins who first advanced him in the French army, and who was now leading an invasion of northern Italy, toppling Austrian satraps and native regimes alike. Morris followed his progress from afar, through the usual scrim of gossip, bias, and misinformation. Time and again, wise heads told Morris that Napoleon was really a coward, and that he owed his victories to luck or the incompetence of his opponents. Morris, catching the bug, would opine that "he will probably now meet the usual fate of French armies east of the Alps"—that is, he would be defeated.[19] Yet somehow, the parvenu and his troops always managed to win. If it was luck, it was a long run of it.

He consoled himself for what had, or hadn't, been said in Hamburg. In Berlin he met again with one of his consolations from Paris, Mme de Nadaillac. There was a baron who was in love with her and wished to marry her, and the king of Prussia wanted her to be his mistress. "It would be ridiculous" for her, Morris admitted, "to succumb now to a *voyageur* who treats everything lightly, and yet such a thing might happen. . . . [T]he struggle between her reasonings and her wishes gives no small interest."[20] In Dresden, Morris met a Mme Crayen, who put up no struggle. The king of Saxony was besotted with her, but she loved the American stranger. They "worship[ped] on the Cyprian altar," and "brighten[ed] the chain together" (one brightens a chain by rubbing it). The "lively sense" of their lovemaking convinced her, Morris wrote boastfully, that she had become pregnant.[21] Balked with Adèle, Morris wanted lovers who were no trouble, either because they were unavailable or available without strings.

In the spring of 1797 he returned to Hamburg. There he saw Adèle, and her supposed fiancé, Souza. Souza, who had just returned from a diplomatic trip to Berlin, told Morris that the Prussians considered him a "great democrat."[22] Morris would puzzle any European—too liberal for monarchists, too conservative for revolutionaries, too skeptical for both. In Hamburg, Morris also ran across a figure from Adèle's past, Lord Wycombe, who only now realized that Adèle had once hoped to marry him. "[H]e seems to be very angry at it, though, in fact, he has nothing to complain of. He seemed a proper subject to work upon, and therefore she exerted herself to get hold of him."[23] To distract himself, Morris carried on with his landlord's two daughters (the younger, he wrote in an image that slides creepily from metaphor back into reality, "begins to feel the gentle hint from nature's tongue").[24]

Adèle evidently feared that she was losing her hold on Souza, because in the summer she applied to the French consular agent in Hamburg for a passport to return home. After the fall of Robespierre, Frenchmen of unapproved political opinions faced less risk of being guillotined. But since France still forbade the return of aristocratic émigrés, Adèle had to present documents showing that she had lived in Paris from 1792 to 1795. These were, of course, forgeries, but the diplomat approved them; corruption was as useful in getting into France as in getting out. She returned to Paris, and left Morris's life forever, in October 1797. Souza married her after all, in 1802—"in order," he told her, "that you would make me laugh."[25] Her son became one of Napoleon's generals. Fanny Burney, who had married one of the Frenchmen marooned in Surrey, found herself "charmed and delighted" when she at last met Mme de Souza.[26]

Morris hardly mentioned Adèle in his diary during his months in Hamburg, never revealingly. This was the long, cool diminuendo of a hot and cold affair—of long absences and furious, furtive lovemaking, of planning governments and hiding from mobs, of sickness, jealousy, and intelligent conversation. Can a man want so much without wanting more? Morris had been happy to woo Mme de Flahaut, but only in competition with Talleyrand, Wycombe, and her husband. His success in a scrum of lovers may have assured him, as Mrs. Plater had after his injury, that he was a whole man; it may have recalled being a brilliant youngest son among hulking older half brothers. But he would not have her alone. Perhaps something about his father's depression and his mother's stubbornness had made the idea of marriage unattractive, or perhaps his father's age during his boyhood had made it seem a state for late-middle-aged men. Only time and circumstances would change his mind.

A far greater star of the morning of the Revolution than the former Mme de Flahaut passed through Hamburg in the fall of 1797. Lafayette had been held in several prisons, ending finally in the Austrian fortress of Olmutz (now Olomuc, in the Czech Republic). After years of stern treatment, in which he wasted away and lost much of his hair, his wife and daughters were allowed to share his imprisonment. Mme de Staël wrote Morris a letter, by turns imperious and flattering, asking him to procure their freedom. "You have influence; [no one is] so stupid as not to consult a man like you."[27] As he had in the case of Paine, Morris doubted the efficacy of a direct demand upon the jailers. "[M]en do not easily allow they have done wrong . . . the most urgent solicitations would perhaps be fruitless; for it would be difficult to comply with them, without admitting the injustice in question."[28] Nevertheless, he applied to the Austrian imperial chancellor. Mercy, he argued, would require no explanations and no excuses. "[S]ince no one has had any right to know why his Majesty, the Emperor, determined to detain [Lafayette] as a prisoner, so no one can assume that of demanding why his kindness has set him at liberty." It would also please an even greater ruler. "Think, also, that forgiveness granted to others is the only unobjectionable title, of which we can avail ourselves before the King of Kings."[29] The emperor himself received a private appeal from George Washington, in the last year of his last term as president. What finally freed Lafayette was not appeals to forgiveness, but French arms. Napoleon and his subordinates, after driving the Austrians from northern Italy and pursuing their armies within sight of Vienna, accepted their demands for peace. One of Napoleon's stipulations was that Lafayette be released. The political position the aging hero represented, of idealistic constitutional monarchy, was so impotent that the French government no longer condemned him. They did not, however, want him in France, so the two nations agreed to set him and his family free in Hamburg. Morris advised him not to speak of the injustices he had suffered: so many had suffered far worse.

Talleyrand had a better recovery from his reverses. Exile had taken him from the English countryside to the woods of the United States, where he made some money in American real estate, and was astonished to see Alexander Hamilton, now retired from the Treasury, working at night in his New York law office (why had he not used his opportunities to make better provision for his future?). Talleyrand was permitted to return to France in the summer of 1796, thanks to the influence of Mme de Staël, and only a year later he became foreign minister, also thanks to her influence, even though no one else liked him ("to enter a government in which nobody wants you," said one admiring observer, "is no mean trick").[30] Now that he was back in power, after experiencing its transience, he would not make Hamilton's mistake. *"Il faut y faire une fortune immense, une immense fortune"* (I have to make an immense fortune, a really immense fortune).[31]

Paine had been freed from prison a month after Morris left France. He attacked George Washington in print for not having demanded his release, and made plans, as Morris had done for Lafayette, for a French invasion of England. He put his hopes on the young General Bonaparte and, in the words of another displaced revolutionary, the Irishman Wolfe Tone, drank "like a fish."[32] Years later, still drinking, he would return to America, his reputation blasted by his criticisms of Washington and Christ, and die in New York, in Greenwich Village. Morris never saw him again.

Morris spent his last year in Europe touring little German cities, then returning to an Adèle-less Hamburg to prepare his journey home. His activities had become somewhat boring, perhaps even to him. But one deserves mention. From the moment he had left France, he had helped French acquaintances in distress. He loaned them money on the most generous terms: "If fortune smile upon you, you will return the money. If not, allow me to treasure the consoling thought that I have alleviated your troubles for a short period."[33] He gave it, without even the pretense of a loan: "The enclosed letter will supply you with what you want. Do not speak of obligations."[34] He gave, what was equally valuable, good counsel. "Try to make everyone understand how necessary it is to forgive, and to forget the past, thinking only of the future."[35] As a geopolitician, he was reckless; as a guide to living, he could be acute.

Morris took inspiration from many of the émigrés he saw. When he first came to Dresden, he found the streets filled with them, fleeing eastward, allowed to stay only three days. (Years later, Adèle remembered posted warnings in German towns against Jews, vagabonds, and émigrés.) "Unhappy people!" wrote Morris. "Yet they are employed in seeing everything curious which they can get at; are serene, even gay. So great a calamity could never light on shoulders which could bear it so well." The weight of suffering, he realized, "is not diminished by the graceful manner of supporting it." Grace, however, spared the sufferers the additional burdens of "spleen and ill-humor."[36]

But whom else did this describe? Who else was habitually serene, even gay? This was the face that Morris had been wearing, and recommending to friends and family members for years. Morris's gaiety came partly from religious belief, for though he honored neither the Sabbath nor the marriage vow, he "hope[d] in the kindness of that Being who is to all his creatures an indulgent father."[37] On the surface of it, this is a paradoxical hope, since divine indulgence is not what émigrés and other sufferers experience. But suffering itself had its lessons. "Do not say, madame," Morris wrote the comtesse d'Albani, one of the many miscellaneous almost-celebrities he had met (she was the widow of "Charles III," pretender to the throne of England), "that life is a sad thing. Without reverses it would soon become insipid, and we find that the happiest mortals are those who have been taught, through some sad experience, the value of this world's goods."[38] In a treatise of moral philosophy, such advice could be enraging. Coming from a man with a stump and a fleshless arm, who so clearly enjoyed this world's goods, it was consoling, even inspiring.

Morris sailed from Hamburg at the beginning of October 1798. Two months later, the ship he was on approached Long Island in the teeth of a nor'wester, and he had one of those encounters that come to self-assured men. "This morning at two o'clock the captain comes to ask my *advice* whether we should stand in for Rhode Island, or stand off. I tell him I will not pretend to *advise*, he must act according to his own judgment, but I will give him my opinion on any state of facts which he may represent."[39] The much-blown traveler landed in Newport and, after more storms and other travails, arrived in New York at the end of the month. On the last Sunday of the year Morris attended divine worship at Trinity Church at the head of Wall Street.

Part 3

Brink of
Revolution

CHAPTER TWELVE

American Passions

ONE OF THE New Yorkers who greeted Morris on his return was Alexander Hamilton, recently promoted to major general and second in command of the United States army. Hamilton wanted his old friend to take a role in the national government—"His talents are wanted," he wrote Rufus King; "men like him do not super-abound"—but Morris told him that he intended to lead a private life.[1]

Morrisania wanted his attention. The best fertilizer, as the proverb says, is a master's footsteps, and his estate had not felt his for over a decade. The roof leaked, so he decided to rebuild the house. He spared no expense, embarking on a course of improvements that would cost him $50,000 to $60,000, or well over half a million today. He entertained generously, if imperiously. "When he spoke," wrote a frequent guest, "he expected the listening ear. On a certain occasion . . . perceiving the attentions of his hearers beginning to flag, he suddenly ejaculated, 'I shall address the tea pot' and he accordingly closed his argument with that silent representative."[2] His determination to live in the style to which he had become accustomed could make his countrymen gape. "[U]pon entering the inn," wrote a traveler who crossed his path, "I found Gouverneur Morris with two French valets, a French traveling companion and his hair buckled up in about a hundred papillottes [paper curlers]. His wooden leg, papillottes, French attendants and French conversation made his host . . . stare most prodigiously and gave me some idea how the natives looked when poor Cook made his entrée at the friendly isles."[3]

He took on a complex civil suit, *Le Guen v. Gouverneur & Kemble*, involving a shipment of East Indian cotton and indigo that had passed through the hands of half a dozen middlemen, one of whom (Isaac Gouverneur) was Morris's uncle. The climactic hearing in Albany lasted seven days and involved eight lawyers, including Hamilton, who was on the opposing side, representing Lewis Le Guen. Morris, wrote one of the lawyers, "at times astonished us with bursts of sublime eloquence—at other times he was flat and uninteresting." Hamilton, "wound up with passion," sometimes went too far. "Hamilton," Morris noted in his diary, "is desirous of being witty, but goes beyond the bounds and is open to a severe dressing."[4]

Outside the courtroom, Hamilton wanted Morris to reenter public life because American politics seemed to be in the gravest state since the ratification of the Constitution, perhaps since the end of the Revolution. Federalists and Republicans had been feuding throughout the second term of George Washington. Morris had urged his idol to stand for office a third time ("[I]t is not given to every man to bend the bow of Ulysses"),[5] but Washington, tired of the political broils, and intent on teaching a last lesson about transferring power in a republic, had stepped down, to be succeeded, in the election of 1796, by his vice president, John Adams. The feuding continued as before. Washington, after trying to maintain a balance between the parties, had steadily found himself drawn to the side of the Federalists. Adams, the target of Jefferson's blurb for *The Rights of Man*, was also commonly reckoned among them. The Republicans were led by Jefferson, now, by a quirk of the Electoral College, vice president, and by James Madison, once the friend and adviser of Hamilton and Washington, now their enemy.

One of the leading Federalists in New York and nationally was Alexander Hamilton. Morris had known him since the Revolution. They had shared several experiences—going to King's College, serving in the Continental Congress—though never at the same time (Hamilton was five years younger). Both men had a self-consciously "realistic" turn of thought, which Morris expressed in the flourishes of his tongue and pen, Hamilton through the relentless thrust of his arguments. Their refusal to be satisfied with airy ideals or soothing phrases was based, in part, on the hard things each had seen in his life. But, as their experiences differed, so did their temperaments. Morris's early injuries were brutal and obdurate, never to be repaired, only graciously lived with. The injuries Hamilton experienced in the West Indies were more insidious. His parents had fastened on him the burden of illegitimacy, and his father had compounded it by abandoning his lover and their children when Alexander was nine years old. His mother's death when he was eleven completed the tale of a bleak and shamed youth. His subsequent rise in the world was meteoric: by the time he was twenty, he was a colonel on Washington's staff; by the time he was thirty-two, he was Treasury secretary. Hard work, it seemed, could fix his and the world's problems. So although Hamilton was witty enough, he, unlike Morris, lacked a true sense of humor: he had too much to do.

The two political parties disputed everything from foreign policy to Hamilton's visionary intention of molding America into a flourishing industrial power (the Republicans equated luxury with corruption, and cherished an agrarian ideal). As sundering as their disagreements was the manner in which they expressed them. Tempers ran as high as differences ran deep. Early in 1798, Representative Matthew Lyon, a Republican from Vermont, spat in the face of Representative Roger Griswold, a Federalist from Connecticut, who in return clubbed him with a hickory cane, all this in the cloakroom and on the floor of the House. The newspapers, as vicious as they were lively, whipped the frenzy up. On another occasion Hamilton, accused by a Republican journalist of secret dealing in government securities when he was Treasury secretary, had felt compelled to reply that the money he had paid his supposed agent had in fact been blackmail, extorted because he had been sleeping with the recipient's wife.

What brought politics to a fever pitch in the second half of the Adams administration was a new strain in America's relations with France, to which the Genet episode had been a mere prelude. The villain of the piece was Morris's old friend Talleyrand. Early in his term Adams had sent three special envoys to Paris to protest French harassment of American shipping. The envoys expected to deal directly with the minister of exterior relations. But, after one fifteen-minute interview with Talleyrand in October 1797, he put them off, while mysterious intermediaries appeared in his stead, suggesting that the United States must pay money—"a great deal of money"—to France and to themselves personally before negotiations could even begin.[6] It was the old story of Le Brun and the debt repayments all over again. Talleyrand and his minions were not trying to affront the United States; they were playing by the rules of diplomacy and public service as they understood them. But the American envoys were shocked, and when they reported the French shakedown to Congress in the spring of 1798, America was outraged. The Federalists, profiting from popular wrath, passed laws against suspicious aliens and Republican journalists, and expanded the army against a French attack, bringing Washington out of retirement to command and making Hamilton his right hand.

Morris arrived in New York just as the war fever had peaked. French setbacks in Ireland and Egypt had caused Talleyrand to moderate his tone; some Americans (including President Adams) began to balk at the cost of a military establishment. If the prospects of a war were fading, however, political warfare raged unabated. The Republicans accused the administration of plotting a military dictatorship, as the first step to a monarchy. The Federalists viewed their enemies as Jacobins; Hamilton, with bellicose jauntiness, explained that the political stakes included "true liberty, property, order, religion and of course *heads.*"[7]

Morris, who would soon be drawn back into politics, would not take part in its bitterness, at least not yet. His time in Europe helped him keep an even keel. Sitting on the rim of a world war, Americans borrowed its ideological terminology for their own disputes. Morris, who had been in the vortex, could not be so facile. Federalists and Republicans might speak of each other as Jacobins and monarchists, ready to make use of guillotines and putsches. But Morris had lost acquaintances to the guillotine, and watched royalists plot vain coups.

He also knew an earlier world of politics. Morris had seen the first stirrings of ideological party strife during his years in Pennsylvania, when the Constitutionalists and the Republicans had fought over the state government and the Bank of North America. (The Pennsylvania Republicans, who had supported a bank and a strong executive, were now Federalists, while the Constitutionalists, suspicious of both, had become Republicans.) But he had sprung out of the older world of colonial New York politics, in which parties formed around rival families, and friendships were also family affairs. One survival of that system was his intimacy with Robert R. Livingston. Local accidents determined Livingston's course: Hamilton, who had worked with the Livingstons to secure New York's ratification of the Constitution, had imprudently boosted Rufus King, newly moved to the state, for a Senate seat that the Livingstons considered theirs. One did not cross a New York grandee without suffering the consequences, and when Jefferson and Madison reached out to the Livingstons as allies, they responded. Morris, for his part, devoted to Washington and detesting the French Revolution, made himself a Federalist once he returned home. Yet Morris and Livingston had been friends since their twenties. The two men maintained their old cordiality.

Morris paid his respects to another old friend, now in disgrace. Robert Morris had been imprisoned for debt before Gouverneur had returned from Europe. The rare claret, the temple erected to hospitality, and all his holdings would not pay a twentieth of his obligations. Gouverneur visited Robert and his wife in their prison in Philadelphia in the fall of 1799. His sketch of his ruined patron is a mixture of clarity and pity. Robert Morris had "behaved very ill," dragging creditors into the depths with him. His wife now "put . . . on an air of firmness which she cannot support, and was wrong to assume." Their visitor kept up a "lively strain of conversation" to distract them from their woes. When the debtors were finally freed, he would do more than that, giving Robert Morris an annuity that would allow the sexagenarian to keep a roof over his head.[8]

At the end of the year, Morris had the duty of delivering Washington's eulogy. He had written Washington in mid-December, urging him to stand as the Federalist candidate for president in 1800 in place of John Adams (Washington was always first in the heart of Morris). Washington never read the letter. He had gone riding in a snowstorm at Mount Vernon, got soaked, and died of an inflamed throat. The city fathers of New York asked Morris to deliver an oration at St. Paul's Chapel, where Washington had gone to worship after his first inauguration, ten and a half years ago. Morris did not consider the speech a great success—"Pronounced my oration badly," he noted in his diary—for eulogy was not naturally his vein. He was always more comfortable as an advocate, when he could employ the sallies for which Washington had once gravely chided him.[9]

The death of Washington removed more than a national icon. The nation lost a symbol of seriousness, and the last psychic brake on unrestrained partisanship. Politics would enter a long period of irresponsibility, punctuated by ugliness.

In the spring of 1800 one of New York's senators resigned his seat, and the state legislature (which then elected senators) picked Morris to fill out the remaining three years of his term. The last time Morris had sat in Congress, almost twenty years ago, the states voted as units, attendance was spotty, and the accommodations, in York at least, were quite grim. Now senators and representatives voted as individuals, and there were three additional states—Vermont, Kentucky, and Tennessee: the emerging frontier, against which Morris had warned at the Constitutional Convention. Accommodations in the new city of Washington, to which the government moved at the end of 1800, were still grim, however. The city was little more than a few public buildings, a few boardinghouses, and swamp; Morris had lived as well in the roadside bugholes of central Europe. In a letter to one of his European friends, the Princess of Thurn and Taxis, Morris described his new abode: "We want nothing here but houses, cellars, kitchens, well informed men, amiable women, and other little trifles of the kind. . . . If, then, you are desirous of coming to live in Washington, in order to confirm you in so fine a project, I hasten to assure you, that fieldstone is very abundant here . . . that there is no want of sites for magnificent hotels; that contemplated canals can bring a vast commerce to this place; that the wealth, which is its natural consequence, must attract the fine arts hither; in short, that it is the very best city in the world for a *future* residence."[10]

Morris was a loyal Federalist in most things. He supported Federalist press restrictions for, although he was proud of his family's role in the Zenger case, he disapproved of journalists who told lies or revealed official confidences, as Paine had done when he worked for the foreign affairs committee. Republicans also supported such restrictions, only wishing them to be enforced by the states, not the federal government (especially when it was controlled by Federalists). But Morris saw that the Federalists were in political trouble. The taxes levied to support a war that had not happened were onerous. "The truth is," he wrote Rufus King, now minister to Britain, "that a direct tax, unpopular everywhere, is really unwise in America, because property here is not productive." The Republicans "have had just cause to complain of the manner in which money is raised, and [since] our expenditure is far from economical . . . no applause is to be expected on that score."[11]

Like many parties in difficult straits, the Federalists fought among themselves. President Adams hoped to repair his fortunes by sending new envoys to France, and by dismantling the army. Hamilton thought that both moves were rash, and that Adams was literally mad. Morris, more charitably, called the president *"unbiegsam"* (unbending).[12] The Republicans, meanwhile, moved with disciplined unity toward their goal, and in the election of 1800 the vote of the Electoral College gave Vice President Jefferson and his running mate Aaron Burr a victory.

The Electoral College was one of the more unusual improvisations of the Constitution Convention. According to the original plan, each elector voted for two men, and the top two vote-getters became president and vice president. In the elections of 1789 and 1792, every elector cast one vote for the Father of his Country. The only suspense concerned who should finish second, which John Adams managed twice to do, though he trailed far behind Washington. In the election of 1796, however, both Adams and Jefferson had finished ahead of their respective running mates, which led to the anomaly of the victorious president having his defeated rival as vice president. Now another anomaly occurred. The Republicans had been determined to let no Federalist slip in between their candidates—with the result that Jefferson and Burr tied.

Burr, who would turn forty-five in early February, had made his career as a lawyer and politician in New York, but Morris's long sojourns in Philadelphia and Europe had deprived him of all but the most recent acquaintance with him. Burr was the son of the Reverend Aaron Burr, president of Princeton, and the grandson of the Reverend Jonathan Edwards, the great preacher and philosopher. Credulous observers made of these religious antecedents an aristocratic pedigree that impressed Burr's contemporaries and gave Burr his imposing self-assurance.[13] New Englanders probably were impressed by Burr's family history, though it is doubtful that Morris or the Livingstons, to say nothing of the Randolphs and the Pinckneys, cared much about a pair of dead Congregationalist divines. As for Burr, he was confident because of his qualities—intelligence and charm—and his achievements—a brave war record and the love of beautiful women.

One attainment Burr lacked was any definite political program or philosophy, and this now gave many of the defeated Federalists hope. The tie in the Electoral College was to be broken by the House of Representatives. States would vote as units, and everyone's quick count showed that the Republicans controlled eight state delegations, and the Federalists six, with two split. If Federalists in the House supported Burr, the deadlock would continue. If Burr could then coax some well-placed Republican congressmen to his side, Jefferson might be supplanted by a possibly better man.

Adèle de Flahaut had disliked Jefferson, calling him *"faux et emporté"* (false and hotheaded).[14] Ordinary Federalist politicians detested him; "they consider Mr. Jefferson," Morris wrote, "as infected with all the cold blooded vices."[15] (How did the hot head of the Frenchwoman's Jefferson run with the cold blood of the Federalists' Jefferson? By expressing sweeping sentiments with the detachment of an intellectual.) But Morris had always gotten along with him well enough. When Jefferson surrendered his main duty as vice president, presiding over the Senate, Morris would write the Senate's valedictory tribute, praising his "intelligence, attention and impartiality."[16] Burr he judged to be an unknown quantity, on whom it was pointless to build hopes.[17] In any case, the Republicans had wanted Jefferson, and they were the majority. "Since it was evidently the intention of our fellow citizens to make Mr. Jefferson their President," Morris wrote Hamilton from Washington in mid-December, "it seems proper to fulfill that intention."[18]

Hamilton believed that Burr was a completely known quantity. From mid-December on through the month of January 1801, he sent a stream of letters from New York to Morris and other Federalists denouncing Burr as a bankrupt, a Bonaparte, and a political corsair. Hamilton claimed not to hate Burr; the two men socialized occasionally, and, in the small legal world of New York, they also appeared in the same courtroom (they had both been lawyers for Lewis Le Guen). But he hated the idea of Burr holding high office. Burr, he wrote Morris, is "daring enough to attempt every thing, wicked enough to scruple nothing."[19]

Neither Hamilton's onslaught nor Morris's doubts had any effect on the Federalists in Washington. "They appear to be moved by passion only," Morris wrote Hamilton early in January. "You, who are temperate, *in drinking*"—a jest at Hamilton's sex scandal—"have never perhaps noticed the awkward situation of a man, who continues sober after the company are drunk."[20]

Those few Federalists who did not want to intrigue with Burr hoped to get assurances from Jefferson. In the middle of February, after the House had begun balloting—the deadlock there would hold for thirty-five ballots—Jefferson ran into Morris outside the Senate chamber (the Capitol was as yet barely begun; Congress met in the passage that now connects the Rotunda to the Senate). Years later, when asked what they had said, Morris politely refused to reveal it. "[I]t was . . . that sort of conversation where, among gentlemen, there is so much confidence implied, that it would be indelicate to cite facts. . . ."[21] Jefferson's memory of the encounter was that Morris told him he could end Federalist resistance by pledging to keep the funding of the public debt, to keep up the navy, and to keep lesser Federalist officeholders in their posts. Jefferson remembered making no promises. Other Federalists approached Jefferson's allies with the same proposals, and some believed they got satisfaction, though Jefferson always insisted that he had commissioned no one to bargain for him. Then as now, Washington insiders claimed to know more than they in fact did, while Jefferson, who was not quite *faux*, as Mme de Flahaut thought, was nevertheless capable of not always hearing what he himself said. However it was, enough Federalist die-hards abstained on the thirty-sixth ballot to give Jefferson ten states and victory.

In the interval between the Federalist collapse and Jefferson's inauguration, Morris answered a letter from Robert Livingston. Livingston had missed standing in Burr's shoes, for when the Republicans were looking for a New Yorker to run with Jefferson, he had briefly been considered. Perhaps to assuage his disappointment, Livingston had written that if Morris had been Jefferson's running mate (a neater trick than Talleyrand coming back into office), the House would have made him president. Morris gracefully waved the hyperbolic compliment aside, then turned to recent events. "The election by the House of Representatives will doubtless have excited heats, and animosities, at a distance. Here the most perfect good humour prevailed, from beginning to end." With the writer, perhaps; of whom else was he thinking? He had known all along, he claimed, that the pro-Burr Federalists "would be disappointed, and, therefore, [I] looked on with perfect composure. Indeed, my dear friend, this farce of life contains nothing, which should put us out of humour."[22]

The election of 1800 had been the United States's first peaceful transition, not from man to man, as had happened in 1796 when Adams succeeded Washington, but from party to party. It had, however, been a closer call than Morris let on: the Republican governors of Pennsylvania and Virginia had thought of dubious outcomes in which they would be obliged to call up their militias. Nor had the peaceful result allayed ill feeling. Most Federalists felt the rage of losers. President Jefferson intended that they should continue to feel it, for though his inaugural address, delivered on March 4 ("too long by half," Morris wrote in his diary),[23] contained a generous sentence—"We are all republicans, we are all federalists"²⁴— he wrote privately that he would "sink federalism into an abyss from which there shall be no resurrection."²⁵

Morris escaped the general mood not only because of his natural cheerfulness but because of an almost casual insight into the function of partisanship. Political parties were not mentioned in the Constitution, because they were thought to be bad things. Madison, in his *Federalist* essays, called them "factions"; Washington, in his Farewell Address, had warned against them. The framers (including Madison and Washington) had almost immediately set two parties up, but they could not acknowledge what they had done. More precisely, none of them could acknowledge the legitimacy of the party that was not his. Federalists thought their opponents were undermining the state; Republicans thought their opponents were perverting it. The difference between Jefferson's inaugural address and his private thoughts was not an instance of hypocrisy. His public statement was truly generous, but it dealt in generalities: all Americans, he was saying, supported the principles of freedom and constitutionalism. He expected Federalist Party members of goodwill, however, to join his party, which understood the proper balance of these principles. Parties as such would then wither away.

In an 1800 letter to Rufus King, months before the crisis in the House, Morris virtually stumbled upon a more profound understanding of the role of opposition. "*Nil desperandum de Republica* [Don't despair of the Republic] is a sound principle. Let the chair of office be filled by whomsoever it may, opposition will act as an outward conscience, and prevent the abuse of power."²⁶ Morris's observation is politically prescient: it brings parties into the checks and balances of the Constitution. It is psychologically acute as well, for the phrase "outward conscience" is large with implication. Parties will generate a morality of partisanship, keeping each other honest. Morris's thought was more important than anything he had said at the Constitutional Convention, and a worthy appendix to everything that had been said there. Not being of a systematic turn of mind, he never elaborated it; perhaps he never fully appreciated it. In the poisonous atmosphere of the next fourteen years, no one, including even himself, would act on it consistently.

In their meeting outside the Senate chamber, Morris had not asked Jefferson to maintain the integrity of the judicial branch, which was just as well, since it was one of the new president's goals to pare the judiciary back. From Jefferson's point of view, he was simply restoring the status quo. On the eve of his inauguration, in February 1801, the lame duck Congress had passed a Judiciary Bill adding seven district and sixteen circuit judges. The Republicans thought these last-minute appointments were pure Federalist patronage ("an hospital for decayed politicians," said John Randolph, a young Republican congressman from Virginia).[27] Morris himself admitted in a letter to Livingston that this was one motivation: "That the leaders of the federal party may use this opportunity to provide for friends and adherents is, I think, probable, and if they were my enemies I should not condemn them for it. . . . They are about to experience a heavy gale of adverse wind. Can they be blamed for casting many anchors to hold their ship through the storm?"[28] But Morris had backed the Judiciary Bill because it brought impartial justice "near to men's doors. . . . Depend on it that, in some parts of this Union, *justice* cannot readily be obtained in the State courts." Morris's grandfather had been removed from his judgeship by a local oligarch, and Morris believed an expanded federal judiciary would diminish the power of contemporary local bullies.

When the new Republican majorities in Congress proposed a bill to disband the new federal courts, Morris became alarmed. The Constitution (Article III Section 1) stated that "Judges, both of the supreme and inferior courts, shall hold their offices during good Behavior. . . ." This provision had been adopted to give judges independence; wasn't abolishing their jobs a way of controlling them? Morris, speaking in the Senate, characterized the Republican proposal thus: "[Y]ou shall not take the man from the office, but you may take the office from the man; you shall not throw him overboard, but you may sink his boat under him; you shall not put him to death, but you may take away his life."[29] If the judiciary had no independence, then the legislature was unchecked, and the French Revolution had shown where that could lead (perhaps the politics of Europe offered a useful parallel after all). "[S]ee . . . what has happened in your own times," he told the Senate. By 1790, "the only question" in France "was, who will become the despot."[30]

Morris's rhetoric did not prevent him from going to tea at the White House, where he found Jefferson "very civil, but with evident marks" of discomfort—not surprisingly, since Morris had just accused his party of wishing to become despots. The wife of Secretary of State James Madison, the plump and beautiful Dolley, struck him as having "good dispositions"—she was friendly, perhaps flirtatious—which he attributed to "the shriveled condition" of her husband.[31] When a new Judiciary Bill repealing the old one passed in March 1802, Morris wrote Livingston that "[w]e have here as yet nothing of importance except destroying the Constitution."[32] Morris took his defeat lightly, because that was his temper, but the seeds of disaffection had been planted.

The New York legislature failed to reelect Morris to a full term at the end of 1802, so that he struck his last blow for Federalism as a lame duck. Talleyrand helped give him his opportunity. The Frenchman was now working for Napoleon Bonaparte, the First Consul, and their foreign policy was simple: peace in Europe, expansion in North America. The object of France's desire was Louisiana, the inner watershed of the continent that France had given to Spain in the middle of the eighteenth century. In 1800, Bonaparte and Talleyrand forced Spain to sign a secret treaty giving it back. Spain was a feeble, and therefore a good neighbor to the United States, but the prospect of Napoleonic France occupying the mouth and the west bank of the Mississippi was something else entirely. In preparation for the French takeover, the Spanish officials still running the colony from New Orleans denied Americans the right to navigate the river. Hoping to pick up western votes, congressional Federalists urged Jefferson to respond aggressively. "No nation," Morris told the Senate, "has a right to give another a dangerous neighbor without her consent."[33] He made a prediction. "There must be [war] either with France or England." If the United States fought France (plus Louisiana), the western states would be ruined; if it fought England, the eastern states would be. "[L]et the war be with whichsoever of those nations it may, one half of the United States must be peculiarly injured."[34]

He also made what was, along with his encouragement of the New-burgh near-mutiny, the worst argument of his public life. France would encourage slave revolts from Louisiana, "stimulat[ing] with a prospect of freedom the miserable men who now toil without hope." But slaves must believe "that it is impossible for them to become free. Men in their unhappy condition must be impelled by fear and discour-aged by despair. Yes. The impulsion of fear must be strengthened by the hand of despair."[35] How had the man who had railed against the three-fifths rule and the slave trade, and their corrupting effect on re-publican institutions, come to this point? Morris was ever prey to the speaker's vice of following the flow of his own words. The repetition of his argument, after the "Yes," shows him in the act (the speech was taken down by shorthand). But Morris's willingness to offer the argu-ment in the first place sprang from a related vice of his—saying un-pleasant truths in the most offensive way possible. He had not wanted to give slaveholders an inflated stake in the government, but they had won it. Very well—he would make them appeals suited to their na-tures. Whatever his reasons, it was a wicked argument, and if he had come to the point of saying such things, it was just as well that he was leaving public life.

This period marked the sour end of his relations with Lafayette. The hero's wife wrote him a letter stating that she would repay the 100,000 livres Morris had loaned her in 1793 with 53,000 livres, citing a new French law that established conversion rates for debts con-tracted during the revolutionary inflation. She was hiding behind the law, and Lafayette was hiding behind her. Morris let the matter drop. "I only wish them a clear conscience," he wrote. "Unhappily, that they will not have, and will ever bear me, in consequence, a sincere hated. The ungrateful man never thinks of his benefactor without a pang, and how should one not detest the object that causes such suffering and lowers one in one's own eyes?"[36]

His Senate years saw his fiftieth birthday approach and pass, and he occasionally felt his age. He called his dancing at one dinner party hobbling, and wrote that only the smallness of the party excused "the ridiculousness of this attempt."[37] But he found yet another lady friend, Sarah Wentworth Morton, a Boston poetess whom he met when he was visiting Philadelphia (the City of Brotherly love had always been kind to him). Her verses had earned her the titles the "American Sappho" and the "American Mrs. Montagu." Lady Mary Wortley Montagu was not on the level of Sappho, and Mrs. Morton was not on the level of either. But the new country was proud of her efforts. Gilbert Stuart painted three portraits of her, including one teasing composition in which a bust of George Washington (one of her subjects) looks on solemnly while the lady slips a bracelet on her lovely wrist.[38]

Mrs. Morton also had her share of troubles, for her husband, Perez Morton, a successful lawyer and orator, had had an affair, seven years after their marriage, with her younger sister, Frances, who then killed herself after bearing his child. This lurid episode was discussed in the Boston newspapers, and in a novel, *The Power of Sympathy*, written by William Brown, one of the Mortons' neighbors. "Oh, why did Willy do such a thing?" Sarah's mother asked Brown's mother. "The names are fictitious," Mrs. Brown replied.[39] The considerate Mr. Brown had changed "Morton" to "Martin."

An intelligent woman with an unsatisfactory husband was, as ever, an attractive combination. Morris made his approaches; Mrs. Morton claimed she was "indisposed." Morris knew that was *"en règle"* (part of the game).[40] The game progressed, and Morris dined with both Mortons in Boston in the summer of 1803. "[M]onsieur," he wrote, "was cordial, all things considered."[41]

The problem of Louisiana was solved by Robert Livingston, whom Jefferson had made minister to France. Napoleon abruptly decided that Europe offered a better field for his energies, and Talleyrand told the startled American that the heart of the continent was for sale. After some dickering, the deal was done for $15 million. Most Federalists, who had wanted to use Louisiana as a stick with which to beat

Jefferson, were unhappy when he bought it. But Morris was proud of his friend's success, and he did not quibble at the cost. "A few millions more or less . . . really seems unworthy of notice."[42]

No politician ever retired with more satisfaction or fewer regrets than Morris. He thought the Constitution was tottering, or already fallen, but he refused to be alarmed. "I have made up my mind to float along as gently as I may."[43] His equanimity rested, in part, on his limitations. He lacked the lifelong follow-through of a Washington; if his advice went unheeded, his pride was touched, and he shrugged off the problem along with the affront. If the founding of the state had rested on him, or men like him, it would not have happened. But devotion to public life is not an unmixed blessing. Many politicians are persistent troublemakers, especially if their pride is wedded to their ambition.

A week after the Fourth of July, 1804, one of Morris's nephews came to Morrisania to tell him that Alexander Hamilton had been killed that morning in a duel, by the vice president of the United States. Aaron Burr had not been unaware of the harsh things Hamilton had said of him during the endgame of the election of 1800; Hamilton had repeated them all again that spring when Burr, hoping to provide for himself after his vice-presidential term ended, ran for governor of New York, and went down to defeat. At last, Burr had had enough. The gentlemen began a correspondence, and met for an interview at Weehawken, across the Hudson from Manhattan.

The duel was not simply a personal feud, however. Burr and his Federalist admirers had been in contact throughout Jefferson's first term. But the Federalists were by now even more desperate than they had been after the election of 1800. Peace and prosperity, capped by the coup of the Louisiana Purchase, guaranteed Jefferson's reelection. A band of Federalist die-hards in New England plotted a secession of the North, and thought they had Burr's support. Hamilton, hearing of their schemes, was appalled.

The next day, July 12, Morris went down to the city and learned that Hamilton was still alive, in a house on Greenwich Street, where he had been taken after being shot (Burr was unharmed). "Go there," Morris wrote in his diary, in clipped rhythms recalling his days in

France. "When I arrive he is speechless. The scene is too powerful for me, so that I am obliged to walk in the garden to take breath. After having composed myself, I return and sit by his side till he expires." When the doctors opened the body, they found that Burr's bullet had snapped a rib, pierced the liver, and lodged in the spine. "A most melancholy scene—his wife almost frantic with grief, his children in tears, every person present deeply afflicted, the whole city agitated, every countenance dejected. . . . I am wholly unmanned by this day's spectacle."

Morris was asked to give the eulogy, and the next day he talked it over with one of Hamilton's legal colleagues. They ran over the difficult points of Hamilton's life: his illegitimate birth; his character flaws ("indiscreet, vain, and opinionated"—Morris might have recognized them); his unpopular opinions. There was the irony of Hamilton's death: "He was in principle opposed to dueling, but he had fallen in a duel. I cannot thoroughly excuse him without criminating Colonel Burr, which would be wrong. . . ." Wrong for two reasons: because in dueling, Burr had only been following the gentleman's code; and because Morris did not want to encourage the incensed mourners to riot. On top of everything else, there was no time to memorize anything lengthy. "The corpse is already putrid, and the funeral procession must take place to-morrow morning."

The next morning, the funeral procession began two hours late. It ended at Trinity Church, where Morris spoke in the open air, inaudible to nine tenths of the crowd. "Get through the difficulties tolerably well; am of necessity short. . . . I find that what I have said does not answer the general expectation. This I knew would be the case; it must ever happen to him whose duty it is to allay the sentiment which he is expected to arouse. How easy would it have been to make them, for a moment, absolutely mad!"[44]

The duel blasted both Burr's future and the secession plot. But the underlying political wounds were not cauterized. It would be easy to make Americans, for years, absolutely mad.

CHAPTER THIRTEEN

Work and Love

*I*N HIS RETIREMENT from public life, Morris wrote Mme
de Staël, urging her to visit America. "As soon as you arrive,
you will come to Morrisania, partake what our dairy af-
fords, and refresh yourself. [You may] gather peaches, take walks,
make verses, romances; in a word . . . do whatever you please. When
my hermitage shall have lost its attractions, you shall establish yourself
in the city, where, by the aid of a good cook, you will contrive to live
very well. Here, as elsewhere, people amuse themselves with discussions, *bon mots,* slandering their neighbors and the like. Life is everywhere much the same in the long run."[1] So he tempted her with the
pastoral ideal of urban sophisticates, old as Horace and Virgil: the
country retreat, never sundered from the place in town.

Morris spent much of the first decade of the new century, however,
traveling through true country—the wilderness of western and northern New York. He gratified his love of boating, and inspected his land
investments along the Genesee and St. Lawrence rivers. Where the
Oswegatchie River, a tributary of the St. Lawrence, flows over a rock
formation called the Natural Dam, he built himself a summer house,
with two-foot-thick stone walls, that still stands. There he sampled "a
most delicious syrup made from the maple tree," and the "finest fishing
for trout that I ever yet saw."[2] But he was also exploring a matter of
public business and national benefit—the possibility of a western canal.

Throughout Morris's youth, most New Yorkers lived on Long Island, and in New York City and the Hudson Valley; a few brave souls
had ventured down the Mohawk River. The great barrier to westward

movement was the Iroquois Confederacy, six well-organized and aggressive native tribes that had historically good relations with the crown. The Revolutionary War removed this difficulty, since most of the Iroquois sided with the British, whose defeat left them subdued or exiled. While Morris was in France, some developers had begun to open up the new landscape. William Cooper, a self-made land speculator from New Jersey, founded Cooperstown in central New York, and, thanks to its success, served in Congress, sent his sons to Yale and Princeton, and hosted Talleyrand at his rural estate. But travel to western New York was onerous, as it was to every place in the United States beyond the Alleghanies. Enough settlers had made it over the mountains to westernmost Virginia and North Carolina that two new states, Kentucky and Tennessee, had been created for them. But their easiest contact with the outside world was not back through their home states, but down the Mississippi, and through New Orleans.

Tempted by the possible gains and undaunted by the actual difficulties, Americans dreamed of canals. One visitor to Mount Vernon, between the war and the writing of the Constitution, recalled that canals and interior navigation were George Washington's "constant and favorite theme. . . . Hearing little else for two days from the persuasive tongue of this great man, I confess completely infected me with the canal mania."[3] Not all of Washington's acquaintance were infected. James Madison explained the great man's mania by saying that "a mind like his, capable of great views . . . cannot bear a vacancy."[4] In New York, Cadwallader Colden, a colonial official who was a contemporary of Morris's father and grandfather, had beaten Washington to the idea by fifty years. As early as 1724, he pointed out that there were two possible routes across New York into the interior: one taking the Mohawk west to Oneida Lake, then curving northwest by the Oswego River to Lake Ontario; another continuing directly west to Lake Erie. The most natural path to the coast from western New York was down the St. Lawrence River. But in 1724, when Colden wrote, the St. Lawrence was controlled by France, the enemy, and therefore to be avoided. After the American Revolution, when the St. Lawrence was controlled by Britain, the former enemy, New Yorkers would seek to avoid it for the same reason.

Morris had the canal mania during the Revolutionary War. When the Council of Safety sent him, in 1777, from Kingston to Fort Edward to consult with General Philip Schuyler, he had held forth on the subject. In the words of one of the officers who was present, "Mr. Morris, whose temperament admitted of no alliance with despondency . . . frequently amused us by descanting with great energy on what he termed the 'rising glories of the Western World.' One evening in particular . . . he announced, in language to which I cannot do justice, that at no very distant day the waters of the great western inland seas [i.e., the Great Lakes] would, by the aid of man, break through their barriers and mingle with those of the Hudson."[5] This memory was recorded half a century after the fact, when public figures and their friends were vying for the parentage of a good idea, but the story is not inherently unlikely—"descanting with great energy" certainly sounds like Morris, and the hope was by no means unique to him.

During his European sojourn, Morris had seen canals at work. The low country of Flanders, through which he passed on visits to Antwerp and Amsterdam, was one elaborate web of artificially improved rivers, and the canal bisecting Scotland particularly impressed him. Soon after he returned home, he visited western New York. In July 1800, after the Senate adjourned, he went up the Hudson, and through Lake George and Lake Champlain, to Montreal (the old invasion route, now traveled in peace); then up the St. Lawrence to Lake Ontario, and so westward, to the mouth of the Genesee River, and finally to Niagara Falls and Lake Erie. There he stopped, and returned the way he had come. In his descriptions of what he had seen, he summoned all the language of the romantic sublime.

"There is a brilliance in our atmosphere," he wrote one of his business friends in Hamburg,

> which you can have no idea of, except by going to Italy, or else viewing one of Claude Lorraine's best landscapes, and persuading yourself, that the light there exhibited is a just, though faint copy of

nature. . . . Still less can I pretend to convey to you the sentiment excited by a view of [Lake Ontario]. It is to all purposes of human vision an ocean; the same majestic motion too in its billows. . . . After
one day's repose at Niagara, we went to view the Falls. To form a
faint idea of the cataract, imagine that you saw the Firth of Forth
rush wrathfully down a steep descent, leap foaming over a perpen-
dicular rock one hundred and seventy-five feet high, then flow away
in the semblance of milk, from a vast basin of emerald.

Most enthusiastically of all, he looked at the future—a future pop-
ulated by men. He described his passage, above the Falls up the Niagara River, to Lake Erie.

[I]n turning a point . . . I saw riding at anchor nine vessels, the least
of them above a hundred tons. Can you bring your imagination to
realize the scene? Does it not seem like magic? Yet this magic is but
the early effort of victorious industry. Hundreds of large ships will,
in no distant period, bound on the billows of these inland seas. At
this point commences a navigation of more than a thousand miles
[through the chain of the Great Lakes, to Lake Superior]. Shall I
lead your astonishment up to the verge of incredulity? I will. Know
then, that one tenth of the expense borne by Britain in the last campaign [in Europe] would enable ships to sail from London through
Hudson's river into Lake Erie. As yet, my friend, we only crawl
along the outer edge of our country. The interior excels the part we
inhabit in soil, in climate, in everything. The proudest empire in
Europe is but a bauble, compared to what America *will* be, *must* be,
in the course of two centuries; perhaps of one![6]

Morris was ever contemptuous of the politics of frontiersmen, but
here he foresaw the frontier transformed into civilization. His rhetoric
in this letter is the sublime of progress.

Morris enjoyed traveling through upstate New York for one other
reason: the pleasure of physical activity. In a trip in the fall of 1803, his
voyage down the Oswego River was "dangerous and exciting. . . . [T]he

sea ran so high as to greatly alarm my ship's company." One passenger, he noted happily, "was frightened even to roaring, and, when he got on shore, declared he would rather return home on foot than go again on board of the boat with me."[7] When the party reached Lake Ontario, a storm was blowing, the pilot was laid low by fever, and Morris had to do what the timid captain had begged him to do in the nor'wester off Long Island, and set the course himself. "[W]ith no other resource than my recollection of a former voyage, and, having fixed what I believe to be the spot, we luckily enter the harbor we were making for through a very high surf and by a rocky point, which we narrowly escape."[8] In 1887, when the American Statesman, a series of biographies published by Houghton Mifflin, made the bizarre assignment of Gouverneur Morris to the young Theodore Roosevelt, the only commonality (besides old New York roots) between the caustic wit and the eager, earnest politician was their shared delight in exercise and the outdoors. Morris the cripple and Roosevelt the asthmatic each had a heavy investment in their own strength and recklessness.

Morris was not the only New Yorker considering improvements to navigation. As he traveled through upstate, his friend Robert Livingston, back on the Hudson, was pushing an invention that, in the long run, would be even more significant than a western canal. For Livingston was the backer of Robert Fulton, a painter turned inventor whom Livingston had met in Europe, and in August 1807 they launched a boat powered by a Watt steam engine. The Steam-boat, as New Yorkers proudly and simply called it—it was the only one in the world—plied the Hudson from New York to Albany. In November, Morris dined with a Mr. Walton, of Ballston, a town north of Schenectady, who told him "that, by means of the steam-boat, he can leave his own house on Monday morning and dine with me on Tuesday, do some business in New York on Wednesday morning, and be again at home of Thursday evening," for a four-day round trip, including work and pleasure.[9] At a time when a stage coach from New York to Albany took three days, and a sailboat anywhere from three days to two weeks, depending on the winds, this was revolutionary.

The Lewis and Clark Expedition, which left St. Louis in 1804 and returned two years later after exploring the Missouri and Columbia rivers, was the great adventure of the federal government during the Jefferson administration. It was not a journey of discovery, since French trappers had been traveling most of Lewis and Clark's route for a century and a half (the husband of Sacajawea, their Shoshone guide, was named Toussaint Charbonneau). But their journey was bold, colorful, and patriotic all at once, and stirred the national imagination. The real steps toward national growth, however, were being taken by old aristocrats in upstate New York, exploiting the tamer landscape of their home state. Lewis and Clark traversed the wilderness, much of which remains wilderness today. If a canal to Lake Erie could be dug, however, the heart of the continent would blossom.

Jefferson himself was mindful of the economic opportunities closer to home. In December 1806, his annual message to Congress touched on roads and canals. Republican thrift had built up a surplus in the Treasury, and Jefferson proposed spending it on internal improvements, if a constitutional amendment allowing such appropriations should be passed. (He did not think the "general welfare" clause of the Preamble gave sufficient sanction.) "By these operations," Jefferson wrote, "new channels of communication will be opened between the states . . . and their union [will] be cemented by new and indissoluble ties."[10] In 1808, his Treasury secretary, Albert Gallatin ("an intelligent fellow," Morris would conclude when he met him,[11] not knowing, or forgetting, that Gallatin had once accused him of being a trickster), sent a report to Congress proposing a $20 million program—$280 million today—of road and canal building, cutting across capes and bypassing waterfalls from Maine to Georgia, and from the coast to the Mississippi. New Yorkers hoped that some of this federal largesse might help build their canal.

*I*N THE MIDST of these gathering projects, Morris gathered one of his own. He hired a housekeeper who would become much more. The servants at Morrisania were a motley lot: "wild Irish, some French who have fled Napoleon's conscription—a few cutthroat English, a portion of Americans who disdain subordination—also a small number of

Germans."[12] Housekeepers "of low birth and education" could not maintain order among them; only a "reduced gentlewoman"—that is, a lady of Morris's class who was in need of work—could command their respect.[13] In October 1808, he drove down to New York to engage the services of such a gentlewoman, Miss Anne Cary Randolph.

Mr. Morris and Miss Randolph had met twice before, in the 1780s, when he had been in Virginia managing Robert Morris's tobacco contract. Nancy Randolph, as she was called, was the daughter of Colonel Thomas Mann Randolph, master of Tuckahoe, a plantation on the James River west of Richmond that Morris visited. In his letters from Tuckahoe, Morris described the colonel—"a gentleman possessing one of the best fortunes in this country"—and his wife—"an amiable woman . . . not in much good health"[14]—but made no mention of their daughter Nancy—not surprisingly, since she was only a girl (thirteen years old in 1788, the time of his second visit). When he met her again in New York, she was living in a boardinghouse, run by an "old Mrs. Pollock,"[15] on Greenwich Street. Her twenty years' descent, from Tuckahoe to urban indigence, had been as rough as it was steep, and the first stage of it had been a matter of public notoriety.

The Randolphs were a first family of Virginia, as eminent as they were numerous. If they produced no suns like Washington or Jefferson, they supplied many a bright star. Peyton Randolph was the last Speaker of the colonial House of Burgesses, and a delegate to the First Continental Congress. "Under temptations and difficulties," Jefferson once wrote, "I would ask myself what would . . . Peyton Randolph do in this situation?"[16] Edmund Randolph was a delegate to the Constitutional Convention, and Jefferson's successor as secretary of state. Jefferson's mother was a Randolph, as was one of his sons-in-law: two somewhat unusual marriages, since Randolphs preferred to marry their own Randolph cousins, whenever they could. In 1789, such a marriage occurred when Nancy's older sister Judith married her first cousin Richard Randolph. The newlyweds settled at a plantation on the Appomattox River named Bizarre (many Virginia plantations had poetic, even hifalutin, names: one near Bizarre was called Horsdumonde). Nancy soon came to live with them.

Richard Randolph had two younger brothers—Theodorick and John. Of the three, John was the most talented, soon to show a vein of eloquence and invective as bitter as it was brilliant. He was also the oddest—his voice never broke, and he never shaved. "[F]rom my earliest recollection," he once said, "I have remarked in myself . . . a delicacy or effeminacy of complexion that but for the spice of the devil in my temper would have consigned me to the distaff or the needle."[17] In a portrait by Gilbert Stuart, he looks like a strange, flaxen-haired boy. All three brothers were generous, passionate, and undisciplined—a common constellation of traits among Virginia aristocrats. They were also all smitten with Nancy. Nancy Randolph first sat for a painter years later, and the work he produced is not very good, but it does show an impish smile, bright eyes, and an inviting bosom, which must have been even more attractive in her late teens. Theodorick and John each asked her to marry him; Richard, who was in no position to do so, asked her never to marry anyone. She became engaged to Theodorick, whose good luck, however, did not hold, for he died of tuberculosis in February 1792.

The internal affairs of the Randolph family came to general notice that fall. Richard, Judith, Nancy, and John were visiting relatives in September, when Nancy was taken ill; her hosts heard screams in the middle of the night. Rumor soon supplied the explanation: Nancy had been pregnant, and had given birth; slaves had found a dead white baby on a pile of shingles; the father was Richard, who had killed the infant by exposing it. "To refute the calumnies," Richard published an open letter in the *Virginia Gazette and Advertizer* in April 1793, announcing that he would appear at the next session of the county court, where his accusers, he demanded, should "stand forth and exert themselves" to convict him of a crime.[18] He seems to have thought he could bluff the gossips into silence. Instead, when he appeared at court he was arrested.

Richard Randolph had to hire lawyers, and the lawyers he hired were the greatest defense team that has ever appeared in an American court: Patrick Henry and John Marshall. They conceded nothing, not even that a child had been born, or that Nancy had been pregnant. The seasoned Henry examined the witnesses. He demolished one woman who testified that she had seen Nancy, naked and round-bellied, through a crack in her door. "Madam, which eye did you peep with?" Henry asked, then turned to the audience and declared, "Great God, deliver us from eavesdroppers!"[19] The young Marshall, a Richmond lawyer, argued the case to the jury, carefully examining every damning detail and showing that it had an innocent explanation (Richard and Nancy were publicly affectionate; but if they had had a guilty connection, would they not have feigned indifference?). Judith testified to the innocence of her husband and sister. The slaves who had found the dead child were forbidden, by Virginia law, to testify against white men in a felony matter. The jury barely deliberated, acquitting Richard Randolph of all charges.

Nancy Randolph, therefore, was also innocent of incest and murder. But her life had nevertheless been blighted at the age of eighteen. Henry and Marshall, in contesting the assertion that any child had been born, also introduced testimony implying that, if one had, the father was Theodorick. Yet even if Nancy had been impregnated by her dying fiancé, rather than by her brother-in-law, she was hardly marriageable. If no man would have her, she would have to live the remainder of her life as a family dependant.

Further clouds gathered round Bizarre. Richard died in 1796, of a sudden fever, leaving Judith and two young sons, the elder of them a deaf-mute. The responsibility of running the plantation fell to John— no light thing, since tobacco prices were in a long, steady decline. Nancy's widowed sister and her brother-in-law could not have been pleasant company, for Nancy or for each other. Judith admitted that hers was a "gloomy disposition."[20] For a time, John could direct his spice of the devil to politics. Elected to the House of Representatives in 1798 when he was only twenty-five, he became, after his cousin Jefferson reached the White House, chairman of the Ways and Means Committee. Representative Randolph was an extreme, and extremely quotable, Republican: the issue of the Hamilton-Burr duel pleased him—"It reminded me of a sinking fox pressed by a vigorous old hound"—and he judged Morris's eulogy, which he read in the newspa-

pers, "wretched."[21] In 1805, however, he bungled an important political task, impeaching but failing to win the conviction of Justice
Samuel Chase, the most aggressive Federalist on the Supreme Court.

In the straitened circumstances of Bizarre, Nancy Randolph was a
small but real burden to her sister and her brother-in-law. She was an
emotional burden as well, for she was the only one of the Randolphs at
Bizarre who seemed determined to live, relishing her rare opportunities to visit, and craving news from the "Beau Monde."[22] In the spring
of 1805, smarting from political failure, John asked Nancy to leave.

Over the next three and a half years, she drifted north. How she
managed to live is unclear, though it is clear that she lived badly. In a
letter to John from Newport, Rhode Island, she asked for $50 (he did
not send it). How Morris learned of her situation is also unclear. In
August 1808, in upstate New York, he met a "Mr. Bell from Virginia,"
with whom he conversed "pleasantly"; perhaps he recounted something.[23] After meeting Miss Randolph at old Mrs. Pollock's, Morris
went back upstate, where he spent the winter. Was he already hoping
for more than a housekeeper? Unfortunately his diary at this period
tells more about his travels than his personal relationships. Morris was
observant, and an intelligent, unhappy woman would have attracted
his notice. He was available, having left Mrs. Morton to her poetry
and her husband years before. While he was in Schenectady, he had a
sobering experience, an illness so alarming that he made a will. The
ailment passed, though when he was in Albany, he experienced a sym-
bolic death, the temperature falling so low that the ink froze in his pen.
The first event, if not the second, must have reminded him of the passing years. It was twenty years since he had met Adèle de Flahaut,
twelve since she had passed out of his life.

He returned to Morrisania in February of the new year, and wrote
Nancy a series of letters. He wished her to begin her new employment.
"Pride may exclaim 'Miss Randolph cannot descend to the rank of a
servant under whatever name, or however elevated and distinguished.'
Pride is such a wrangling disputant that I will not argue with him."[24]
He also set the stage of their personal relationship. "I once heard, but
have no distinct recollection, of events which brought distress into

your family. Dwell not on them now. If ever we happen to be alone you shall tell your tale of sorrow when the tear from your cheek may fall in my bosom."[25] This was an offer of friendship. But did he expect Miss Randolph to fall into his bosom along with her tears? He was fifty-seven years old and rich; she was thirty-four years old and poor. Did he intend her for a kept woman? "[A]las! Time in taking away the ardor has not wholly quelled the rashness of youth. I can only answer that I will love you as little as I can."[26] He added that no illicit connection with his housekeepers had ever existed, or been suspected—". . . certainly I have never approached . . . them with anything like desire."[27] Morris was laying out the terms of their intercourse: he was taken with Miss Randolph, and intended to pursue her, but he promised to pursue her honorably.

He also gave her, what he gave so well, words of encouragement. He spoke of virtue, "which I do not use in the tea-table sense that calls a woman virtuous though she have the malice of a dozen devils . . . but to express a pure heart, a chastened spirit, fortitude, benevolence, charity." This was indirect praise, singling out qualities he saw in her, whatever Virginia gossips had said sixteen years ago. He concluded with his life-long credo: "The incidents of pleasure and pain are scattered more equally than is generally imagined. The cards are dealt with fairness. What remains is patiently to play the game, and then to sleep."[28]

Morris was attracted to Nancy Randolph, as he had been to other women, by the combination of spunk and suffering, which allowed him to be both a fellow struggler and a benefactor. His previous serious lovers had suffered from bad marriages, for which he had offered himself as recompense. Nancy Randolph had, in some ways, suffered more than they had; if he offered himself to her now, he would find no marriage barring a possible union. In April 1809, he wrote in his diary that he brought "Miss Randolph of Virginia" home to Morrisania.[29]

Morris made one effort to check if there were any other bar to their happiness. Nancy had surely told him her version of the events of September 1792, and he surely believed it. But early in December 1809 he wrote Richard Randolph's surviving lawyer. Patrick Henry had gone before the highest Judge; John Marshall was now Chief Justice of the

Supreme Court. Morris presented his situation as a party matter: " . . . connected [as I am] with so many worthy men as fill the Federal ranks," Republicans would naturally seek to "affix a stigma" on Morris, or "on any one of us, however inconsiderable he may be personally considered. Now it is from consideration for friends I esteem . . . that I [write]."[30] Why so many considerations? Was it verbal wordplay, or nervousness as he neared his goal? What "reputation," Morris asked, had Miss Randolph left in Virginia? The Chief Justice answered judiciously. Virginians had disagreed about the case, but the circumstances were "ambiguous," and Judith Randolph, "who was most injured by the fact if true," had let Nancy live under her roof for twelve years.[31]

Morris now made haste. On Christmas Day, he entertained a party of friends and in-laws at Morrisania. One of them was Isaac Wilkins, his old Tory brother-in-law who had returned from his exile in Nova Scotia to be an Episcopal clergyman. "Many of the family whom I expected," the host wrote in his diary that night, "are detained by the weather. I marry this day Anne Cary Randolph—no small surprize to my guests."[32]

The new couple had their portraits painted, in the following year, by a traveling English artist, James Sharples. Sharples's portrait of Mrs. Morris made her look like the cat that ate the canary. Like all previous portraitists, Sharples failed to capture her mercurial husband. What he did get, in the subject's penetrating gaze, was his intelligence and sarcasm. Mr. Morris seems to know what the viewer is thinking, and he does not care one whit.

The marriage was an unpleasant surprise to Morris's nephews and nieces, who had expected one day to divide the estate of the aging bachelor. One of them, Mrs. Gertrude Meredith of Philadelphia, was bold enough to express her chagrin in a letter to him. Morris's reply was sweetly lethal. "[I]f the world were to live with my wife, I should certainly have consulted its taste; but as that happens not to be the case, I thought I might, without offending others, endeavor to suit myself. . . ."[33] Morris had consulted the Supreme Court, but no lesser tribunal.

CHAPTER FOURTEEN

War Comes Again

*G*OUVERNEUR MORRIS'S political quiescence during this long period of canal-planning and wife-taking sprang from a cheery pessimism. He thought the affairs of the nation were in the hands of incompetent men with bad principles, and this made him easy of mind and light of heart. The political bitterness that brought death to Alexander Hamilton had festered for years. Vice President Burr was indicted for murder in New York and New Jersey, though he was not prosecuted, since no jury of gentlemen would convict a duelist. In 1807, Burr was tried for treason, on account of his plottings in the Louisiana Territory, which were so deep and indefinite that historians still have not explained them; he was acquitted. Napoleon's turn from the New World to the Old plunged Europe into war, and finally economic war. Each belligerent great power—France by the Berlin Decrees, Britain by the Orders in Council—sought to prevent neutrals from trading with its enemy. America's response was to make it a crime for Americans to trade with anyone, driving the commercial states of the Northeast to despair.

Through all these crises the Republican Party maintained itself in office, led by its great Virginians, whom Morris disdained without exception. He thought Jefferson an amiable and otherworldly theorist; his opinion of the "shriveled" James Madison, who succeeded Jefferson as president in the election of 1808, was lower, and would sink lower still. For James Monroe, who had replaced him as minister to France, and who now seemed to be the next Virginian in line for the White House, he felt nothing but contempt. When Jefferson favored

Monroe with an appointment, Morris, recalling Matthew 21:42, wrote that Jefferson had showed his Christian spirit, for he "has taken special care that a stone which the builders rejected should become the first of the corner."[1]

Morris believed that when the policies of Virginia Republicanism had been crowned by unignorable failure, then the people would reject them. "[N]ations, like individuals, are not to be reasoned out of vice, much less out of folly, but learn wisdom and virtue in the school of affliction. . . . [R]ascals are more likely to repent at the gallows and whippingpost, than at the gaming table and dramshop."[2] Until the instructive crisis came, he would keep his thoughts to himself, and a small circle of relatives and friends. "I consider it a vain task to preach to unbelievers."[3] He woke from these pleasant hopes of doom only when national politics became entangled with the progress of New York's canal.

New York's official canal-planning began in a spirit of bipartisan cooperation. In March 1810, the state legislature appointed a seven-man commission to report on the feasibility and cost of such a project. All factions in the state were represented, the leading Republican commissioner being the mayor of New York City, DeWitt Clinton. The forty-one-year-old Clinton had already been in politics for twenty-two years. His mentor was his uncle, George Clinton, who had been governor of the state for so long that he had earned the title "The Old Incumbent," and was now serving the second of two terms as vice president. Tall, intelligent, and imperious, DeWitt Clinton had lofty ambitions for his city and state, both economically and intellectually. He studied Indian languages and archeology, and helped found local learned and artistic societies. Morris was skeptical of these latter endeavors. When one of his dinner companions excused his late arrival by saying that he had been detained at a meeting to found a Philosophical Society, Morris asked where would they find the philosophers?[4] But the aging Federalist and the rising Republican saw eye-to-eye on the issue of economic development. The legislature named Morris chairman of the Canal Commission, in recognition of his eminence and his enthusiasm.

In the summer of 1810 the commissioners set out across the state to examine possible routes. Most of them traveled to Oswego by water, and they had a miserable time. DeWitt Clinton's journal echoes Morris's accounts of central Europe a decade earlier. Clinton complained of "drunken people in the adjacent room . . . crickets in the hearth . . . rats in the walls . . . dogs under the beds . . . the whizzing of mosquitoes about our heads, and the flying of bats about the room."[5] Morris, the more experienced traveler, went by carriage to Niagara Falls, taking his bride with him, in an early version of the classic honeymoon trip (a second carriage carried his French cook). The commissioners rendezvoused at Lewiston on the Niagara River. Morris's diary implied that there were disagreements among the commissioners—he worried whether the "most correct" opinions would prevail[6]—but they were soon composed, and never aired. The commissioners thought of themselves, and presented themselves to the public, as a phalanx of the state's elite, united in a common purpose.

On their way back east, the Morrises added religion to business by visiting a community of Shakers on the Massachusetts border. This sect had been founded in the eighteenth century by Mother Ann Lee, an Englishwoman who claimed to be the female Christ, and who taught communism, trance dancing, and celibacy. The couple heard a sermon that urged them "to abandon worldly pursuits, pleasures, and enjoyments, and, more especially, the conjugal pleasures. . . ." Morris found this last an "unnatural (and therefore impious) doctrine."[7]

The following year Morris presented the commission's findings to the legislature in a report that was polemical and poetic by turns. He argued for a route going all the way to Lake Erie, scorning the shortcut to Lake Ontario. "[A]rticles for exportation, once afloat on Lake Ontario, will, generally speaking, go to Montreal, unless our British neighbors are blind to their own interest, a charge which ought not lightly to be made against a commercial nation."[8] He pointed out the dangers of feeding a canal with water drawn from rivers, which are subject to floods and droughts. "[I]n the spring, the careful husbandman and miller will open every ditch and sluice to get rid of that water which, though at other times a kind friend and faithful servant, is then

a dangerous enemy and imperious master."[9] Happily, New York could
feed its canal from its numerous lakes. Morris introduced into the report a hobbyhorse of his: the notion that the entire canal could be an
inclined plane, slanting gently down from Lake Erie to the Hudson.
This was a daydream, ignoring the need for locks and aqueducts to
surmount local changes in elevation, and once professional surveyors
so concluded, Morris would drop the notion. He made another prediction, however, which must have struck observers as no less fantas-
tic, but which turned out to be reasonably correct. "There is no part of
the civilized world in which an object of such great magnitude can be
compassed at so small an expense."[10] Morris thought the canal could
be dug for $4 million (over $50 million today). Who would pay? A private company, Morris argued, could not raise the money. "Few of our
fellow citizens have more money than they want.... But the public can
readily, at a fair interest, command any reasonable sum." The borrower
should be the federal government, since more states than New York—
including states not yet created—would profit. "[T]hose who partici-
pate in the benefit, should contribute to the expense.... The wisdom,
as well as the justice of the national legislature, will, no doubt, lead to
the exercise on their part of prudent munificence."[11]

That DeWitt Clinton would sign such a document showed how far
his family, and the Republican Party, at least in New York, had come.
DeWitt's uncle George had opposed the Constitution; once it was ratified, he became the strictest of constructionists. In February 1811, as
vice president, he broke a tie vote in the Senate on rechartering the
Bank of the United States; the elder Clinton voted no, on the grounds
that chartering a bank was not a power expressly granted to the federal
government. Now his nephew was willing to use federal money to dig
a canal.

The next step was to present the plan to Congress, but Morris sand-
wiched into his duties as canal commissioner the writing of another
report, this time on the street plan of New York City. The small town
in which he had studied law and taken his first steps in politics had
grown to a population of 96,000, and pushed north to Houston Street,
two miles beyond Manhattan's wedge-shaped tip. New York City

might lack philosophers, but it had energy, and it was in the process of passing Philadelphia to become the nation's largest city. In 1807, the state had appointed Morris to a three-man commission to plan for the city's growth beyond Houston Street. Now their report, unsigned but marked with his prose rhythms, forsook the gnarled streets of the old Anglo-Dutch town for a vast grid of 12 parallel avenues running eight miles up the length of the island and 155 streets at right angles to them. Hills, streams, and marshes would be overlaid; old roads and paths that meandered across the grid would be abandoned. (The only significant survival was the slanting former Indian trail of Broadway, and the commissioners had wanted to abolish even that.)

The plan was an implicit critique of the baroque star patterns that the designers of Washington, D.C., had envisioned for the streets of the nation's capital. The city of capitalism would be based on economy, not Italianate affectation. "Straight-sided and right-angled houses," wrote Morris, "are the most cheap to build, and the most convenient to live in."[12] So the planners envisioned nearly two thousand rectangular city blocks, each divided into rectangular lots. Morris's two plans, for the canal and the streets, shared a determination to cut through natural obstacles for human use. They had another link: if the canal to Lake Erie were dug, then the produce of the heartland would flow to the world through New York City, making additional streets all the more necessary.

In December 1811, Morris and Clinton went to Washington at the behest of their state to lobby. They called at "the palace"—the White House—and met with congressmen (a "mess of democrats; a pleasant society enough, though not select").[13] The appeal they presented to President Madison, though probably written by Morris, reflected the self-assurance of both men. "We do not assign reasons in . . . support [of a canal], because they will not escape your penetration; neither do we solicit your patronage, because we rely on your patriotism."[14] Though Madison told the New Yorkers he was an "enthusiast" for canals, he was "embarrassed" by constitutional "scruples" about paying directly for New York's.[15] Gallatin, the Treasury secretary, found a compromise solution: a land grant of 4.5 million acres in northern Indiana, whose revenues would fund the project. Shortly after the New Year, Madison submitted an omnibus canal bill to Congress including Gallatin's suggestion, and praising the New York canal for its "honorable spirit of enterprise."[16]

Yet the bill died in committee. In a report to the state legislature in the spring of 1812, Morris and Clinton urged New York to go it alone, "making a manly and dignified appeal to her own power."[17] The rebuff still stung, however, and the lobbyists assigned a reason, "operating with baneful effect, though seldom and cautiously expressed. The population and resources of the state of New York furnish no pleasant reflections to men, whose minds are imbued with state jealousy."[18] At the Constitutional Convention the delegates in apportioning representation had put New York in fourth place for population, behind Virginia, Massachusetts, and Pennsylvania, and tied with Maryland. In the 1810 census, New York had become the largest state in the Union. In the First Congress, New York had had only six representatives; in the Twelfth, it had twenty-seven. A canal would add wealth to numbers.

Morris and Clinton refrained from saying what the political consequences of New York's growth might be. The Republican Party's success at the national level had been based on an alliance of Virginians and New Yorkers, attempted in every election since 1800 with a vice-presidential candidate from New York (Aaron Burr in 1800; George Clinton in 1804 and 1808). But Virginia had always been the senior partner. Now in 1812 DeWitt Clinton was considering the top spot for himself. At home, Clinton was happy to work with Federalists; nationally, he was willing to pick a fight with fellow Republicans. President Madison might overlook Clinton's ambitions in the name of the spirit of enterprise, but other politicians were more gimlet-eyed.

There was yet another reason for the failure of the canal bill, however—the approach of war. Britain and France both had adopted a bullying attitude to the remote neutral nation, but Britain, thanks to its navy, had more opportunities to bully. First Jefferson, then Madison had tried every means of resistance that was pacific, or purely defensive, and Morris had mocked them for it. They believed, he said, "in defence of territory by reduction of armies, and in vindication of rights by appointments of ambassadors";[19] they wanted to repel the British navy "with a mosquito fleet of gun-boats."[20] With the failure of every alternative, Madison felt driven toward war. A new generation of his party, meanwhile, was eagerly demanding it. In 1811, a crop of fire-eating southerners and westerners had entered Congress, among them John C. Calhoun of South Carolina, age twenty-nine, and Henry Clay of Kentucky, age thirty-four (Madison, by contrast, had turned sixty in 1811). These were the frontiersmen whom Morris had always feared, but who only now attained real power; Clay was elected Speaker during his first term in the House. A typical warhawk, Calhoun spoke fervently about "the laws of self-preservation" and "the shield of honor";[21] he also thought Canada could be overrun in only four weeks. The lone Republican voice opposing the firebrands belonged to the increasingly alienated John Randolph. "There is a fatality, Sir, attending plenitude of power. Soon or late, some mania seizes upon its possessors; they fall from the dizzy height, through the giddiness of their own heads."[22]

Morris saw the wheels of war in motion when he was in Washington lobbying. One day he stayed in his room, "los[ing] thereby the opportunity of hearing Mr. Randolph make a much admired speech"—one of his desperate anti-war philippics.[23] A week into the new year, "a thumping majority" passed a bill to raise a 25,000-man army.[24] In this state of things there was no time for canals.

In the spring of 1812 Vice President George Clinton died at the age of seventy-two. Once again, Morris was asked to deliver a eulogy. In May, DeWitt Clinton visited him at Morrisania, to talk about his late uncle, and current politics. Morris's advice to him was momentous, coming from the author of the Constitution. "[I]n the degenerate state to which democracy never fails to reduce a nation, it is almost impossible for a good man to govern, even could he get into power, or for a bad man to govern well." Morris's solution was to call for a Convention of northern states to "consider the state of the nation," and propose repeal of the three-fifths rule. "[T]he southern states must then either submit to what is just or break up the Union." DeWitt Clinton, he believed, "acknowledge[d] the force of these observations," though he could hardly proclaim them as a political platform.[25] Two weeks later, Morris eulogized the Late Incumbent; always his severest critic, he felt his speech was badly delivered and "better received than such speaking deserved."[26]

Morris's politics from mid-1812 on defined a contradiction. The canal he had been working for would be an agent of consolidation, uniting vast tracts of the country economically, just as the Constitution, which he had written twenty-five years earlier, had united it politically. Yet now the economic nationalist was proposing constitutional changes in the form of demands, and welcoming disunion if the demands were rejected. As late as 1811, he had been content with the serene cynicism of the past decade. "As in war so in politics, much must be left to chance; or, in other words, to combinations of which we are ignorant."[27] In private life, the cynic traveled, made money, and enjoyed himself. "I . . . enjoy from my window the exhilarating view of approaching spring," he wrote early in 1812 after turning sixty. "Oh, my friend, had we also a renewed spring of life. . . ."[28] What changed his mind only months later?

All his life Morris believed that men acted only under the threat of disaster. If times were peaceful, it was useless to reason with them. But when disaster struck, then men must act. The impending disaster now was war with Britain, compounded by loss of opportunity. Morris had urged Lafayette to go to war two decades earlier, but France was a great nation. The United States, with no army, scarcely any navy, and no national bank, was preparing to take on the greatest power on earth. In doing so, it would ignore Morris's canal. Faced with such folly, Morris was ready to act again. In June 1812, Congress declared war on Great Britain. (Ironically, London had just repealed its obnoxious Orders in Council, but word of the deed reached Washington too late for second thoughts.) "I believe, sir," wrote Morris in a letter at the end of the month, "that men of honor and worth must prepare for scenes more serious than electioneering."[29]

All the talk of conquering Canada was quickly shown up as empty rant. In Detroit, an American army surrendered ignominiously to a smaller British force. On the Niagara River, another American army, commanded by Stephen Van Rensselaer, the lord of the manor of Rensselaerwyck and a member of the Canal Commission, failed in an attack on Queenston on the Canadian side when the New York militia would not leave the state. The only ally the United States had in its warmaking was distant France, but on October 19 Emperor Napoleon evacuated Moscow, to begin his long, disastrous retreat. Morris, studying his maps, had predicted that Napoleon would evacuate on October 20; "the varlet was off a day sooner than I supposed."[30] For once, his low opinion of Bonaparte proved to be correct.

In the election of 1812 Morris helped throw Federalist support to DeWitt Clinton, who tried to unseat Madison by being all things to all men, telling Federalists that he opposed the war and Republicans that he would prosecute it more vigorously. He carried the usual Federalist bastions (New England, Maryland, Delaware) as well as New York, but Pennsylvania held firm for Madison, and gave him his margin of victory. Morris had foreseen that, too: "Pennsylvania . . . may be led to cover with her broad shield the slave-holding states: which, so protected, may for a dozen or fifteen years exercise the privilege of strangling commerce, whipping Negroes, and bawling about the inborn inalienable rights of man."[31]

But electioneering, as he had said, was not his real concern. He thought the war was wicked, that paying for it was equally so, and that Federalists who supported the war shared in its wickedness. Latecoming successes in 1813, such as the recapture of Detroit, or naval victories at sea and on the Great Lakes, did nothing to change his attitude. The war was wicked because, despite all the talk of the rights of neutral nations to trade and sail the seas, it was in fact "a war of conquest,"[32] which "complete[d] the guilt of those by whom this country has so long been misgoverned."[33] Paying for the war was wicked because "the debt . . . is void, being founded in moral wrong. . . ."[34] As for any "federalist, whose vote may in any wise support this war," he would be guilty of "treason" to his party, and his country. But he would be guilty of worse; his deed "would be an act of impiety as well as treachery."[35]

Morris's passionate polemics were occasionally brightened by profound insights. The danger of having an independent mind is going off half-cocked; the benefit is seeing what others miss. In the divisions of the War of 1812 he saw a great sectional split. "Time . . . seems about to disclose the awful secret that commerce and domestic slavery are mortal foes; and, bound together, one must destroy the other. I cannot blame Southern gentlemen for striving to put down commerce, because commerce, if it survives, will, I think, put them down. . . ."[36] He was ahead of time by half a century, but he was truly ahead of it. He also indulged in gossip almost at the level of his old French friends. "I supposed him," he wrote of President Madison in early 1813, "to be out of his senses, and have since been told that he never goes sober to bed. Whether intoxicated by opium or wine was not said. . . ."[37]

Morris's specific wartime suggestions went far beyond the election advice he had offered DeWitt Clinton. At his blackest, he hoped for a revolt of New England. "I hear some of the brethren exclaim, 'O Lord! O Lord! why, this is civil war!' Unquestionably it is civil war. And what of it?" If New York would not join in, then he hoped New England would invade it, and take it out of the Union by force. "[T]he prick of the Yankee bayonet will make you skip like squirrels."[38] At the very least, the Constitution that he had written had to be overhauled. "The present form," he admitted, "was good, but has been so much perverted that it can hardly be restored to what it was. If, therefore . . . good citizens mean that posterity should inherit freedom"—the goal of the Preamble—"they] must persuade [them]selves not merely to permit, but to effect a change."[39] Even though he might be tearing up his life's greatest achievement, Morris believed he was being true to his life's course. "It seems to me I was once a member of Congress during a revolutionary war. . . . We once had hearts—hearts that beat high with the love of liberty."[40] His heart was beating again.

He did all that "a gouty, one-legged old man"[41] could do, speaking at public anti-war meetings in New York and White Plains in the summer and fall of 1812, and expressing his opinions thereafter in a stream of letters, not just to the usual friends and family but to officeholders: Timothy Pickering, the Federalist senator from Massachusetts, who agreed with him; and his friend Rufus King, Federalist senator from New York, who would not go so far as to welcome Yankee bayonets in their state.

In the midst of war and disaffection, Morris became a father. On February 9, 1813, Gouverneur Morris II was born. Nancy was thirty-eight; Morris had just turned sixty-one. Children cannot literally renew the spring of life, and liveliness, which they can renew, in Morris's case needed no refreshing. But he loved the strange, late addition to his existence. In the fall of 1813, on a trip upstate, he wrote a letter to Nancy, in rhyme:

> *Kiss for me, my love, our charming boy.*
> *I long to taste again the joy*
> *Of pressing to his father's breast*
> *The son and mother. Be they blest*
> *With all which bounteous Heaven can grant;*
> *And if among us one must want*
> *Of bliss, be mine the scanty lot.*
> *Your happiness, may no dark spot*
> *Of gloomy woe or piercing pain*
> *Or melancholy ever stain.*[42]

In a lifetime of loving letters, this was one of the few that he had written to people who were happy. His relatives were not happy to see the wealthy old man reproduce; one of them, punning on the Russian marshal who had beaten Napoleon, nicknamed the child "Cutusoff."[43]

That same fall, Napoleon made what seemed to be his last stand at Leipzig, and lost. In 1791, on the same night that Louis XVI had made his doomed flight to Varennes, his younger brother, the comte de Provence, was able to escape to Flanders. Now the survivor was restored to the throne of France as Louis XVIII. In April 1814, Morris delivered an oration in New York celebrating the return of the Bourbons and "the Deliverance of Europe from the Yoke of Military Despotism." This speech he allowed himself to call "tolerably well written" and "in part, well delivered."[44]

Eager to conclude a war that one side considered a sideshow and the other considered a curse, Britain and America had sent peace commissioners to the Belgian city of Ghent. Yet while they wrangled, the war still dragged on. When the British tried to invade northern New York by the old route of Lake Champlain, they were decisively beaten at Plattsburg. When they tried to move up Chesapeake Bay, they chased Madison and the government from Washington, burned the White House and the Capitol, and were only stopped outside Baltimore. Former President Jefferson wrote his protégé a letter of consolation: "Had General Washington himself been now at the head of our affairs, the same event would probably have happened."[45] Happily for the Virginians, Morris never saw this communication, and thus was unable to comment on it.

CHAPTER FIFTEEN

Revolution Deferred

*I*N 1814, THE MORRISES resumed contact with Nancy's estranged family. The Randolphs were in a bad way. John had been turned out of Congress by a son-in-law of Thomas Jefferson who had moved to his district expressly to still his flamboyant anti-war voice; the defeated politician brooded and read Byron. In the spring of 1813, the plantation house at Bizarre had burned down, and Judith had to move into a house in a nearby town across the street from a tavern. Judith's elder son, St. George Randolph, was not only a deaf-mute; his awareness, growing with his natural urges, that there could never be a woman in his life had driven him insane. The family's hopes focused on the younger son, Tudor, who was a student at Harvard. But there, he showed signs of tuberculosis, the same disease that had killed his uncle Theodorick.

Nancy had not seen her sister Judith since she had left Virginia. She had seen her cousin John only once, in December 1811, when she had accompanied Morris on his canal-lobbying trip to Washington. Then Morris had urged Randolph to call on Nancy—not, it seems, from any hope of effecting a reconciliation between the two of them, but to ensure that a decent civility be shown her, and him. Randolph had complied. In the summer of 1814, Morris made a more expansive gesture, suggesting that Tudor come to Morrisania for a visit, and that his mother and uncle see him there. They would find "good air, milk, vegetables, and fruit . . . a comfortable house, an affectionate sister, and a good friend."[1] Tudor arrived at Morrisania in August, looking so ill he was put to bed; when he had a hemorrhage, the Randolphs were asked to come as soon as possible.

Judith and John arrived in late October. At first all went well. The Bizarre Randolphs greeted their successful transplanted kinswoman with seeming warmth. John, as the man of the family, following the protocol of the day, formally gave his sister-in-law and his nephew permission to stay at Morrisania for as long as they wished. A mishap occurred after John left for a boardinghouse in New York City; his carriage hit a pile of stones and overturned, and he was badly shaken. Everyone at Morrisania came down to New York to visit the other ailing Randolph.

On All Hallow's Eve, John sent Nancy a letter, care of her husband. John began by announcing that the eyes of man and God were upon her; then he got down to specifics. Mrs. Morris had "impos[ed] upon the generous man to whose arms you have brought pollution." Nancy was in fact a double murderess, having killed not only her own child, found on the shingle pile in 1792 ("your hands . . . deprived of life that of which you were delivered"), but also Richard Randolph. This new charge he justified by his own suspicions—"My brother died *suddenly*"—and by those of Tudor, who "imparted to me the morning I left Morrisania his misgivings that you had been the perpetrator of that act." He added other charges, lesser only by comparison, such as that she had had an "Othello" (a slave lover) at Bizarre, and that she had lived as a *"drab"* (a prostitute) after leaving it. Now "[c]hance has again thrown you under my eye. What do I see? A vampire that, after sucking the best blood of my race, has flitted off to the North, and struck her harpy fangs into an infirm old man." Randolph forecast her future deeds from her past. She might carry on "lewd amours" behind her husband's back, or kill him and their son, even as she had killed Richard and her child. "If he be not both blind and deaf, he must sooner or later unmask you unless *he too die of cramps* in his *stomach.* You understand me. . . . Repent before it is too late."[2]

One key to the virulence of this letter is its similarity with John Randolph's day-to-day rhetoric. There may be no understated way to tell a man that his wife is a killer, and that he may be her next victim, but if there were, Randolph was not the man to choose it. His speeches in Congress were furnished from the same wardrobe of tropes—*pollution, Othello, vampire, harpy*—that he used in this letter. "Sir, [the question of slavery] is not a *dry rot,* which you can cover with the carpet until the house tumbles about your ears; you might as well try to hide a *volcano* in full *eruption;* it cannot be hid; it is a *cancer* in your face" (italics added).[3] He spoke that way because he thought that way. All his life his language was vivid, his temper aggressive, and his imagination morbid.

Another ingredient that went into writing the letter may have been opium. Morris might scribble down rumors of Madison's opium use. Randolph had been using the drug since 1810, when a horse crushed the toes of his right foot. On his way to Morrisania, he had fallen down a flight of stairs at an inn, hurting an ankle and a shoulder; then he had his carriage accident. A weak body, bad luck, and bad medicine were unhappy companions for a bitter mind.

John claimed a solid source of information in Morris's own family—David B. Ogden, a nephew, and Martin Wilkins, a great-nephew. These two relatives had visited Randolph when he was recuperating in his New York boardinghouse. Their motives for resenting Nancy were obvious: it was Wilkins who had made the joke about "Cutusoff." Ogden could ill afford to be cut off. A local politician and a land speculator, who was prominent enough to be painted by John Trumbull (his face is dark, fleshy, and intelligent—not unlike Morris's, except for the lack of sparkle), Ogden was in several kinds of debt to his uncle. In a memo to himself, John Randolph wrote that Ogden told him that Gouverneur II was the son of a servant, not of Gouverneur. John might not be considered a reliable note-taker, but Ogden witnessed the memo.

In all his accusations, John did not say who he thought had been the father of the child Nancy had borne in 1792. He scoffed at the idea that it could have been Theodorick—"long before his death . . . he was reduced to a mere skeleton"[4]—and he said that Richard would have "perish[ed] on the same gibbet by your side" if the prosecution had been more aggressive. But he held Richard guilty only of disposing of the body, to protect his sister-in-law. No doubt he believed that a woman who would copulate with slaves and paying customers would have had no dearth of lovers.

Nancy fell ill after getting John's letter, then fought back. She wrote warning letters to Wilkins and Ogden, then produced, in January of the new year, a forty-page answer to John, which she copied and mailed to interested parties in Virginia. She asked the obvious questions about his "filthy accusations":[5] if she was "a negro's concubine," why had he let his nephew Tudor stay with her? If she was "a common prostitute" and "the murderess of her own child and of your brother," why had he politely greeted her when he arrived at Morrisania? She reminded him that he had once courted her, though thanks to his "stormy passions," "mean selfishness," and "wretched appearance," he had failed. She admitted that she had given birth in 1792, but insisted that the baby was stillborn, and that the father was Theodorick. "I was betrothed to him, and considered him as my husband in the presence of . . . God." John's tales of prostitution were all lies, though "if suffering could have driven me to vice, there was no want of suffering."

She defended her husband, for whom John professed concern. "I loved my husband before he made me his wife. I love him still more now that he has made me the mother of one of the finest boys I ever saw; now that his kindness soothes the anguish which I cannot but feel from your unmanly attack." She finished with a Shakespearean reference. "I trust you are by this time convinced that you have clumsily performed the part of 'honest Iago.'" Nancy was like her cousin in one thing: Randolphs did not pull punches.

There may have been moments during this deadly catfight when Morris wondered what sort of family he had married into. His preferred manner, where his own interests were at stake, ran to *suaviter in modo*. To Wilkins and Ogden he wrote bland letters expressing the assurance that of course they would defend the reputation of his wife. When Judith Randolph wrote from Virginia, protesting that she had had nothing to do with John's, or Tudor's, performance, Morris replied that he would "vindicate your honor."[6] To a friend in Virginia, he wrote that he would not sue John, since that would only spread his libels. His "communications gave me no concern, for Mrs. Morris had apprised me of the only fact in his possession, before she came to my house, so that her candor had blunted the point of his arrow." That only fact would have been the stillborn child. He offered his own thoughts on Nancy's accusers: they "hate her because she is happy."[7]

John Randolph hated Morris for the same reason. He and Morris were not utterly unalike. They opposed the war; they were aristocrats; they were unusual. But there the resemblance ended. Morris was rich, a father, and happily married to the last of his many lovers. Randolph was financially pressed, single, childless, and sexless. Morris, who had a peg leg, enjoyed himself. Randolph, who had crushed toes, took opium. A gloomy mind could not miss the contrast.

FAMILY BUSINESS did not distract Morris from public business. In October 1814, the Massachusetts legislature had called for a Convention of delegates from the New England states, to consider the state of the nation and their region. On December 15, the delegates met in the State House in Hartford, Connecticut, a building as light as it is dignified, under the gaze of a Gilbert Stuart portrait of George Washington. With a few late additions, the Convention had twenty-six delegates from three states (Massachusetts, Connecticut, Rhode Island), two counties in New Hampshire, and one county in Vermont. They were thus following, in truncated form, the campaign advice Morris had given DeWitt Clinton two years earlier. In a letter written just before Christmas, Morris praised the Convention in the language of the Magi as "a star in the East . . . the day-spring of freedom and glory. The madmen and traitors assembled at Hartford will, I believe, if not too tame and timid, be hailed hereafter as the patriots and sages of their day and generation."[8]

The Hartford Convention met in secret for three weeks, opening each session with a prayer. (During one of their deadlocks the delegates to the Constitutional Convention had rejected Benjamin Franklin's suggestion that they pray because they did not want to give the appearance of desperation, and because they had no funds to pay a clergyman.) Almost half of the delegates had served in Congress or in high state office; the rest were local figures—state legislators, probate court judges. They are better known to history by their relatives: Connecticut sent a nephew of Morris's old colleague, Roger Sherman; Massachusetts sent the father of Henry Wadsworth Longfellow. The leaders had a reputation as moderates: George Cabot, the presiding officer, said his purpose was to keep "hot-heads from getting into mischief,"[9] while Harrison Gray Otis, who worked on all the important committees, was called "a hare trembling at every breeze."[10]

The recommendations the Hartford men offered on January 5, 1815, were cloaked in moderation. They proposed seven amendments to the Constitution. Three were immediate reactions to the war: no declarations of war except by a two-thirds vote in both houses of Congress; no interdiction of trade with any country except by the same margin; and no general embargos lasting more than sixty days. Three amendments were partisan assaults on the Republicans: no new states admitted without a two-thirds vote in both houses of Congress (thus raising the bar for future Kentuckys and Tennessees); no foreign-born federal officeholders (a slap at such Republicans as the Irish Matthew Lyon and the Swiss Albert Gallatin); a one-term limit on the presidency, and no consecutive presidents from the same state (to break the seemingly endless chain of two-term Virginians). Only one amendment addressed an issue that had been discussed in Philadelphia in 1787: the Hartford men opposed the three-fifths rule.

More controversially, the convention asked that states be allowed to divert taxes collected for the federal government to their own defense. The convention complained of a federal policy that left the New England seacoast undefended (Britain occupied half of Maine), while the state militias were conscripted to fight battles on the Canadian frontier. But letting states defend themselves was a first step toward letting them conduct their own foreign relations. Most radical was the coda of the Hartford Convention: a call for a second convention in Boston in June if these proposals were rejected. That convention "must act as such urgent circumstances may then require."[11] This was the threat that converted suggestions into demands. The mutinous officers at Newburgh had said nothing balder.

The Hartford men were playing for time. They wanted to see what, if anything, the peace commissioners had agreed upon at Ghent. The British were known to have made exorbitant demands, insisting on an independent nation for their Indian allies in the American Northwest. The northwest border, which the Louisiana Purchase had pushed to the Rockies, would then be rolled back to Ohio. "The British ministers," Morris wrote sarcastically when he read this demand, have discovered "that our copper-colored brothers are human beings. . . . Take care, my good friend, that they do not make a similar discovery respecting our ebony-colored brethren."[12] The Hartford men also awaited news from the South. A British expedition had landed in Louisiana in December with the evident intention of taking New Orleans. If the federal government could not defend the mouth of the Mississippi, New England hard-liners expected the west to join them in disaffection. "If the British succeed," wrote Senator Timothy Pickering in January "—and if they have tolerable leaders I see no reason to doubt of their success—I shall consider the Union as severed."[13]

The Gouverneur Morris of 1787 would have scoffed at most of the Hartford Convention's proposals. In Philadelphia he wanted the president to take the lead in foreign policy, seeing him as "the general guardian of the national interests."[14] Though embargos had not been a topic of much discussion, he had strongly supported other commercial regulations—export taxes, laws favoring American shipping—and it could be assumed that, having no principled objection to lesser measures, he would back stronger ones in more desperate circumstances. The man who had labored for the suffering army at Valley Forge certainly would not have favored giving military power to the states. His speech on the Indians who let guests sleep with their wives had been meant to mock the idea of immigrants easily becoming senators, but he had argued for nothing more exclusive than a fourteen-year citizenship requirement. He had opposed term limits in all cases, as leading to instability. "A change of men is ever followed by a change of measures. . . . Rehoboam will not imitate Solomon."[15] The only points on which the young Morris agreed with the Hartford men were suspicion of new states, and detestation of the three-fifths rule.

When Morris read what the Hartford men had done, he was in fact contemptuous. "They have fallen short," he wrote Rufus King, " . . . and will be laughed at by many."[16] "Such humble language," he wrote another correspondent, had "a squeaking sound." But he understood, and approved of, the threat. If their "modest propositions are rejected," New England would resort to "cannon law."[17]

Why had Morris given up so? The last national issue before the war that had engaged his attention had been the Judiciary Act of 1802, which scaled back the federal courts. Morris often said that he considered the Constitution "dead" from that date.[18] This diagnosis reflected his inattention. The federal judiciary had been pared down, but John Randolph's 1805 attack on the Supreme Court had failed. Chief Justice John Marshall had not begun his long counterattack, but he was known to be no friend to Republican measures. It was not the alleged death of the Constitution caused by the Judiciary Act, but the War of 1812 that drove Morris to desperation.

In our minds the War of 1812 has taken its place in the string of American wars, more inglorious than others perhaps, but also shorter. To Morris and his contemporaries, it was the second war the United States had fought. The Revolution had been a desperate defense of our rights. The War of 1812 was a defense of the right to sail and trade, but it was also an attempt to seize Canada. The Revolution had been led by George Washington. The War of 1812 was being misled by the unmilitary James Madison, and by generals most of whom were as incompetent as he.

Morris saw the War of 1812 as a war of Virginia against the North, specifically New York. "The question to be settled between the Northern and Southern states, reduced to its simple elements, is merely this: Shall the citizens of New York be the slaves or masters of Virginia?"[19] This too was mistaken, as far as Virginia was concerned. Virginia, in the person of Madison, had been dragged into war by the Clays and Calhouns in his party, whom Virginia, in the person of John Randolph, had vainly resisted. But it was true that New York's interest had been neglected to satisfy the greed of other sections of the country.

New York's paramount interest was its canal. The canal would turn upstate hamlets into towns and cities, and New York City, with its grid, into a world city indeed. The canal would reach beyond New York to the Great Lakes, supplying settlers and drawing out their produce in ships of over 100 tons. This was the vision Morris had seen while sailing, shooting rapids, and tending to his properties. Who needed Canada, with such a prospect? But Morris's vision had been set aside for a predator's dream, the quick pounce on a sure thing—only, the sure thing had slipped away in three years of bumbling conflict.

Was this reason enough to break up the nation? A rash man would say so, and the war and the rejection of his canal had made Morris a rash man. "Generally speaking," he had written in the spring of 1814, "wisdom gives moderate counsels, but there are cases in which moderation is dangerous, and even ruinous."[20] Morris's extremism is striking, coming from the draftsman of the Constitution: the southerners who would fulfill his sectional prophecies by taking their states out of the Union could not speak with such perverse authority.

But Morris's willingness to scrap his handiwork also has an intellectual advantage over later critics of the Constitution, as it has over the men of the Hartford Convention in their moderate guise. Both the critics to come and the Hartford men labored to maintain the fiction of legality. John C. Calhoun, his days as a young nationalist past, would argue in the 1830s that states had a right to nullify the operation of federal laws that were oppressive to them. His intellectual heirs of the Confederacy would argue in the 1860s that, the Union being a compact of states, they had a right to secede when a man as obnoxious as Abraham Lincoln was elected president. In the interval until their threat should be called in, the men of Hartford claimed to be "interpos[ing]" the "authority" of their states against "deliberate, dangerous, and palpable infractions of the constitution. . . ."[21] This is tugging the Constitution, like a tablecloth, over disunion as well as union. It is asking permission to leave in a huff; it is pretending that political debate can be conducted by threats. Morris had no patience for such evasions. Having written the Preamble to the Constitution, he knew how it ended: "to . . . promote the general welfare, and secure the blessings of liberty to ourselves and our posterity. . . ." If, as he believed, the federal government was manifestly and deliberately failing to do that, then the Constitution was dead, and that is why as many northern states as possible should leave. Leaving was not constitutional, for the Constitution had failed. "[T]he union, being the means of preserving freedom, should be prized as such," Morris had written Harrison Gray Otis in 1813, "but . . . the end should not be sacrificed to the means."[22] Morris might misjudge circumstances. But his moral position is clear.

In February 1815, commissioners from New England made their way to Washington, bearing the results of the Hartford Convention. They were overtaken by other messengers. First came the news from New Orleans: British generals who had beaten Napoleon's troops in Europe had been crushed by frontier Indian fighters. Then came the terms of the Treaty of Ghent, which were surprisingly good: not worth a war (nothing was said of the rights of sailors), but the British had agreed to abandon both their Indian allies and the coast of Maine. If the double news did not exactly mean victory, it meant something equally overwhelming: relief. Accompanied by the sound of ringing church bells, the New England commissioners went quickly and quietly home. Thus ended, wrote Morris, a war "rashly declared, prodigally maintained, weakly conducted, and meanly concluded."[23]

CHAPTER SIXTEEN

Acceptance

THE TREATY OF GHENT had closed the book on almost a quarter century of revolutionary and Napoleonic world war. The book flew open again in the spring of 1815 when Napoleon escaped the island of Elba to which his vanquishers had confined him and rallied the French army. Morris was not alarmed. "Bonaparte," he wrote, "will be quelled, and his associate conspirators brought to condign punishment."[1] One of those conspirators was Charles de Flahaut, Adèle's son, now thirty years old. General Flahaut, as handsome as his mother and with as many lovers, was at the emperor's side at Waterloo, and fled thence to England. No note of this echo of the past reached Morris through the clangor of events. He made his final judgment of the French at the end of the year. "That tract of country always produced a turbulent race. Caesar or Tacitus, I forget which, characterized them as 'too proud to obey, too ferocious to be free.' A firm hand is needful to govern them. Their ruler must flatter their vanity, and punish severely the slightest attempt to diminish his authority. . . . [L]ike a vicious horse with a cart," France "may kick and plunge, but the whip and the spur well applied will tame her."[2] The observer of two revolutions had no general theory to cover both cases. Americans in distress could assert their natural rights, but Frenchmen were too volatile to be allowed the privilege.

With the return of peace, New Yorkers turned their thoughts back to a canal. Morris once again advised New York to go it alone, suggesting that the Canal Commission be empowered to issue $5 million in bonds, backed by the state. As each stretch of the canal was completed, it should be opened to navigation, and the tolls used for upkeep and interest on the debt. He was as confident as he had been before the war that the "natural effect" of the work would be to "make New York mistress of the union."[3] Washington was not as alarmed as it had been by this prospect, for the war seemed to have purged it of regional jealousies. In Congress, Calhoun introduced a canal bill, intended to combat every "low, sordid, selfish and sectional spirit."[4] Madison, however, had not been purged of his scruples; his last act as president was to veto the bill as "contrary to the established and consistent rules" of constitutional interpretation.[5] New York went ahead anyway, without the federal government's help, and on July 4, 1817, DeWitt Clinton, now governor, presided over a groundbreaking at Rome, a village a hundred miles northwest of Albany whose name reflected the state's hopes.

Morris did not see the ceremony. But he did not need progress on his cherished canal to sweeten his political temper. In the postwar world, he executed one more political reversal, as dramatic as any of his earlier ones, and became an advocate of stoicism and acceptance. Having written the Constitution after one war, and abandoned it during the next, he embraced it again in peace.

Not that he approved all the policies coming out of Washington. His correspondence chiefly concerned finance, "a matter which," as he wrote Rufus King, "from the course of my life, I ought to know something about, if I be not a very stupid fellow."[6] After letting the Bank of the United States lapse, Congress wished to charter another. In 1781, Morris had helped found the Bank of North America when the country was in desperate need of credit, but now he thought the proposed national bank would be inflationary, and he opposed it. "The first bank in this country was planned by your humble servant," but "what was medicine then would be poison now."[7] It was proposed to pay off the war debt with a land tax, and many Federalists supported this move as a matter of fiscal responsibility. Morris opposed this, too. Direct taxes, he lectured Rufus King, are "ungracious and tormenting, and when pushed are no longer taxation but confiscation."[8] He saved his choicest words for protective tariffs, which raised prices and artificially stimulated manufacturing. Why, he asked, should "those who till the soil . . . be laid under heavy contribution to support the scum of England and Ireland who come out to live in ease and idleness as mechanics[?] We already have . . . poor children who can be pent up, to march backward and forward with a spinning jenny, till they are old enough to become drunkards and prostitutes."[9]

But all these measures were follies of peacetime, and Morris was now once more at peace with America. His mood found expression in his advice to his party. Burned by the bad timing of the Hartford Convention, the Federalists turned to one of their more moderate voices, Rufus King, as their presidential candidate in 1816. King, the transplant from Massachusetts, had been living at his farm in Jamaica, in the county of Queens, for years. He was by now a downstate rural grandee, like Morris. In the spring of 1816, Morris wrote him a jocular letter of congratulation. "I . . . am pleased to learn, that you stand a candidate for the government. The office, could it be restored to what we made it by the Constitution, is of great dignity." But now, like a warship with its upper deck removed (cut down "from a seventy-four to a razee"), "it is not worth your acceptance. I feel, therefore, and applaud your selfdenial. . . ."[10] Since King had absolutely no chance of winning—he would carry only three out of nineteen states against the next Virginian president, James Monroe—it was gracious of his friend to mock the office for which he contended.

Morris's real strategy for the election of 1816, politeness aside, was revealed in a letter some months later to a Federalist Committee of Correspondence in Philadelphia. The Committees of Correspondence before the Revolutionary War had been designed to stir up revolutionary sentiment; much of Morris's correspondence during the War of 1812 had had the same purpose. The Federalist Committee of Correspondence of 1816, however, was an ordinary campaign organization, designed to view with alarm and point with pride. Morris told them to spare their efforts.

"[T]he best course you can pursue is to leave . . . the whole ground" to the enemy. "If you come forward, Democrats"—still a term of abuse, especially among Federalists, but soon to become the legitimate name of Jefferson's heirs—"will stifle their feelings to support their party, not so much because they love it, as because they hate you. If you leave them to themselves, they will split and abuse each other."

This was Morris speaking in the voice of Machiavelli, counseling non-resistance as a political ploy. Then he shifted to a different tone. "But, gentlemen, let us forget party, and think of our country. That country embraces both parties. We must endeavor, therefore, to save and benefit both." He recurred to a pet theory of his—that there was no point preaching in time of peace, since men would only listen at the approach of a crisis. "[W]hen it arrives, the people will look out for men of sense, experience, and integrity." Now he gave the argument a twist that, if it was not new for him—he had always had friends and associates across party lines, from DeWitt Clinton to Robert R. Livingston to Peter Van Schaak—was certainly fresh after the rancor of the last four years. "Such men may, I trust, be found in both parties; and, if our country be delivered, what does it signify whether those who operate her salvation wear a federal or a democratic cloak?"[11]

Morris was not the only Federalist who was willing to let the old feuds alone. Worn out by strife, defeat, and their own mistakes, so many supporters of the minority party decided to work with the triumphant Republicans that the postwar period came to be known as the era of good feelings, and Rufus King's hapless race for the White House was the last presidential effort any Federalist would make. Morris's attitude, however, was notable coming from one who had been so bitter. His advice now contradicted his insight after Jefferson's election that political losers could serve as the outward conscience of the winners. But he correctly estimated the Federalists' ability to play that, or any other role. When he was courting Nancy Randolph, he had told her that the cards of life were fairly dealt, and that our lot was to play them, then sleep. As with men, so with political parties. It was time for Federalism to fold its hand.

He ended the letter with a self-portrait, and a credo. "Perhaps the expression of these sentiments may be imprudent; but, when it appears proper to speak truth, I know not concealment." That was certainly true of him, whether he spoke truth or (as he sometimes did) folly. "It has been the unvarying principle of my life, that the interest of our country must be preferred to every other interest."[12] He had defined the country's interest very erratically on occasion, but he had always sought it.

In his poison pen letter to Nancy, John Randolph had called Morris an "infirm old man." His constitution was naturally stronger than Randolph's, and his wits had always been steadier. But infirmities had begun to dog him, and in 1816, when he turned sixty-four, he had reached the age at which his own father died. Morris's chronic ailment was gout, the inflammation of the joints caused by deposits from the kidneys. James Gillray, the great turn-of-the-century English caricaturist, did a famous cartoon of gout as a demon biting a bare foot. Gout was a disease associated with high living, and the upper classes who could afford to indulge themselves. Morris was a likely candidate on both counts. Gout had "paid . . . its first call" on him when he was living in France.[13]

In the summer of 1816, Morris described himself, in a letter to a companion of his Hamburg days, as "only peep[ing] out occasionally from the threshold of my hermitage." The letter is an envoi, a counterpart, on the personal plane, of his advice to the Philadelphia Federalists. "I lead," he wrote, "a quiet and, more than most of my fellow-mortals, a happy life." Praise of his wife led him to thoughts about marriage. "The woman to whom I am married has much genius, has been well educated, and possesses, with an affectionate temper, industry and a love of order. That I did not marry earlier is not to be attributed to any dislike for that connection. On the contrary it has long been my fixed creed that as love is the only fountain of felicity, so it is in wedded love that the waters are most pure." This was a challengeable statement, especially by anyone who had met the writer in Europe, where his only experience of wedded love had been loving the wives of other men. Morris was evidently aware of the difficulty, for he immediately addressed it. "To solve the problem of my fate it was required to discover a woman . . . who could love an old man." This begs several questions: why should his amorous fate have been a problem? Why could it only be solved when he was old? Still, he had found such a woman, and he had loved her for more than seven years, despite an extraordinary effort to destroy their happiness.

He turned to their son. "The sentiments of a father respecting an only child render his opinions so liable to suspicion that prudence should withhold them even from a friend. I will only say, therefore, that some who would have been more content had he never seen the light"—the Ogdens, the Wilkinses, and the Merediths—"acknowledge him to be beautiful and promising."

He closed with himself. "You may, then, opening your mind's eye, behold your friend as he descends, with tottering steps, the bottom of life's hill. . . ." From the time of his carriage accident, any instance of tottering had been a bitter humiliation, a failure of hard-won self-control and élan; but now gout and the years forced it on him. "[L]ooking back, I can, with some little self-complacency, reflect that I have not lived in vain. . . ."

This boast demands examination. However base and foolish the statesmanship of the War of 1812 had been, the statesmanship of the Revolution and the Founding had been glorious. Morris belonged to a generation of leaders who were proud of what they had done, and intensely anxious that their deeds be remembered. In that context and in that company, could he say that he had not lived in vain?

He was no philosopher. His thoughts occurred in bursts, in letters and speeches, and he wrote no coherent account of them. But that was true of most of his peers. His enemy Madison and his friend Hamilton had, with some help from John Jay, written *The Federalist,* a treatise that still repays study. Wise as it is, it is an occasional performance, and each author squirreled important insights (sometimes changing his opinions) in other documents. Washington, Jefferson, and the other founders wrote in the same scattershot fashion. The only one to assemble anything like a *Summa* was Paine, in *The Rights of Man* and *The Age of Reason*—but Paine had been only erratically useful to his two adopted homelands.

What Morris thought, here and there, and never quite swept together, was that God, all-powerful and virtually unknowable, rules the world, and directs events as He sees fit. Liberty is a blessed state, although some nations, by virtue of their temperaments, cannot safely enjoy as much liberty as others. Even the citizens of the freest do not pay much attention to reason, unless a crisis drives them to it. Experienced governors, who ought to be in office at all times, might then be called upon. In good times or bad, men should enjoy the rights to work, write, and worship (this was the only sense in which Morris would have thought that all men are created equal). If this collection of principles is not consistently inspiring, it is free from cant, as good as the principles of most of Morris's peers, and better than those of most of his French friends.

Good principles make a man admirable; a good style makes him arresting. Morris's sparkling prose still shines after two centuries. Reading it, we hear a voice—so vivid, we imagine the speaker has just left the room, and so delightful that we want him to come back. The moral source of his style is confidence: he knows who he is, and that he is right; he knows, from long experience, that he will please most of his auditors; and he does not care about those he does not please.

Morris performed two special services as a public man. As Jefferson immortalized the Continental Congress's view of first principles, so Morris had applied his finish to the Constitutional Convention's view of fundamental law. Morris did not leave his country on paper: he worked to plan a canal that should make it bloom. A handful of other men might have buffed the Constitution almost as smoothly, but he was the one who did it; a handful of New Yorkers pushed for the Erie Canal—he was one of the most eloquent and energetic. For the rest, he gave many hours of intelligent and industrious labor as a New Yorker, a financier, and a diplomat. This more than compensates for his bad ideas and outrageous advice.

He performed one more service that became known only after his death. His diary bore witness to another Revolution and Founding that did not go so well. Many other writers have told France's story, but his record—published in extracts in the nineteenth century, and fully only on the eve of World War II—is indelible.

Yet there is another sense in which he had not lived in vain. Morris was an important founding father, but he was something else, useful in a different way to his friends and acquaintances. He was a gentleman. In his case, that is a moral even more than a social term. Born to riches and power, he had also learned to live well. Nature gave him a buoyant and appreciative temperament, but he had fostered those qualities, despite severe trials. His conduct, from his teens on, is marked by courage, courtesy, and warmth—by affection for his friends, sympathy for the afflicted, and disdain for bullies. His example is still useful. The founding fathers can show us how to live as citizens. Morris can show us how to enjoy life's blessings and bear its hurts with humanity and good spirits. "At sixty-four," he concluded his letter, "there is little to desire and less to apprehend. Let me add that, however grave the form and substance of this letter, the lapse of so many years have not impaired the gayety of your friend. Could you gratify him with your company and conversation, you would find in him still the gayety of inexperience and the frolic of youth." [14]

His gout became crippling in the fall. His diary entries ceased early in October, with the first frost, and he made a new will at the end of the month. David Ogden and Martin Wilkins were not mentioned. Another nephew got a bequest, and yet another was told that if the principal heir, Gouverneur Morris II, should die young, he might inherit the estate, so long as he assumed the Morris name and arms. He gave his wife a life interest in his property, plus an annuity of $2,600 a year ($32,500 today). If she married again, her annuity would be increased to $3,200, "to defray the increased expenditure, which may attend that condition." [15]

"Sixty-four years ago," he said as death approached, "it pleased the Almighty to call me into existence—here, on this spot, in this very room; and now shall I complain that he is pleased to call me hence?" [16] The end was painful. He suffered a blockage of his urinary tract, and he tried to clear the obstruction with whalebone, no doubt from one of his wife's corsets. But he had known pain before. On his last day, November 6, he quoted poetry—not his own, but Gray's *Elegy Written in a Country Churchyard:*

> *For who, to dumb Forgetfulness a prey,*
> *This pleasing, anxious being e'er resigned,*
> *Left the warm precincts of the cheerful day,*
> *Nor cast one longing lingering look behind?* [17]

Postscript

*M*ORRIS DIED leaving one project, and a few old colleagues, behind him.

The Erie Canal, begun by Governor DeWitt Clinton on July 4, 1817, was finished in 1825, two years ahead of schedule. Clinton, still governor, poured a ceremonial bucket of Lake Erie water into the Atlantic at Sandy Hook, off New York Harbor. The volume of commerce that the canal was soon carrying fulfilled the most sanguine hopes of its projectors. At night, wrote one observer, the "flickering head lamps" of the boats making their way across the heart of New York shone like "swarms of fireflies."[1] The produce of a continent went out past Sandy Hook to Europe and the world, enriching New York all the more. Whatever their political opinions, Morris and his fellow patricians had made a confident bet on their country and their city, which was paid back manyfold.

Deploring the illiberality of both Bonaparte and the restored House of Bourbon, the marquis de Lafayette was a marginal figure in French politics for many years. In 1824, at the age of sixty-seven, he returned to the country he had served more successfully than his own for a triumphal visit. When he saw Houdon's statue of Washington (which had used Morris for the body model), he said it was the very image of his hero. Six years later, in 1830, there was a second French Revolution, and the tricolor flew again, though this time much less blood flowed. Lafayette, who took an active part, saw the reestablishment, at the end of a long life, of a constitutional monarchy, the ideal of his youth. Talleyrand came out of retirement, at the end of an even longer life, to help the new regime over several international rough spots. In his last days he was reconciled to the Catholic Church. While receiving extreme unction, he told the attending priest, "Do not forget I am a bishop."[2]

In the United States, the remnants of Morris's generation gave way to a new cohort of leaders. In 1820, one of the last founders to hold office, Rufus King, argued passionately against allowing slavery in the new state of Missouri. So a survivor of the Philadelphia Convention looked ahead to the issues that would produce the Civil War. John Randolph did his best to make civil war inevitable, by linking the cause of states' rights to the institution of slavery; his passionate polemics made a convert of the young nationalist John C. Calhoun. Contrary to the end, Randolph freed all of his own slaves in his will. Released from the burden of leadership, James Madison spent a quiet retirement. In 1831 the historian Jared Sparks asked him for his views of the man who had written the Constitution that Madison had done so much to prepare and expound. Madison could scarcely have been unaware of Morris's low opinion of him as an officeholder, though happily he had been spared knowledge of the details. The estimate he gave Sparks was as generous as it was just.

Morris also left a ghost story. One night, so the story went, when Nancy was staying at his north country summer house, two horsemen banged on the front door, demanding a treasure that her husband had taken while he was in France. At this, Morris stepped from a portrait on the wall and waved the riders away. After they fled, he led Nancy to the hidden treasure. The story captures this truth: if Morris in death could have faced down ruffians and been generous to his wife, he would certainly have done so. At the end of the twentieth century, the people living in his old summer house still reported mysterious bangings on the front door.[3]

The real treasure Morris had hoped to leave his wife and son was diminished by a very real ruffian, his nephew David Ogden. Morris had endorsed one of Ogden's mortgages, which left his estate liable for a load of debt—more than $100,000, according to Nancy. She was reduced to the severest economies. She forewent her annuity. She sued to recover debts that her husband had not bothered about. She sued to remove an executor of the estate who had mismanaged some land sales. She was sued by her lawyer, a son of Alexander Hamilton, for legal bills that she considered exorbitant. She rented out the farms of Morrisania, and fretted when her tenant's cows broke into her corn. The struggle was unremitting, but by the time Gouverneur II reached his majority, she was finally able to pass on to him his father's estate, free and clear.

She had read her husband's diaries, with aching eyes, at night after her son was in bed. Some passages, evidently sexual, have been crossed out, possibly by her, though considering what remains the censor had a light hand. We will never know what she censored from her own past. She had claimed, in her correspondence with John Randolph, that Theodorick was the father of her child, and that the baby was stillborn. Yet Richard Randolph, her brother-in-law, had loved her, and many desperate men and women have killed newborns. What we can say is that the inferences John drew from her alleged crimes were false. She loved her husband and son. More galling to John, she had endured. She died age sixty-two in May 1837.

Gouverneur Morris II had the long Morris nose and his father's commanding stature (so much for David Ogden's tales about his paternity). Like his father, he was interested in transportation, serving as president of railroad companies, the next stage of development after canals. As the tracks of the Harlem line pushed up through his patrimony, he profitably sold off swathes of it. In 1841, he gathered the remains of his parents and of earlier Morrises and buried them at St. Ann's, an Episcopal church he had built in honor of his mother. A year later, once again following his father, he married a Virginian, Patsey Jefferson Cary, one of Nancy Randolph's nieces. The last bottle of Marie Antoinette's imperial Tokay was drunk in Morris's house in 1848.

New York City grew beyond Gouverneur Morris's imagining, filling his grid, the rest of Manhattan, and four surrounding counties. What was once Morrisania now lies in the South Bronx. The Number 6 train stops at 138th Street and Brook Avenue, laid over the south-running brook that once divided the estate in two. 138th Street is a commercial strip, poor but bustling, dotted with fast-food restaurants and cheap clothing and furniture stores. Depending on the closest holiday, the fire escapes of the tenement housing above the storefronts are hung with Puerto Rican, Haitian, or Mexican flags. A few blocks east and north stands St. Ann's Church (the little blue and white metal sign that Episcopalians hang in front of their houses of worship also identifies it as *Iglesia de Santa Ana*)—all that remains in the Bronx, aside from a few place names, of the Morrises.

The building is capacious but plain, reflecting a simple era of Episcopal worship. All the eccentric Morrises of the seventeenth and eighteenth centuries are listed on a tablet on the rear wall of the sanctuary. Set in the floor, beneath an iron grate, is a stone that was inscribed first by Morris's widow, then by his son. Nancy wrote:

> *Conjugal affection*
> *Consecrates this spot where*
> *the Best of men was laid*
> *untill a vault could be erected*
> *to receive*
> *his precious remains*

Gouverneur II added, more conventionally, a tribute to

> *the wife and mother*
> *in memory of whom*
> *this church*
> *was erected*
> *to the God she loved*
> *by filial veneration*

In the yard outside, the state of New York erected a stone tablet with a list of Gouverneur Morris's accomplishments, which can be read from the sidewalk, if anyone wished to. At the end of a short, leaf-strewn path, his vault lies half-sunken in a slope of the yard; beside it stands an elm tree, spared from blight by remoteness from its fellows, whose crown spreads like a huge umbrella.

New York has been attacked again, as it was when Morris was a member of the Provincial Congress. He knew his share of destruction, sometimes firsthand, sometimes at one remove, from evacuating Kingston to reentering Philadelphia; from the Prussian artillery within earshot of Paris to Napoleon rampaging across Europe. If he thought his country's warmaking was wickedly at fault, he would not hesitate to counsel revolution. If he thought it was in the right, he would do his work wherever duty placed him, whether in small towns or among rioting foreign mobs.

No one now knows that. Morris's grave is on no city tour; it is mentioned in only the most comprehensive reference works. The people on 138th Street are of a different culture and class, while the wealthy and educated have forgotten him even more completely than they have his great contemporaries (Hamilton at least is buried in Trinity Churchyard, at the head of Wall Street). Yet of all the founding fathers, he would be the least distressed by their ignorance. Despite many trials, he savored life. He did it by following the formula he offered one of his correspondents: "To try to do good, to avoid evil, a little severity for one's self, a little indulgence for others—this is the means to obtain some good result out of our poor existence. To love one's friends, to be beloved by them—this is the means to brighten it."[4] He had enjoyed his life. Let the passersby enjoy theirs.

Notes

Morris has been fortunate in his biographers and editors. Jared Sparks was given access to Morris's papers by his widow, and his three-volume work—*The Life of Gouverneur Morris, with Selections from his Correspondence and Miscellaneous Papers*—contains generous selections from his letters, diaries, essays, and speeches. Anne Cary Morris, a granddaughter, offers, in her two-volume *The Diary and Letters of Gouverneur Morris,* a narrative scaffold with a somewhat different selection of Morris's writing. Both were edited for the sake of prudery and conciseness. Beatrix Cary Davenport's two-volume work, *A Diary of the French Revolution by Gouverneur Morris,* offers—uncut—the diary that Morris began in Paris on March 1, 1789, and continued until January 5, 1793, when he wrote that "[t]he situation of things is such that to continue this journal would compromise many people" unless his entries became so brief as to be "insipid and useless. I prefer therefore the more simple measure of putting an end to it" (Davenport II, p. 598). Davenport includes numerous letters that fill out the record.

The biographies by Daniel Walther (1932; trans. 1934), Howard Swiggett (1952), Max M. Mintz (1970), and Mary-Jo Kline (1978) are listed in the Bibliography, and gratefully cited in these Notes. In 1887, the twenty-eight-year-old Theodore Roosevelt was commissioned to do a biography of Gouverneur Morris, but found that the Morris family "won't let me see the old gentleman's papers at any price. I am in rather a quandary"—Edmund Morris, *The Rise of Theodore Roosevelt* (New York: Random House, 1979), p. 379. Roosevelt made good use of public documents and his own talents, but I have not relied on his book (which was published in 1888).

Much of Morris's story is in French. I have translated the conversation and poetry that appear in Sparks, Anne Cary Morris, and Davenport, but have mostly relied on their translations of his letters, the speech he wrote for Louis XVI, and his proposed French constitution. The American impressions of the prince de Broglie, the marquis de Chastellux, and the marquis de Barbé-Marbois, as well as standard modern works on the period—Furet and Richet's *The*

French Revolution, Orieux's *Talleyrand*—have been published in English. I had to translate the biographer of Mme de Souza, and was rash enough to translate Rousseau.

I have used the following collections of unpublished papers:

The Papers of Gouverneur Morris: Library of Congress

The Papers of John W. Francis: New York Public Library

The Papers of Robert Morris (Gouverneur's cousin, not the financier): Rutgers University

The Cabell Family Papers: Alderman Library, University of Virginia

All unattributed references to diaries or letters are from the Papers of Gouverneur Morris: Library of Congress.

INTRODUCTION

1. Mme de Damas's letter is in Sparks I, pp. 506–12.

2. Swiggett, p. 331, quoting Abigail Adams—a useful source, since she was an intelligent phonetic speller. Today the residents of the upstate New York town of Gouverneur, founded on land Morris owned late in life, pronounce the name "Gov-ah-*noar.*" Interestingly, Frenchmen of Morris's acquaintance did not consider him French; the prince de Broglie, who met him in America, called him "Governor" (Balch, p. 234); so did the marquis de Chastellux (Chase, p. 167). The upshot of all this would seem to be that the accent is on the last syllable and that the vowels are not Frenchified.

3. Swiggett, p. 42.

4. Morris II, p. 574.

5. Sparks I, p. 284.

6. Ibid., p. 285.

7. Read, p. 202.

8. Mintz, p. 94.

9. Farrand III, p. 92.

CHAPTER ONE

1. Burrows and Wallace, p. 98.

2. This, and other information on the first Morrises, is found in the *New York Post,* "Famous New York Families: The Morrises," May 11, 1901. The quotation marks around dialogue reported two centuries after it was spoken are obviously a narrative convention for relaying a family tradition. But there is no reason, apart from a killjoy spirit, for doubting that tradition.

3. Alexander, p. 9.

4. Burrows and Wallace, p. 155.

5. Ibid.

6. Alexander, p. 5.

7. McAnear, p. 165.

8. Sparks I, p. 5.

9. Franklin, p. 1432.

10. Ibid.

11. Ibid., pp. 1432–33.

12. Jones, p. 140.

13. Mintz, p. 14.

14. Ibid., p. 15.

15. Jones, p. 140.

16. Mintz, p. 15.

17. Ibid., pp. 13–14.

18. Kline, p. 5.

19. Morris II, p. 389.

20. Swiggett, p. 353.

21. Sparks I, p. 17.

22. Mintz, p. 9.

23. Ibid., p. 18.

24. Morris "delighted in Horace"—"Recollections of Gouverneur Morris," John W. Francis Papers.

25. Sparks I, p. 6.

26. Jonathan Landon to Robert Morris, August 27, 1766, Robert Morris Papers.

27. Delafield, p. 75.

28. Farrand III, p. 92.

29. Jonathan Landon to Robert Morris, September 4, 1766, Robert Morris Papers.

30. Davenport I, p. 354.

31. Mintz, p. 31.

Chapter Two

1. Mintz, p. 27.

2. Jones, p. 140.

3. Mintz, p. 26.

4. The standard biography of Robert R. Livingston is Dangerfield. For young John Jay, see Pellew, p. 7.

5. Sparks I, p. 17.

6. Ibid., p. 19.

7. Swiggett, pp. 18–19.

8. Miller, p. 63.

9. Mintz, pp. 40–41.

10. Kline, p. 27.

11. Ibid., p. 26.

12. Kammen, p. 360.

13. Sparks I, pp. 20–21.

14. Ibid., p. 25.

15. Ibid., pp. 23–24.

16. John. W. Francis Papers.

17. Sparks I, p. 26.

18. Burrows and Wallace, p. 224.

19. Kline, pp. 37–38.

20. Mintz, p. 48.

21. Sparks I, p. 40.

22. Mintz, pp. 51–52; Swiggett, p. 27.

23. Kline, p. 43.

24. Mintz, p. 53.

25. Swiggett, p. 26.

26. Mintz, p. 57.

27. Ibid., p. 00.

28. Farrand III, p. 85. Mintz (pp. 169–70) gives the dubious provenance of all three stories; one we owe to former president Martin Van Buren, who heard it from a judge, who heard it from a senator, who heard it from Alexander Hamilton. Swiggett (p. viii) presents a bluff argument for disbelieving them; on the other hand, an academic historian told me that he loved the Washington/Morris/Hamilton version because it was so characteristic of all three men.

29. Bobrick, p. 211.

30. Mintz, pp. 63–65. For the long, tangled career of William Smith, Jr., see Schechter, *passim.*

31. Sparks I, pp. 99–100.

32. Ibid., p. 103.

33. Mintz, p. 70.

34. Ibid., p. 69.

35. Sparks I, pp. 119–20.

CHAPTER THREE

1. Mintz, p. 74.

2. *The Federalist Papers,* p. 38.

3. Mintz, p. 75.

4. Sparks I, p. 125; Kline, p. 78.

5. Davenport I, p. 265.

6. Davenport II, p. 8.

7. Van Schaak, p. 131.

8. Mintz, p. 76.

9. Kline, p. 79.

10. Sparks I, p. 127.

11. Mintz, p. 77.

12. Van Schaak, p. 440.

13. Ibid., pp. 55, 62.

14. Ibid., p. 100.

15. Ibid., p. 129.

16. Ibid., pp. 130–32.

17. Bobrick, p. 271.

18. Ibid., p. 273.

19. Kline, p. 83.

20. Mintz, p. 80.

21. Kline, p. 84.

22. Bobrick, p. 254.

23. Kline, p. 82.

24. Ibid.

25. Mintz, p. 83.

26. Ibid., p. 84.

27. Sparks I, p. 141.

28. Ibid., p. 145.

29. Mintz, p. 85.

30. Pratt, p. 110.

31. Mintz, p. 86.

CHAPTER FOUR

1. Weigley, p. 133.

2. Mintz, p. 88.

3. Kline, p. 106.

4. Swiggett, p. 73.

5. Mintz, p. 126.

6. Swiggett, p. 47.

7. Mintz, p. 89.

8. Kline, p. 170.

9. Flexner, *Revolution,* p. 261.

10. Sparks I, p. 154.

11. Mintz, p. 101.

12. Sparks I, p. 174.

13. Schama, p. 27. Schama is rather contemptuous of Lafayette, and anyone who follows his later career through Morris's eyes will not think well of him. Against this must be set Lafayette's glorious career in America, and George Washington's high opinion of him.

14. Bobrick, p. 295.

15. Mintz, p. 92.

16. Sparks I, p. 151.

17. Mintz, p. 100.

18. Ibid.
19. Sparks I, p. 159.
20. Ibid., p. 158.
21. Mintz, p. 94.
22. Ibid., p. 91.
23. Ibid., pp. 95–96.
24. Kline, p. 102.
25. Weigley, p. 142.
26. Ibid., p. 134.
27. Balch, p. 234.
28. Weigley, p. 152.
29. Swiggett, p. 55.
30. Ibid., p. 43; Kline, p. 160.
31. Mintz, pp. 113–14.
32. Sparks I, p. 217.
33. Ibid., p. 113.
34. Jensen, p. 251.
35. Ibid., pp. 252–53.
36. Rossiter, p. 351.
37. Ibid., p. 358.
38. Kline, pp. 113–14.
39. Ibid., p. 120.
40. Ibid., p. 122.
41. Miller, p. 52.
42. Mintz, p. 102.
43. Ibid., pp. 111, 103, 112–13.
44. Sparks I, p. 184.
45. Mintz, p. 113.
46. Washington, p. 328.
47. Kline, p. 143.
48. Morris II, p. 551.
49. Sparks I, p. 192.
50. Kline, p. 144.
51. Bobrick, p. 194.
52. Sparks I, p. 198.
53. Paine, p. 91.
54. Keane, p. 176.
55. Sparks I, p. 202.
56. See Mintz, p. 119.
57. Sparks I, p. 200.
58. Kline, p. 157.
59. Ibid., p. 148.

60. Sparks I, p. 212.
61. Kline, p. 168.

CHAPTER FIVE

1. Swiggett, p. 78.
2. Kline, p. 172.
3. Sparks I, p. 17.
4. Kline, p. 26.
5. Ibid., p. 107.
6. Swiggett, p. 59.
7. Ibid., p. 66.
8. Ibid., p. 72.
9. Sparks I, p. 223.
10. Mintz, p. 140.
11. Sparks I, p. 224.
12. Kline, p. 176.
13. Mintz, p. 141.
14. Davenport II, p. 247.
15. Davenport I, p. 234.
16. Chastellux, p. 135.
17. Kline, p. 178.
18. Ibid., p. 177.
19. Davenport I, p. 504.
20. Davenport II, p. 64.
21. John W. Francis Papers.
22. Morris II, p. 216.
23. Chastellux, p. 131.
24. Chase, p. 167.
25. Read, p. 202.

CHAPTER SIX

1. Sparks I, p. 230.
2. Ibid., p. 229.
3. Ver Steeg, p. 6.
4. Ibid., p. 37.
5. Mintz, p. 145.
6. See Ver Steeg, pp. 43ff.
7. Mintz, p. 148.
8. Sparks I, p. 220.
9. Kline, p. 202.
10. Morris II, p. 599.
11. Kline, p. 206.

12. Ibid., p. 223.

13. Ibid., p. 216.

14. Keane, p. 217.

15. Ibid., p. 218.

16. Ibid.

17. See McKusker, pp. 80–88. The New York Stock Exchange listed prices in eighths of dollars (bits) until April 2001. See also Koch and Peden, pp. 54–56.

18. Kline, p. 220.

19. Sparks I, p. 239.

20. Kline, p. 249.

21. Ibid., pp. 250–51.

22. Sparks I, p. 249.

23. Mintz, p. 160.

24. Sparks I, p. 251.

25. Mintz, p. 160.

26. Sparks I, p. 251.

27. Flexner, *Revolution,* p. 504.

28. Ibid., p. 507.

29. Sparks I, p. 266.

30. Ibid., p. 264.

31. Van Schaak, p. 372.

32. Kline, p. 299.

33. Paine, pp. 361–62.

34. Sparks III, p. 451.

Chapter Seven

1. Kline, p. 305.

2. Mintz, p. 177.

3. Farrand III, pp. 89–90.

4. Ibid., p. 92.

5. Madison, p. 23.

6. Farrand III, p. 391.

7. Madison, p. 225.

8. Farrand III, p. 92.

9. Madison, pp. 232–33.

10. Ibid., p. 496.

11. Ibid., p. 504.

12. Ibid., pp. 353–54.

13. Ibid., p. 564.

14. Ibid., p. 401.

15. Farrand III, p. 534; Madison, p. 23.

16. Madison, p. 232.

17. Ibid., p. 268.
18. Ibid., p. 246.
19. Ibid., p. 247.
20. Ibid., p. 261.
21. Ibid., p. 275.
22. Ibid., p. 262.
23. Ibid., p. 40.
24. Ibid., p. 227.
25. Ibid., p. 384.
26. Ibid., p. 225.
27. Ibid., p. 392.
28. Ibid., p. 393.
29. Ibid., pp. 450–51.
30. Sparks I, p. 286.
31. Madison, pp. 574–75.
32. Rossiter, p. 379.
33. Ibid., p. 397.
34. Ibid., pp. 353–54.
35. Ibid., p. 383.
36. Ibid., p. 391.
37. Ibid., p. 374.
38. Ibid., pp. 386, 392, 394.
39. Sparks I, p. 284.
40. Rossiter, p. 389.
41. Farrand III, p. 379.
42. Rossiter, p. 374.
43. Ibid., pp. 361, 351. The Articles of Confederation explicitly guaranteed the defense, liberties, and general welfare of the states; Madison's plan implicitly accepted that intention.
44. Farrand II, p. 134.
45. Rossiter, p. 367.
46. Madison, p. 582.
47. Simon, p. 23.
48. Farrand IV, p. 84.
49. Madison, p. 619.
50. Morris II, p. 436.
51. Ibid., p. 527.
52. Syrett V, p. 7.

CHAPTER EIGHT

1. Davis, p. 168.
2. Davenport I, p. xxxiii.

3. Ibid., pp. xxxiii–xxxiv
4. Van Doren, p. 609.
5. Ibid., pp. 639–40.
6. Butterfield, p. 207.
7. Ibid., p. 216.
8. Ibid., p. 222.
9. Ibid., p. 210.
10. Brodie, p. 235.
11. Koch and Peden, p. 395.
12. Ibid., pp. 382–83.
13. Van Doren, p. 760.
14. Butterfield, p. 238.
15. Ibid., p. 310.
16. Koch and Peden, p. 383.
17. Davenport I, p. 36.
18. Ibid., p. 113.
19. Ingersoll, p. 453.
20. Davenport I, p. 516.
21. Ibid., p. 570.
22. Ibid., p. 358.
23. Washington, p. 597.
24. Malone, *Rights,* p. 45.
25. Davenport I, p. 156.
26. Davenport II, p. 166.
27. Davenport I, p. 530.
28. Maricourt, p. 67.
29. Davenport I, p. 286.
30. Orieux, p. 55.
31. Maricourt, p. 167.
32. Ibid.
33. Orieux, p. 55.
34. Maricourt, p. 60.
35. Davenport I, p. 17.
36. Orieux, p. 4.
37. Davenport I, p. 108.
38. Davenport II, p. 302.
39. Ibid., p. 148.
40. Ibid., p. 54.
41. Davenport I, p. 61.
42. Ibid., pp. 111–12.
43. Ibid., p. 66.
44. Ibid., p. 67.

45. Ibid., p. 68.
46. Ibid.
47. Ibid., p. 85.
48. Ibid., p. 98.
49. Ibid., p. 136.
50. Ibid., p. 142.
51. Ibid., p. 148.
52. Ibid., p. 144.
53. Ibid., pp. 158–59.
54. Ibid., pp. 255–56.
55. Koch and Peden, p. 478.
56. Ibid., p. 487.
57. Schama, p. 406.
58. Davenport I, p. 164.
59. Ibid., p. 44.
60. Ibid., p. 292.
61. Ibid., p. 29.
62. Ibid., p. 119.
63. Ibid., p. 157.
64. Ibid., p. 160.
65. Ibid., p. 164.

CHAPTER NINE

1. Davenport I, p. 232.
2. Furet and Richet, p. 126.
3. Davenport I, p. 221.
4. Ibid., p. 223.
5. Ibid., pp. 383–84.
6. Ibid., p. 385.
7. Ibid., p. 387.
8. Ibid., p. 328.
9. Ibid., p. 507.
10. Ibid., p. 235.
11. Ibid., p. 226.
12. Ibid., p. 407.
13. Davenport II, p. 62.
14. Davenport I, p. 293.
15. Ibid., p. 318.
16. Ibid., p. 243.
17. Ibid., p. 245.
18. Ibid., p. 413.
19. Ibid., pp. 260–61.

20. Ibid., p. 237.
21. Ferguson, p. 271.
22. Davenport I, p. 464.
23. Ibid., p. 604.
24. Ibid., p. 493.
25. Davenport II, p. 48.
26. Ibid., p. 55.
27. Ibid., p. 64.
28. Ibid., pp. 119, 123.
29. Ibid., p. 80.
30. Ibid., p. 158.
31. Burke, pp. 92–93.
32. Paine, p. 448.
33. Ibid., p. 539.
34. Ibid., p. 453.
35. Davenport II, p. 156.
36. Ibid., p. 138.
37. Ibid., p. 77.
38. Schama, p. 549.
39. Davenport II, p. 164.
40. Ibid., p. 166.
41. Ibid., p. 207.
42. Ibid., pp. 212–13.
43. Schama, p. 555.
44. Davenport II, p. 211.
45. Ibid., p. 300.
46. Ibid., pp. 266–68.
47. Ibid., p. 250.
48. Sparks III, p. 482.
49. Ibid., p. 483.
50. Davenport II, pp. 322–23.
51. Ibid., p. 318.
52. Rousseau, p. 195.
53. Schama, p. 205.
54. Burke, p. 93.

CHAPTER TEN

1. Swiggett, p. 225.
2. O'Brien, p. 103.
3. Swiggett, p. 226.
4. O'Brien, p. 130.
5. Swiggett, p. 225.

6. Washington, pp. 799–800.

7. Davenport II, p. 403.

8. Ibid., p. 436.

9. Paine, p. 657.

10. Davenport II, p. 368.

11. Ibid., p. 429.

12. Ibid., pp. 444, 449.

13. Ibid., p. 477.

14. Ibid., p. 490.

15. Ibid.

16. Ibid., p. 512.

17. Ibid., p. 517.

18. Ibid.

19. Ibid., pp. 518–19.

20. Maricourt, pp. 150–51.

21. Hemlow and Douglas II, p. 14.

22. Ibid., p. 25.

23. Ibid., p. 22. The Burneys "had wandered out of the sedate drawingrooms of *Sense and Sensibility* and were in danger of losing themselves in the elegantly disordered alcoves of *Les Liaisons Dangereuses*"—Cooper, p. 64.

24. Sparks I, pp. 407–8.

25. Davenport II, p. 531.

26. Ibid., p. 561.

27. Ibid., p. 509.

28. Ibid., p. 507.

29. Ibid., p. 515.

30. Ibid., p. 527.

31. Ibid., p. 566.

32. Schama, p. 640.

33. Keane, p. 349.

34. Ibid., p. 351.

35. Davenport II, p. 597.

36. Paine, p. 388.

37. Davenport II, p. 602.

38. Ibid., p. 492.

39. Maricourt, pp. 159–63.

40. Sparks II, p. 312.

41. Morris II, pp. 43–44.

42. Walther, p. 240.

43. Ibid., p. 242.

44. Davenport II, p. 586.

45. Schama, p. 800.

46. Morris II, p. 48.
47. Sparks II, p. 393.
48. Paine, pp. 670–71.
49. Davenport II, p. 11.
50. Sparks II, p. 393.
51. Davenport II, p. 595.
52. Cobbett, p. 104.
53. Elkins and McKitrick, p. 363.
54. Ibid., p. 369.
55. Morris II, p. 37.
56. Ibid., p. 70.
57. Davenport II, p. 579.
58. Ibid., p. 570.
59. Ibid., p. 571.
60. Davenport I, p. 567.
61. Ibid., p. 129.
62. Morris II, p. 116.
63. Sparks III, p. 489.

Chapter Eleven

1. Morris II, p. 296.
2. Swiggett, p. 293.
3. Maricourt, p. 175.
4. Morris II, p. 81.
5. Ibid., p. 82.
6. Swiggett, p. 297.
7. Morris II, pp. 109–10.
8. Ibid., pp. 134–35.
9. Ibid., p. 138.
10. Ibid., pp. 156, 184.
11. Ibid., p. 129.
12. Diary, June 27, 1796.
13. Morris II, p. 75.
14. Ibid., p. 248.
15. Ibid., pp. 174, 190.
16. Ibid., p. 244.
17. Ibid., pp. 248–49.
18. Ibid., pp. 249–50.
19. Ibid., p. 227.
20. Ibid., pp. 180, 183.
21. Swiggett, p. 320.
22. Morris II, p. 295.

23. Ibid., pp. 295–96.

24. Swiggett, p. 322.

25. Ibid., p. 359.

26. Ibid.

27. Sparks I, p. 440.

28. Ibid., p. 441.

29. Ibid., p. 446.

30. Elkins and MicKitrick, p. 567.

31. Ibid., p. 871, though Cooper (p. 86) argues that this famous story is false.

32. Keane, p. 437.

33. Morris II, p. 85.

34. Ibid., p. 103.

35. Ibid., p. 105.

36. Ibid., pp. 202–3.

37. Ibid., p. 203.

38. Ibid., p. 23.

39. Diary, December 1, 1798.

CHAPTER TWELVE

1. Syrett XXII, p. 192.

2. John W. Francis Papers.

3. Swiggett, p. 365.

4. Goebel II, pp. 88, 86, 83.

5. Sparks III, p. 82.

6. Elkins and McKitrick, p. 572.

7. Syrett XVIII, p. 329.

8. Morris II, p. 378.

9. Ibid., p. 380.

10. Sparks III, p. 130.

11. Ibid., p. 128.

12. Morris II, p. 396.

13. "Aaron Burr had 100,000 votes from the single circumstance of his descent from President Burr and President Edwards"—John Adams to Thomas Jefferson, November 15, 1813, Cappon, p. 399.

14. Davenport I, p. 256.

15. Morris II, p. 401.

16. Malone, *Ordeal,* p. 458.

17. See Morris II, p. 397.

18. Sparks III, p. 132.

19. Syrett XXV, p. 272.

20. Sparks III, p. 134.

21. Ibid., p. 256.

22. Ibid., p. 154.

23. Morris II, p. 405.

24. For discussions of this famous phrase, see Elkins and McKitrick, p. 753, and Joseph J. Ellis, p. 182.

25. Elkins and McKitrick, p. 754.

26. Sparks III, p. 128.

27. Adams, *Randolph*, p. 58.

28. Morris II, p. 405.

29. Sparks III, p. 371.

30. Ibid., p. 375.

31. Morris II, p. 417.

32. Ibid., p. 422.

33. Sparks III, p. 409.

34. Ibid., p. 415.

35. Ibid., pp. 417, 414.

36. Morris II, p. 412. George Morgan presents a balanced discussion of this quarrel, pp. 394–96.

37. Morris II, p. 388.

38. Flexner, *Agony*, pp. 311–12.

39. Milton Ellis, p. 362.

40. Swiggett, p. 362.

41. Ibid., p. 363.

42. Sparks III, p. 203.

43. Morris II, p. 453.

44. Ibid., pp. 456–58.

Chapter Thirteen

1. Sparks III, p. 243.

2. Diary, August 14, 1808; September 1, 1808. For the history of Morris's upstate house, see Rossie et al., pp. 12–13.

3. Watson, p. 246.

4. Flexner, *New*, p. 82.

5. Sparks I, p. 497.

6. Sparks III, pp. 142–44.

7. Morris II, pp. 439–40.

8. Ibid., p. 440.

9. Ibid., p. 507.

10. Malone, *Second*, p. 555.

11. Morris II, p. 536.

12. Crawford, p. 201.

13. A[nne] C[ary] Morris to Joseph C. Cabell, October 14, 1831, Cabell

Family Papers; Gouverneur Morris to Anne Cary Randolph, March [n.d.] 1809.

14. Swiggett, p. 137.

15. Anne Cary Morris to Josesh C. Cabell, October 14, 1831.

16. Koch and Peden, p. 590.

17. Crawford, pp. 116–17.

18. Ibid., pp. 77–78.

19. Ibid., p. 92.

20. Ibid., p. 145.

21. Adams, *Randolph,* pp. 83–84.

22. Crawford, p. 148.

23. Diary, September 17, 1808. Swiggett (pp. 395–96) has another theory.

24. Gouverneur Morris to Anne Cary Randolph, March [n.d.] 1809. In courting Nancy as an employee, and something more, Morris wrote her three letters in March 1809, whose arguments I have, in arranging thematically, taken out of sequence: March 3, 9, and a letter whose first page has been removed from the letterbook (March n.d.).

25. Gouverneur Morris to Anne Cary Randolph, March 3, 1809.

26. Gouverneur Morris to Anne Cary Randolph, March 9, 1809.

27. Gouverneur Morris to Anne Cary Randolph, March n.d. 1809.

28. Gouverneur Morris to Anne Cary Randolph, March 3, 1809.

29. Swiggett, p. 399.

30. Gouverneur Morris to John Marshall, December 2, 1809.

31. Crawford, p. 197.

32. Diary, December 25, 1809.

33. Swiggett, p. 403.

Chapter Fourteen

1. Morris II, p. 431.

2. Sparks III, p. 216; Morris II, p. 472.

3. Sparks III, p. 251.

4. John W. Francis Papers.

5. Cornog, p. 111.

6. Morris II, p. 520.

7. Ibid., p. 521.

8. *Journal of the Senate,* p. 66.

9. Ibid., p. 69.

10. Ibid., p. 73.

11. Ibid., p. 75.

12. Burrows and Wallace, p. 421.

13. Morris II, p. 536.

14. *Public Documents,* p. 59.

15. Ibid., p. 60.
16. Ibid., p. 64.
17. Ibid., p. 63.
18. Ibid., p. 61.
19. Morris II, p. 431.
20. Ibid., p. 509.
21. Adams, *Madison,* p. 394.
22. Adams, *Randolph,* p. 206.
23. Morris II, p. 535.
24. Ibid., p. 536.
25. Ibid., p. 541.
26. Ibid.
27. Ibid., p. 527.
28. Ibid., p. 537.
29. Ibid., p. 543.
30. Ibid., p. 548.
31. Ibid., p. 543.
32. Ibid., p. 573.
33. Ibid., p. 543.
34. Ibid., p. 551.
35. Ibid., p. 549.
36. Ibid., p. 552.
37. Ibid., p. 548.
38. Ibid., p. 559.
39. Ibid., p. 566.
40. Ibid., p. 564.
41. Ibid., p. 566.
42. Swiggett, p. 418.
43. Ibid., p. 417.
44. Morris II, p. 565.
45. Adams, *Madison,* p. 1071.

Chapter Fifteen

1. Crawford, p. 227.
2. Ibid., pp. 234–40.
3. Adams, *Randolph,* p. 184.
4. Crawford, pp. 235–36.
5. Ibid., pp. 245–53.
6. Swiggett, p. 435.
7. Ibid., p. 426.
8. Morris II, p. 575.
9. Adams, *Madison,* p. 1111.

10. Ibid., p. 1113.
11. Ibid., p. 1115.
12. Morris II, p. 568.
13. Adams, *Madison,* p. 1117.
14. Madison, p. 567.
15. Ibid., p. 349.
16. Morris II, p. 578.
17. Ibid., p. 579.
18. Ibid., p. 578.
19. Ibid., p. 557.
20. Sparks III, p. 304.
21. Dwight, p. 361.
22. Sparks III, p. 290.
23. Morris II, p. 588.

Chapter Sixteen

1. Sparks III, p. 340.
2. Ibid., p. 341.
3. Ibid., p. 347.
4. Adams, *Madison,* p. 1283.
5. Ibid., p. 1285.
6. Morris II, p. 594.
7. Ibid., p. 599.
8. Ibid., p. 594.
9. Ibid., p. 598.
10. Sparks III, p. 355.
11. Ibid., p. 361.
12. Ibid.
13. Morris II, p. 499.
14. Ibid., pp. 600–601.
15. Swiggett, p. 441.
16. Morris II, p. 602.
17. Ibid.

Postscript

1. Gordon, p. 56.
2. Cooper, p. 374.
3. Swiggett, p. 447; *Gouverneur (N.Y.) Tribune Press,* "Historic Morris 'Mansion' on the Mend," March 4, 1992.
4. Morris II, p. 43.

Bibliography

Adams, Henry. *History of the United States During the Administrations of James Madison.* New York: Library of America, 1986.

———. *John Randolph.* Armonk, NY: M. E. Sharpe, 1996.

Alexander, James. *A Brief Narrative of the Case and Trial of John Peter Zenger,* ed. Stanley Nider Katz. Cambridge: Harvard University Press, 1963.

Balch, F. W., trans., "Narrative of the Prince de Broglie," *Magazine of American History,* I (April 1877).

Chastellux, marquis de. *Travels in North America,* trans. Howard C. Rice, Jr. Chapel Hill: University of North Carolina Press, 1963.

Cobbett, William. *Peter Porcupine in America,* ed. David Wilson. Ithaca, NY: Cornell University Press, 1994.

Cooper, Duff. *Talleyrand.* New York: Grove Press, 1997.

Cornog, Evan. *The Birth of Empire.* New York: Oxford University Press, 1998.

Crawford, Alan Pell. *Unwise Passions.* New York: Simon & Schuster, 2000.

Dangerfield, George. *Chancellor Robert R. Livingston of New York.* New York: Harcourt Brace, 1960.

Davenport, Beatrix Cary. *A Diary of the French Revolution by Gouverneur Morris,* 2 vols. Boston: Houghton Mifflin, 1939.

Davis, Joseph S. *Essays in the Earlier History of American Corporations.* Cambridge: Harvard University Press, 1917.

Delafield, Julia. *Biographies of Francis Lewis and Morgan Lewis.* New York: A. D. F. Randolph & Co. 1877.

Dwight, Theodore. *History of the Hartford Convention.* Freeport, NY: Books for Libraries Press, 1970.

Elkins, Stanley, and Eric McKitrick. *The Age of Federalism.* New York: Oxford University Press, 1993.

Ellis, Joseph J. *American Sphinx.* New York: Alfred A. Knopf, 1997.

Ellis, Milton. "The Author of the First American Novel," *American Literature,* 4 (January 1933).

Farrand, Max, ed. *The Records of the Federal Convention.* New Haven: Yale University Press, 1937.

Ferguson, E. James. *The Power of the Purse.* Chapel Hill: University of North Carolina Press, 1961.

Flexner, James Thomas. *George Washington in the American Revolution.* Boston: Little, Brown, 1968.

———. *George Washington and the New Nation.* Boston: Little, Brown, 1970.

———. *George Washington: Anguish and Farewell.* Boston: Little, Brown, 1972.

Franklin, Benjamin. *Writings.* New York: Library of America, 1987.

Furet, François, and Denis Richet. *The French Revolution,* trans. Stephen Hardman. New York: The Macmillan Company, 1970.

Goebel, Julius, Jr., ed. *The Law Practice of Alexander Hamilton.* New York: Columbia University Press, 1964–81.

Gordon, John Steele. *The Great Game.* New York: Scribner, 1999.

Hamilton, Alexander, James Madison, and John Jay. *The Federalist Papers.* New York: New American Library, 1961.

Hemlow, Joyce, and Althea Douglas, eds. *Fanny Burney: Journals and Letters.* Oxford: Oxford University Press, 1972.

Ingersoll, Charles J. *Recollections, Historical, Political, Biographical and Social.* Philadelphia: J. B. Lippincott & Co., 1861.

Jensen, Merrill. *The Articles of Confederation.* Madison: University of Wisconsin Press, 1959.

Jones, Thomas. *History of New York During the Revolutionary War.* New York: New-York Historical Society, 1879.

Journal of the Senate of the State of New-York. Albany: S. Southwick, 1811.

Kammen, Michael. *Colonial New York—A History.* New York: Charles Scribner's Sons, 1975.

Keane, John. *Tom Paine.* Boston: Little, Brown, 1995.

Kline, Mary-Jo. *Gouverneur Morris and the New Nation 1775–1788.* New York: Arno Press, 1978.

Knox, Katharine McCook. *The Sharples: Their Portraits of George Washington and His Contemporaries.* New Haven: Yale University Press, 1930.

Koch, Adrienne, and William Peden. *The Life and Selected Writings of Thomas Jefferson.* New York: Modern Library, 1944.

Madison, James. *Debates in the Federal Convention of 1787,* ed. James McClellan and M. E. Bradford. Richmond, VA: James River Press, 1989.

Malone, Dumas. *Jefferson and the Rights of Man.* Boston: Little, Brown, 1951.

———. *Jefferson and the Ordeal of Liberty.* Boston: Little, Brown, 1962.

———. *Jefferson the President: Second Term 1805–1809.* Boston: Little, Brown, 1974.

McAnear, Beverly. "An American in London," *Pennsylvania Magazine of History and Biography,* 63 (April 1940).

McKusker, John J. *How Much Is That in Real Money?* Worcester, MA: American Antiquarian Society, 2001.

Maricourt, baron André de. *Madame de Souza et Sa Famille.* Paris: Emile-Paul, 1907.

Miller, John C. *Alexander Hamilton: Portrait in Paradox.* New York: Harper & Brothers, 1959.

Mintz, Max M. *Gouverneur Morris and the American Revolution.* Norman, OK: University of Oklahoma Press, 1970.

Morgan, George. *The True Lafayette.* Philadelphia: J. B. Lippincott Co., 1919.

Morris, Anne Cary. *The Diary and Letters of Gouverneur Morris,* 2 vols. New York: Charles Scribner's Sons, 1888.

O'Brien, Conor Cruise. *The Long Affair* . Chicago: University of Chicago Press, 1996.

Orieux, Jean. *Talleyrand,* trans. Patricia Wolf. New York: Alfred A. Knopf, 1974.

Paine, Thomas. *Collected Writings.* New York: Library of America, 1995.

Pellew, George. *John Jay.* New York: AMS Press, 1972.

Pratt, George W. *An Account of the British Expedition Above the Highlands of the Hudson River. . . .* , N.p.: Ulster County Historical Society, 1977.

Public Documents Relating to the New-York Canals . . . New York: William A. Mercury, 1821.

Read, Elizabeth. "The Chews of Pennsylvania," *Magazine of American History,* 4 (March 1880).

Rossie, Fowler, Edwards, DeKalb, and Hammond. *Centennial Souvenir History of Gouverneur.* Watertown, NY: Hungerford-Holbrook Co., 1905.

Rossiter, Clinton. *1787 The Grand Convention.* New York: The Macmillan Company, 1966.

Rousseau, Jean Jacques. *Lettre à D'Alembert.* Paris: Garnier-Flammarion, 1967.

Schama, Simon. *Citizens.* New York: Alfred A. Knopf, 1989.

Schechter, Barnet. *The Battle for New York.* New York: Walker & Company, 2002.

Simon, James F. *What Kind of Nation: Thomas Jefferson, John Marshall, and the Epic Struggle to Create a United States.* New York: Simon & Schuster, 2002.

Sparks, Jared. *The Life of Gouverneur Morris, with Selections from his Correspondence and Miscellaneous Papers,* 3 vols. Boston: Gray & Bowen, 1832.

Swiggett, Howard. *The Extraordinary Mr. Morris.* Garden City, NY: Doubleday & Company, 1952.

Syrett, Harold C., et al., eds. *The Papers of Alexander Hamilton* 26, XXX vols. New York: Columbia University Press, 1961–87.

Van Doren, Carl. *Benjamin Franklin.* New York: Viking Press, 1938.

Van Schaak, Henry C. *The Life of Peter Van Schaak.* New York: Appleton & Company, 1842.

Ver Steeg, Clarence L. *Robert Morris, Revolutionary Financier.* Philadelphia: University of Pennsylvania Press, 1954.

Walther, Daniel. *Gouverneur Morris Witness of Two Revolutions,* trans. Elinore Denniston. New York: Literary Digest Books, 1934.

Washington, George. *Writings.* New York: Library of America, 1977.

Watson, Elkanah. *Men and Times of the Revolution; or, Memoirs of Elkanah Watson.* New York: Dana & Company, 1856.

Weigley, Russell F., et al., eds. *Philadelphia: A 300-Year History.* New York: W. W. Norton & Company, 1982.

Index

Richard Brookhiser is the author of *America's First Dynasty: The Adamses, 1735–1918* (2003); *Alexander Hamilton, American* (1999); *Founding Father: Rediscovering George Washington* (1996); and *The Way of the WASP* (1991), all published by The Free Press. He is a Senior Editor at *The National Review* and a *New York Observer* columnist. He contributes to such publications as *American Heritage* and *The New York Times,* and he lives in New York City.